WOMEN AND RELIGION
IN OLD AND NEW WORLDS

WOMEN AND RELIGION
IN OLD AND NEW WORLDS

EDITED BY
SUSAN E. DINAN AND DEBRA MEYERS

ROUTLEDGE
NEW YORK AND LONDON

Published in 2001 by
Routledge
29 West 35th Street
New York, NY 10001

Published in Great Britain by
Routledge
11 New Fetter Lane
London EC4P 4EE

Routledge is an imprint of the Taylor & Francis Group.

Printed in the United States of America on acid-free paper.
Design and typography: Jack Donner

10 9 8 7 6 5 4 3 2 1

Library of Congress Cataloging-in-Publication Data

Women and religion in old and new worlds / edited by Susan E. Dinan and Debra Meyers.
    p. cm.
  Includes bibliographical references and index.
  ISBN 0–415–93034–0 (hardcover : alk. paper)—ISBN 0–415–93035–9 (pbk. : alk. paper)
    1. Women in Christianity—Europe—History. 2. Women in Christianity—
America—History. I. Dinan, Susan E. II. Meyers, Debra.

BV639.W7 . G46 2001
270.6'082—dc21   00–051710

CONTENTS

ACKNOWLEDGMENTS

The authors and editors would like to thank the copyright holders for their permission to reproduce the following articles: "Nuns, Kurakas, and Credit: The Spiritual Economy of Seventeenth-Century Cuzco," *Colonial Latin American Review* 6 (1997), pp. 185–203; "Recovering the Religious History of Dutch Reformed Women in Colonial New York," *de Halve Maen* 64 (1991), pp. 53–59; and "Anglicans, Catholics, and Nonconformists after the Restoration, 1660–1720," *Women and Religion in England 1500–1720* (New York: Routledge 1996), pp. 185–208.

We have incurred great debts of gratitude while putting together this collection of essays. First, we would like to thank all of the contributors for their diligence, patience, and promptness. We would also like to recognize the editorial assistance provided by Jeanie Attie, Jean Pedersen, and Allyson Poska. Thanks are also due to Jodi Bilinkoff and Merry Wiesner-Hanks for their early support for this project and their words of wisdom. Moreover, Routledge assigned us an anonymous reviewer who carefully read this collection and made numerous very helpful comments. Brendan O'Malley and Jeanne Shu at Routledge have proven thoughtful and efficient editors.

Finally, we would also like to thank our husbands Benson Hawk and Jay Meyers for their encouragement and support; it is to them that we dedicate this volume.

Introduction

Susan E. Dinan and Debra Meyers

WHILE THE EARLY MODERN CHRISTIAN CHURCH often acted as a vehicle for enforcing female subordination, it also provided opportunities for women to exercise authority and facilitate change as they redefined themselves and their positions within the Church, their families and communities. Indeed, women—Protestant and Catholic alike—were historical agents. The era of the European Reformations was one of enormous social transformation as western Christendom experienced a schism that resulted in a multitude of Christian churches and sects in the place of one Roman Catholic Church. The Roman Church, however, did not continue with business as usual; it re-created itself with a clearly articulated theology and a new, educated and disciplined corps of male and female reformers. Certainly both the Protestant and Catholic Reformations changed social attitudes about gender and behavior. By examining gender we hope to gain a better understanding of early modern society in western Europe. Toward that end, this comparative transatlantic anthology brings together some of the diverse experiences of Christians in Europe and the Americas during the post-Reformation era.

We have organized this book along two axes. First, we have structured it geographically. We compare four regions from the Old and New Worlds: Spain and New Spain, France and New France, the Netherlands and the New Netherlands, and England and New England and Maryland. This geographical framework asks the reader to consider the continuities and discontinuities between the Old and New Worlds. Second, this collection examines several related themes across national, continental, and denominational boundaries. At the intersection of these two axes is an examination of how gender influences religious experience and how religion influences gender construction. Consequently, the essays explore the relationships between lay and religious women, of similar and different faiths, and the interactions between women and men in churches, communities, and families. Women had unique experiences in distinct places and this volume seeks to highlight how women of various social strata and of different religious affiliations shaped and in turn were shaped by their faiths. Our focus is on ordinary women, some anonymous and some better known, who used religion to organize their daily lives and to make their everyday experiences meaningful. By studying the expectations women held concerning their faiths and their ability to serve their families, both spiritual and biological, we hope to draw attention to some of the distinctions between Catholic and Protestant experiences within the Atlantic community. Ultimately, we believe that one of the anthology's greatest contributions to historiography will be to apply a comparative transatlantic approach to the study of gender and religion.

REVIEW OF THE LITERATURE

This collection and other recent work on women's history are products of the social history movement of the 1970s. Social historians of the 1970s used new methods and documents to answer different kinds of questions about people of the past. They moved away from narrative political history to uncover the lives of ordinary people with a sympathetic eye toward race, class, and gender as factors in change over time.

In their quest for inclusion, feminist historians of the early 1970s also framed our understanding of gender and its historical significance. Ultimately, historians sought to determine not only how societies controlled women, but also ways in which women asserted their agency. Joan Kelly's pivotal 1977 article asked the question "Did Women Have a Renaissance?" and concluded that they did not enjoy the same cultural and social advancements as did men.[1] With this essay Kelly encouraged historians to question the universality of historical periodization and invited a reworking of traditional understandings of gender relations and the place of women in history. Similarly, Joan Scott's early work asked historians to question not only periodization, but also the arbitrary gendered categories of politics and war that comprised traditional male history. Ultimately, Scott called for a complete rewriting of history. Scott argued that women must arrogate the construction of historical understanding to wrest the production of knowledge about women away from their oppressors. Women could only obtain power and authority if they chose to rewrite the old (male) political history using new categories of analysis. Alternatively, Caroll Smith-Rosenberg and Bonnie Smith rejected the traditional view that women were merely victims of male oppression and assigned them roles as historical agents of change. Smith-Rosenberg's "The Female World of Love and Ritual" and Smith's *Ladies of the Leisure Class* focused on the distinctive world of women set apart from men in a "separate sphere."[2] They emphasized women's centrality as historical actors who created a more or less autonomous culture of their own that both epitomized female creativity and challenged the dominant male society. Using women's own words culled from letters and diaries, these authors suggested that the history of women could only be truly understood as separate from men's history because the traditional male categories of politics and events did not reflect women's reality. Collectively, Kelly, Scott, Smith-Rosenberg, Smith, and other feminist historians encouraged readers to rethink historical periodization and to apply gender as a category of analysis. Moreover, they opened new paths for research by legitimizing the use of unconventional sources (diaries, advice books, literature, and physicians' documents) to uncover the lives of previously ignored historical figures. Thus, the feminist historians of the 1970s called for an expansion of what was understood as historical to include female as well as male subjects and subjectivity.

The field was further enriched when gender historians insisted religiosity also be reintegrated into the matrix of analysis. Historians including Jo Ann McNamara, Peter Brown, Caroline Bynum, Natalie Zemon Davis, and Merry Wiesner reminded readers that religion is a critical analytical category when studying the past. Since the essays in this volume are heavily indebted to these historians' contributions to our understanding of gender and religion, a short survey of their work should prove useful.

Women's historians of the 1970s and 1980s often considered the church an oppressive institution. However, some did offer a more optimistic assessment of society during the golden age of early Christianity in late antiquity. Jo Ann McNamara, for instance, compared pagan women's lives to those of women in the early church and suggested that Christian females experienced greater rights and freedom of choice.[3] Historians like McNamara and Peter Brown often argued that immediately after the death of Christ, Christians were preoccupied with the imminent end of the world and thus ignored socially constructed gender roles that placed women in subordinate positions.[4] This golden age waned as soon as the Christian Church modified its sole focus on the spiritual hereafter and began to build a hierarchic temporal institution that embraced traditional gender norms placing women in a submissive position.

Caroline Bynum, however, found a surprising amount of female autonomy within the Christian Church in the High Middle Ages. In *Holy Feast and Holy Fast* Bynum challenged traditional assumptions about the medieval church when she asserted that women found empowerment in the unconventional excessive fasting of Christian ascetics.[5] Bynum tossed aside the generally accepted interpretations of female asceticism as world renunciation that was the product of misogynous cultural constraints. Instead, she suggested that women acted as historical agents and responded within their cultural constraints (much like the women studied by Caroll Smith-Rosenberg and Bonnie Smith) and thus shaped their own religious experiences. Medieval ascetic women's struggle to control their bodies was an effort to utilize one of the only means available to them in order to create their own spirituality and personal power. Bynum stressed the agency of her female subjects who shaped their own piety while redefining women's roles within the church, family, and community. Moreover, Bynum introduced historians to new sources (iconography, hagiography, miracle chronicles, and male texts with descriptions of food practices and metaphors) and research methods to uncover the lives of religious women.

Like their medievalist counterparts, Natalie Zemon Davis and Merry Wiesner have successfully used religion as a means to understand women's experience in the early modern period. Their work looks to religion, and especially the Reformation, as a fundamental factor in determining gender relations. In her writings, such as *The Return of Martin Guerre*, Davis seeks to reconstruct the worlds of early modern people of common origin in order to pull individual lives, particularly the lives of women, from obscurity.[6] Davis argued that the Reformation was neither good nor bad for women by demonstrating that the connections between gender and religion were far more complex than this simple dichotomy implied. Historians such as Roland Bainton and Nancy Roelker had claimed that the Protestant Reformation improved the position of women and both cited as evidence the role of noble and other elite women in bringing reformed ideas into Catholic territories. By way of contrast, Davis uncovered a more complicated situation in Lyon, France. In her study of Catholic Lyon before and during Huguenot rule (1559–1572) Davis discovered that the Catholic Church neglected the needs of women, that the Catholic convents lacked vitality, and that many literate and well-off women converted to Calvinism. Davis also found that the new female converts soon realized that Protestant men did not treat Protestant women as their equals any more than

than the Catholics had. Davis recognized that the Calvinist and Catholic churches offered their female members different—not necessarily better—life options while also demonstrating that women used both churches in an effort to gain access to knowledge and power.[7] Davis's analysis is particularly rich because of her interdisciplinary approach to historical research. Along with utilizing new sources, Davis pioneered new ways of reading traditional sources with the methods of many disciplines. These include the tools of gender and women's history to research and develop her female characters, sociological methods to study the structure and subtleties of village life, and anthropological methods to elucidate the cultural constructs of the sixteenth century.[8]

In "Beyond Women and the Family: Towards a Gender Analysis of the Reformation" Merry Wiesner examined the centrality of gender to religious change. She focused her analysis on the unequal distribution of authority and power within the church and on modes of female expression. Like Joan Scott, Wiesner believed that gender history should focus on the organization of relations of power; both authors use a Foucauldian notion of power and hence seek to analyze the social spaces of power relations. Wiesner's focus is on women's access to power, be they nuns or bathhouse attendants, and women's fierce defense of their autonomy and authority. One benefit of gender theory is its flexibility in application to different historical fields.[9] Power and gender are everywhere and ever changing and therefore historians need a flexible theoretical methodology to illustrate their many relations.

All of the essays in this collection are informed by the work of Davis and Wiesner. Like Davis the authors examine women's unique expectations and experiences in different Christian faiths, and like Wiesner they look broadly at social structures and imperatives that shaped the lives of lay and religious women. In their recent works both Davis and Wiesner have embraced a more global perspective—applying gender analysis to men and women in Europe and elsewhere—and thus they serve as ideal models for our efforts in this volume.[10] Many contributors to this anthology accept the interdisciplinary perspectives and methods of the historians discussed above. Consequently, they use both unconventional and traditional primary sources in inventive ways. In order to uncover ordinary women's voices from the past, contributors consider sources such as convent account books, published works written by women, funeral sermons, travelers' accounts, wills, court records, personal correspondence, prescriptive literature, and church records. Each of the contributors to this volume share basic assumptions about the importance of gender as a category of historical analysis and use methodologies of women's and gender history while pointing out that women were not submissive recipients of religion. Contributors, of course, did not find that all women had the same degree of agency. Geography, religious beliefs, place of origin, age, marital status, wealth, race, and many other factors mitigated or contributed to the role that gender played in shaping religious experience and female agency. Although this concise volume cannot hope to depict the experiences of all women in the early modern transatlantic community, it does afford an innovative framework for examining and comparing the place of religion in the lives of women.

CONTINUITIES AND DIVERGENCES: GEOGRAPHY, DENOMINATION, SOCIAL STATUS, AND RACE

The goal of this collection of essays is to encourage readers to think about the similarities and differences between early modern women of different regions, religions, and social classes. In the section below we compare geographical areas in the Old and New Worlds in order to highlight places of divergence and continuity in women's experiences. The major themes embraced by all of the essays include the ability of individuals, be they nuns, wives, or criminals, to shape religious experiences, the importance of social class in determining the roles individuals will play within their church, and the creation of formal and informal spheres of sacred activity.

Although women in Spain, France, and their colonial counterparts in the New World shared a common faith, their experiences as Catholic women were very diverse. The four essays in this collection that examine these regions are primarily interested in the lives of women religious, both those in convents and less formal religious communities. Convents in the sixteenth and seventeenth centuries were technically cloistered institutions where nuns remained on the interior segregated from the external secular world. The reality, however, is more complex and more interesting. Convents in both Spain and Peru functioned as important centers of social, political, economic, and familial power. Examining nuns in Spain, Allyson Poska and Elizabeth Lehfeldt conclude that cloisters functioned as a permeable boundary. Although convents were places in which women practiced spiritual devotion and chastity, they were also important institutions within the local community in which nuns interacted with the laity. For instance, convent patronage was an important way to demonstrate wealth and to forge a link with nuns who were, in effect, powerful local lords controlling large parcels of land and considerable amounts of wealth. The convents' financial transactions brought nuns into regular contact with the secular world as nuns witnessed property sales and contract negotiations. Poska and Lehfeldt also compare the experiences of nuns to those of laywomen and illustrate how lay piety, like convent spirituality, was shaped within a culture of narrow expectations for female religiosity but nonetheless was expressive of women's needs.

Kathryn Burns comes to a similar conclusion in her study of convents in the Spanish colony of Peru. Burns argues that the parlors of Peruvian convents, rooms in which nuns sat on one side of a grille to converse with the laity on the other side, were busy centers of exchange. Colonial convents were important financial institutions; the nuns' dowries supported the convent and functioned as a source of local credit. Convents managed significant endowments and functioned as lenders to their secular neighbors who were interested in investing to improve their properties and businesses but who faced considerable difficulties accessing money in the cash-poor colony. Spanish and colonial convents shared the same system for making loans. As in Spain, financial transactions brought the nuns into contact with lay society and the economic power of the nuns made them an invaluable local resource, one that could not be entirely segregated from the outside world.

As Poska, Lehfeldt, and Burns demonstrate, convents in Spain and Peru were institutions for the nobility and upper classes and convent connections were very important for elite families who derived spiritual and economic benefits from them. Spanish convents were often quite open in their relations with the outside world. Wealthy women used convents as places for spiritual retreats and nuns were occasionally dispatched from their convents to assist laywomen in their homes. Ultimately, Spanish nuns had more freedom of movement and more direct contact with the secular world than did the nuns of Peru. Convents also reflected the hierarchy of the secular society beyond its walls. Only the daughters of elites could become fully professed choir nuns, and less wealthy women could only enter convents as lower status lay sisters, as servants to the choir nuns. In fact, Poska and Lehfeldt assert that women of more modest means were in fact "pushed" into joining communities of *beatas* instead of convents because they could not afford convent dowries. The same situation existed in France where wealthy families hesitated to allow their daughters to enter unenclosed religious communities but willingly placed them in convents of the Ursulines and Visitandines where they could become professed nuns.

Although there are many parallels between the experiences of nuns in Spain and Peru, there is a major point of divergence: race. In Peru the consideration of wealth in the dynamics of convent life was complicated by considerations of race. Those most involved in financial negotiations on both sides of the convent grille were white, either Spaniards or criollos (American-born descendants of Spaniards). Just as their families were the dominant power outside the convent, these nuns controlled positions of power within the convent. Burns notes that women of Andean descent never rose to important roles within the convents; even the *kurakas*, the families of the powerful Incan lords, could not produce a mother superior. Their darker skin restricted them to wearing the white veil of novices and servants within the convents. Interestingly, although familial wealth in Peru could override the social stigma of an illegitimate birth and white illegitimate women could rise in the convent ranks, women of color of legitimate birth could not do the same. The black veil of the fully professed nuns was available only to women deemed white; rarely did a woman of Andean race obtain a black veil, and none ever rose into the convent's leadership ranks. Moreover, although Andeans could borrow money from the convents, they borrowed much smaller amounts than did their white counterparts. Burns convincingly argues that the convents of Peru both created and reinforced the boundaries that separated criollos and Andeans.

Susan Dinan's and William Foster's French and Quebecois subjects were not nuns, but *filles séculières*, who shared a religious vocation and simple vows but did not formally profess a religious calling with solemn vows. This was a very important distinction by the later sixteenth century because the Council of Trent had dictated that all nuns reside inside cloisters. As Poska, Lehfeldt, and Burns demonstrate, enclosing nuns did not mean that they were isolated from the secular world, but their ability to move and work in the world was definitely limited. *Filles séculières*, however, were not required to remain inside convent walls and could engage in active vocations like teaching and nursing. As Dinan and Foster show, the seventeenth century witnessed a flowering of communities of women who evaded the dictates of Trent in order to perform good works. Both Dinan's Daughters of Charity in France and Foster's Congrégation Notre-Dame in Montreal used their communities to aid their neighbors in the seventeenth century. However, their neighbors differed dramatically. Whereas the Daughters of Charity's mission to cater to the poor and sick was limited to France and Poland in the seventeenth century, members of the Congrégation had a mission to educate French immigrants, English captives, and local Indians in Montreal. Both communities were seeking to strengthen the resolve of Catholics and convert others, be they Huguenot or Iroquois, but the circumstances in which they catechized were dramatically different.

Louise de Marillac, founder of the Daughters of Charity with Vincent de Paul, and Marguerite Bourgeoys, founder of the Congrégation

Notre-Dame, came from wealthy families. However, it was young women from artisan and farming families who entered their innovative communities and brought with them practical skills and work experience. Unlike the nuns in Spanish or Peruvian convents, these poorer women were used to working hard and sought lives of service, not contemplation. The Daughters of Charity performed a wide range of social services including visiting the sick and poor in their homes and creating schools for poor girls, but they are most noted for their work as hospital administers and nurses. The Congrégation Notre-Dame, on the other hand, was a teaching community. Bourgeoys brought her Congrégation to Canada to convert the natives to the Catholic faith, but when this proved unfeasible, she directed her efforts at educating Canadian immigrants and their children. Central to both communities' mission was an active vocation of serving those in need, as Christ and his apostles had done in their own day.

Although gender history is an outgrowth of women's history, it is imperative to remember that gender is not exclusive to women. What makes gender histories rich is their exploration of the interaction of women and men in public and private worlds. In Roman Catholic Spain, France, and their colonial outposts, women's religious communities were not exclusively female. In Spain and Peru men used convents as financial institutions and visited the nuns to negotiate loans and business deals. In France men were instrumental in the formation of religious communities like the Visitandines (François de Sales) and the Daughters of Charity (Vincent de Paul). Moreover, the Daughters of Charity had regular contact with men as they visited the houses of the poor, nursed the sick (including soldiers), and attended prisoners and galley slaves. However, it is in Quebec where the local women religious had the most contact with men. William Foster examines the very unusual demographics of Montreal where he finds the sisters of the Congrégation Notre-Dame employing men as short- and long-term servants and educating boys within their community. In both cases it was the women who were the superiors of the men; nuns directed the work of male indentured and permanent servants and taught boys who also worked as the community's domestic servants—work that was not expected of female pupils. Foster finds that the situation in Montreal got more difficult for its men when local Indian women entered the Congrégation. Unlike the Andean women in Peru who were kept out of the upper echelons of convent life, the Iroquois women in Montreal could become leaders within their religious community. Foster highlights the troubles that race caused for white men. Although men managed to work as servants to white "sisters" of roughly similar social class, it ultimately proved impossible for them to be under the direction of Indian "savages" and the number of men in the Congrégation dwindled.

In contrast to the studies conducted by Poska, Lehfeldt, Burns, Dinan, and Foster that examine institutionalized female spirituality, the articles by Carlson, Goodfriend, Crawford, Brown, and Meyers explore women's spirituality in Protestant-dominated countries where women had fewer opportunities for a professional religious vocation. Marybeth Carlson suggests that early modern political and religious upheavals at the state level in the Netherlands provided women with opportunities to exert a level of authority that had previously been denied them. This window of opportunity for women was precipitated by a breakdown of traditional political and religious structures. Women were involved in community governance and wielded genuine influence in churches that needed their individual talents and financial resources. Carlson sketches the pious lives of several prominent female religious leaders, such as Anna Maria van Schurman, Antoinette Bourignon, and Elizabeth Strou-ven, who served their communities by providing medical services and poor relief much like their Roman Catholic counterparts in France. In fact, in the Dutch Reformed Church (called the Public Church by contemporaries) some women served as unofficial deaconesses in charge of supervising poor relief for their congregations. Yet, Joyce Goodfriend found that Dutch women in the New World principally expressed their piety in the domestic sphere. Carlson's female theologians, like Anna Maria van Schurman, and founders of religious sects, like Antoinette Bourignon, appear to be noticeably absent in the Dutch colony of New Netherland. In the New World "shrewd" female traders "routinely participated in the marketplace," but they did not play as prominent a role in the religious community or church as they had in the Netherlands. Goodfriend suggests that these women generally expressed their spirituality in the home by reading the Bible and devotional books, teaching children, attending church, and making charitable donations to the poor or contributing to the building or refurbishing of religious spaces.

Why did Dutch women in the Old World rise to positions of greater power than their New World counterparts? There are several possible explanations including denominational differences and the ability or inability to enforce social norms by the existing church or political institutions. Significantly, in Carlson's essay the most prominent female religious leaders or female religious communities were not directly associated with the Dutch Reformed Church. Outside of a few unofficial deaconesses of the Reformed Church, Carlson's female religious leaders were members or founders of pietistic sects, such as the Labadists, or they associated themselves with the Roman Catholic Church. It might be reasonable to assume that the ability to rise above the normal level of spirituality in the Old World, for the most part, may have rested on a woman's willingness to begin or join a minority sect. The lack of Dutch pietistic and Catholic sects in the New World might account for the corresponding lack in prominent female religious leaders and theologians. More importantly, perhaps the frontier environment allowed the Reformed Church and/or the state to enforce regulations against such behavior. It is quite possible that in the ethnically diverse colony of New York the threat of acculturation and the loss of Dutch customs may have produced a more conservative environment that limited women's access to power.

Of course, there were many similarities between the Dutch women in the Old and New Worlds. Religion was vital to both groups of women and they contributed to their chosen sects by teaching children and financially supporting their institutions. Additionally, Dutch women in both the Old and New Worlds were far more likely to be full church members than their male counterparts. Perhaps the majority of Dutch women who associated themselves with the Dutch Reformed Church in the Old and New Worlds focused their pious behavior in the domestic sphere, as Goodfriend describes.

Patricia Crawford's essay also explores how political and social disturbance can create opportunities for women. During the political and religious upheavals of the seventeenth century, English women from middling and wealthy families dedicated more of their time to pious devotion, and English Protestant, Puritan, and Roman Catholic women all shared patterns of piety, according to Crawford. They read devotional books, wrote diaries and spiritual autobiographies, financially and spiritually supported the clergy, participated in church in greater numbers than their male kin, "looked after the 'church stuff,'" instructed children, and provided relief to the poor. Whether Protestant, Puritan, or Roman Catholic, their piety brought their families "honor" and ensured the continuation of their sects. Additionally, personal piety not only provided women with consolation, but it served to justify their involvement in political protest and their choice to defy their own husbands. Crawford also points to the many differences between religious sects in early modern England. Roman Catholic women—like their counterparts in other countries—could opt to join a religious order on the continent or embark on a pilgrimage to holy shrines. Neither of these options was open to Protestant women. English Catholic women also differed from their Protestant counterparts in their attitudes toward the body. Catholics traditionally welcomed physical suffering (including fasting) as a sign of their piety, whereas Protestants did not embrace the Catholics' need for "pain, suffering, and sacrifice" for they were "uncomfortable with rituals of humiliation." Protestant women, according to Crawford, were far more interested in daily introspection and establishing a disciplined, godly family than embracing the Catholics' penchant for physical suffering.

Like Crawford, Sylvia Brown sees the authority gained by English Puritan women in New England as derived from their personal piety. Here too, personal piety both provided women with consolation and justified their involvement in the social and political arenas. Drawing on literary examples from both Old and New England, Brown complicates the assumptions of previous historians that the only "good" early modern woman was a silent woman, and consequently that a speaking or writing woman was, by definition, radical. She argues that orthodox Puritan culture used and approved of women's words—but only in specific circumstances and with qualifications. Her essay sets out the local contexts that determined when women's words were acceptable to the male religious establishment. Brown suggests that the important distinction was not between women's speech and women's writing, but rather between women whose words upheld the authority and the orthodox interpretation of Scripture, and women who circumvented authority and orthodoxy by invoking personal revelation. In other words, distinctions were made between "women of the Word" and "women of the Spirit." Puritans themselves had difficulty distinguishing between the two, as the trial of one transgressing "woman of the Spirit," Anne Hutchinson, shows. Even conservative Puritans acknowledged the necessity of a personal experience of grace, and of the Spirit's assistance in interpreting Scripture. Women like Hutchinson were therefore dangerous—not because they opposed the dominant religious culture, but because they revealed the inherently contradictory and potentially explosive assumptions upon which it was based.

Sylvia Brown also agrees with Patricia Crawford's argument that English women had a duty to "build up the number of the godly" by converting their ungodly husbands, teaching their children, and evangelizing to a wider audience by publishing pious literature. And while Crawford and Brown suggest that English women were often at the helm of pious and holy households (particularly when men were absent), Debra Meyers found significant differences between English Protestant and Roman Catholic household authority figures in Maryland. Drawing on seventeenth-century literature and the surviving last wills and testaments, Meyers explores the religiously heterogeneous population and discovers that English women of different faiths had distinct experiences within their churches, communities, and families. Women who accepted John Calvin's notion of predestination (Particular Baptists, Presbyterian, and Puritans) lived very different lives from their counterparts who did "good works" throughout their lives to gain eternal salvation. For these "Predestinarians" marriage was a patriarchal institution in which women were obedient to their husbands and held little or no power and authority in the family. Families that believed that any human could freely choose to have faith in God and begin to work toward gaining eternal salvation by doing good works (referred to as "Free Will Christians" in this essay) constructed very different family power structures. English Free Will Christians, such as the Arminian Anglicans, Quakers, and Roman Catholics, considered marriage a partnership and women held positions of authority both in the family, their churches, and the larger society.

Thus, Crawford, Brown, and Meyers suggest that for English women in both the Old and New Worlds membership in particular sects was often related to female members' views toward the body, access to opportunities to join religious orders, and the position women were allowed to hold within the family, their churches, and the society. Moreover, although nearly all of the English sects did not willingly permit women to debate theology or take on positions of authority in the church, women found ways to circumvent male dictates. Women in New England discussed and wrote about Scripture and theology provided they did not claim divine revelation, as the ill-fated Anne Hutchinson did. Wealthy Roman Catholic women, like Henrietta Maria Neale in Maryland, funded the building of chapels and maintained a prominent position within their Catholic communities. Additionally, pastors encouraged Protestant English women to keep spiritual diaries to chronicle their thoughts, prayers, and deeds. The diaries served as measures of spiritual growth as well as a place for contemplation and pious expression.

English Anglican, Puritan, and Catholic women shared many common forms of piety, but there were differences in spiritual expression between wealthy and poorer women within each faith. Not surprisingly, wealthier women had more time for prayer and acts of piety. More privileged women were also much more likely to be literate and thus were able to read Bibles and pious texts on their own. Overwhelmingly, our contributors emphasize the fact that economic status fundamentally informed their subjects' level of religious empowerment. The same class distinctions applied to Reformed Dutch women. Those of middling social ranks were generally literate, but the poor were not. Certainly, literate women whose faiths placed a high priority on reading the Bible would have access to more power and authority than their illiterate sisters would. Economic divisions were even more pronounced in Catholic nations where wealthy families were able to offer their daughters the option of entering a convent. Convent dowries, although considerably less than marriage dowries among the upper classes, were costly and varied according to the status of the convent. Poorer women, however, only had access to convents as lay sisters who were servants to the wealthier choir nuns. A life of religious devotion was the province of women from at least fairly privileged families as poor women in Catholic countries rarely had the opportunity to profess themselves to a life of spiritual pursuit. The vow of poverty that nuns took was definitely a right of the wealthy and not the poor.

Regardless of denomination or place of residence, social status determined the scope of religious experiences and defined to a large degree which "sacred spaces" men and women inhabited. Not only were there the obvious differences between what spaces women were allowed to occupy depending upon their statuses as nuns, *filles séculières,* or laywomen, but local cultures and personal initiatives further differentiated women's experiences. What made a space sacred for early modern women varied widely depending upon the woman's status within their religion, family, and community. As the essays indicate, individuals often determined and constructed sacred spaces. For instance, English and Dutch Catholic women created priest "holes" to hide clerics within their homes. They also transformed household rooms into sacred chapels for the celebration of illegal masses. Converting parts of a home into sacred space was not just the province of Catholic women. Protestant Reformed Dutch women decorated their homes with religious motifs in an effort to bring some of the Dutch Reformed Church into their private abodes. Kathryn Burns suggests that the nuns of Cuzco provide a counterexample as they reformed the parlor of their convent into a center for local banking and trade. With this action, the nuns transformed a private and sacred space into a public and commercial one. Clearly, women could deem spaces sacred when it suited their needs and could render them more secular, or at least more commercial, when they considered this more beneficial. Catholic and Protestant women created sacred spaces according to very different expectations but both undertook the same fundamental task. In both faiths there were places in which women determined the sanctity of a space; this was not determined for them by a church official or a familial patriarch.

Women not only created and dismantled sacred spaces, they also transcended them. This is most apparent in the cases of Catholic nuns and sisters. Members of female religious orders like the Spanish and Peruvian nuns mentioned above lived enclosed lives within a cloister. Formal church doctrine stated that nuns could not exit the convent gates. However, women did not systematically practice the restrictive enclosure that the Council of Trent demanded. Both male and female laypersons frequently visited the convents and it was not impossible for nuns to leave their cloisters for the outside world. As several of the essays demonstrate, convents and homes of religious congregations were important sites of exchange of people, money, and information. William Foster, for instance, argues that French Canadian convents were not exclusively female environments; rather, they were sites of education, poverty relief, and confinement. Within these religious communities men and women, European and Indian interacted under the authority of the mother superior. Perhaps the Daughters of Charity best demonstrate the malleability of *clausura*. The Daughters' liminal status as semi-religious and semisecular women left them with an unusual degree of freedom in the early modern world. The Daughters used this freedom to avoid enclosure and to work in the world as teachers and nurses while sharing temporary vows of poverty, chastity, and obedience. Catholic women were able to violate formal doctrines of enclosure because they were important actors in their local communities and their neighbors were dependent upon them for their services. Additionally, the bishops and priests of the Catholic Church were unwilling or unable to impose church doctrines upon all women religious since that would require them to live within the walls of a convent.

Men, as well as women, asserted their power when they created sacred spheres. Spaces were not uniformly sacred and church officials often divided and prioritized them. Spanish churches segregated women and children from men. Priests invited men to the front of the church to best experience the ceremony and the sacrament, and they left women and their potentially noisy offspring in the back of the church far removed from the miracle of the mass. In the New Netherlands, Reformed men also sat in a distinct part of the church separated from the women and children. Segregation was not only physical, but it was also more abstractly expressed. Marybeth Carlson explains that church officials encouraged women to join the Dutch Reformed Church in the Netherlands and New Amsterdam where they comprised the majority of members. However, once inside the Public Church, women had no voice in its affairs. Church officials commonly separated women from formal sites and avenues of church power by excluding them from positions of authority within the church. This should not, however, lead us to conclude that women were powerless in asserting control over sacred and secular realms.

In conclusion, while generalizations must be made carefully with particular attention paid to the varieties of experiences among women from diverse cultural backgrounds, this introduction has pointed to some important geographical and denominational differences and continuities in the lives of early modern women. Not surprisingly, women's choices and opportunities varied according to their race, denomination, and place of residence. Still, perhaps the most pivotal factor contributing to the variations in women's religious experiences was social status. Regardless of where a woman lived or what faith she professed, her economic and racial status largely determined her access to power and authority in her family, church, and society. As agents of historical change, both Protestant and Roman Catholic women frequently transcended their denominational or cultural restrictions and created meaningful spiritual lives. Early modern Protestant and Catholic women in the Old and New Worlds had access to religious power and often used this to redefine their roles in the church, family, and community.

NOTES

1. Joan Kelly-Gadol, "Did Women Have a Renaissance?" in *Becoming Visible: Women in European History*, ed. Renate Bridenthal, Claudia Koonz, and Susan Stuard (Boston, Mass.: Houghton Mifflin Company, 1987), 175–201.

2. Caroll Smith-Rosenberg, "The Female World of Love and Ritual," *Signs* 1, no. 1 (1975): 1–29; Bonnie Smith, *Ladies of the Leisure Class: The Bourgeoises of Northern France in the Nineteenth Century* (Princeton, N.J.: Princeton University Press, 1981).

3. Jo Ann McNamara, "Wives and Widows in Early Christian Thought," *International Journal of Women's Studies* 2 (1979): 575–92.

4. Peter Brown, *The Body and Society: Men, Women, and Sexual Renunciation in Early Christianity* (New York: Columbia University Press, 1988).

5. Caroline Walker Bynum, *Holy Feast and Holy Fast: The Religious Significance of Food to Medieval Women* (Berkeley, Calif.: University of California Press, 1987).

6. Natalie Zemon Davis, *The Return of Martin Guerre* (Cambridge, Mass.: Harvard University Press, 1983).

7. Natalie Zemon Davis, *Society and Culture in Early Modern France* (Stanford, Calif.: Stanford University Press, 1975).

8. Natalie Zemon Davis and Arlette Farge, *A History of Women in the West:*

Renaissance and Enlightenment Paradoxes (Cambridge, Mass.: Harvard University Press, 1993).

9. Merry Wiesner, "Beyond Women and the Family: Towards a Gender Analysis of the Reformation," *Sixteenth Century Journal* 18 (1987).

10. Natalie Zemon Davis, *Women on the Margins: Three Seventeenth-Century Lives* (Cambridge, Mass.: Harvard University Press, 1995); Merry Wiesner-Hanks, *Christianity and Sexuality in the Early Modern World: Regulating Desire, Reforming Practice* (New York: Routledge, 2000).

Spain
and the
New World

Redefining Expectations

Women and the Church in Early Modern Spain

Allyson M. Poska and Elizabeth A. Lehfeldt

EVEN DURING THE POLITICAL AND RELIGIOUS TURMOIL of the early modern period, a Spanish woman's religious experience was first and foremost determined by her own piety and the route(s) that she chose to manifest that piety. Despite the religious monopoly of the Catholic Church, Spanish women had many options when it came to expressing their religious devotion. A woman could live a good Christian life by conscientiously fulfilling her duties as wife, mother, and member of the parish. She attended mass, raised children, and did charitable works in her community, all of which accrued to her spiritual benefit. Women who felt the call of a religious vocation that transcended customary social and familial demands could enter one of the many female religious orders that proliferated in early modern Spain. There they could devote their lives to prayer and contemplation, employing their piety on behalf of those in need. Other women sought a more affective spirituality. They adopted the intense spiritual life of *beatas*, lay holy women who devoted their lives to prayer and charity outside of the confines of both marriage and convent.

In Spain's highly stratified society, not all of these options were available to all women. In particular, wealth determined how many of these options were open to any particular woman. Noble and upper-class women could use their wealth and power to enter the most exclusive convents. They could also influence the religious settings of their communities by founding monasteries, convents, and chapels. Even outside the convent, most expressions of piety required money, as funerary masses, charitable gifts, weddings, and baptisms all involved some expenditure. Thus, access to resources played an important role in a woman's choice of religious expression. For instance, many upper-class women may have had a limited portion of their families' wealth available for religious expression, as a result of the creation of entailed estates, known as *mayorazgos*. In families whose estates were entailed, one designated heir (usually a male) inherited the majority of the estate. However, only the most distinguished Spanish families were granted the right to *mayorazgos*. Spanish law required that the rest of the population distribute familial wealth using partible inheritance, in which each child, male and female alike, received an equal portion of the estate. Thus, even in the poorest families, a daughter received a fair allotment of family property that could be used for religious purposes if she so desired.

A woman's ability to use her wealth for religious activities also depended greatly on her marital status. Often, married women had only limited access to familial wealth. Legally a married woman maintained ownership over her dowry, her *arras* (a marital gift from husband to wife), and half of everything that the couple acquired during the marriage. Spanish law required that her property remain separate and that it could not be dissipated without her consent. However, the reality was that the woman's property became the couple's common property under her husband's control throughout the marriage, and she could not access her wealth without his permission. Unmarried women over twenty-five and widows had considerably more authority to dispose of themselves and their income as they saw fit. Many widows acquired considerable wealth during their marriages and they had almost complete freedom to administer it as they wished.[1]

Any examination of the interaction of Spanish women and the institutional church during the early modern period must also take into account the gender expectations articulated by the elites in Spanish society. Although we know that Spanish women actively engaged in a variety of pursuits from farming to writing novels, traditional gender norms still saw a woman's place as one of relative seclusion and silence. The advice of ecclesiastics and other moralists of the day instructed women to be chaste and obedient. As daughters, Spanish women were urged to avoid the dangers of the outside world. Families were instructed to keep careful watch over these young women, who were not supposed to leave the home unsupervised. While at home, they were to be schooled in those skills and behavior that would make them good wives. Juan Luis Vives (1492–1540), humanist and the author of one of the most influential behavioral guides for Spanish women, *The Education of a Christian Woman* (1524), urged women to look to the Virgin Mary for the model of chastity, silence, and obedience.[2] These words of advice were rooted in the culture's larger concerns about honor and female virginity. Particularly in the upper classes, families derived much of their sense of honor, identity, and respect from their ability to regulate the sexuality of their female members. Any threat to the integrity of a daughter's sexuality could result in diminished marriage prospects and a loss of social status for the entire family. Early modern moralists emphasized the discipline of obedience for Spanish wives. Advice manuals like Fray Luis de León's *La perfecta casada* (The Perfect Wife) (1583) emphasized a husband's authority and sought the creation of wives who were the perfect helpmates and whose work benefited the overall stability and prosperity of the household. Widows were a thorny category for moralists who urged them to protect their chastity and submit themselves to some form of male authority, either by remarrying or by entering a religious institution.

Underlying the advice of these and other early modern moralists was a fundamental mistrust of female nature. Women, considered the weaker and imperfect sex, were inconstant, gossipy, fickle, and sexually avaricious. While these men believed that their admonishments on behalf of the strict regulation of women would protect women from unwanted sexual advances and other threats, they also sought to protect women from themselves and men from women's lascivious and unpredictable nature. From their perspective, women's public manifestation of these dangerous and entirely unchristian traits created social disorder, and thus women required the constant supervision of men.[3]

LAY PIETY

Most women chose the life of a good Christian laywoman, using the traditional roles of wife and mother as the basis of their religious lives. Historians have long assumed that the Spanish Catholic Church, bolstered by the terrifying arm of the Inquisition, left Spanish laywomen cowed and submissive when it came to both social behaviors and religious expression. However, recent research has revealed the fluidity of the relationship between women and the Church. Even at the height of the Catholic Reformation in Spain, laywomen were integral in defining their own religious experience. Their piety was deeply influenced by traditional, extraecclesiastical modes of expression, as well as institutions that were both church-sanctioned and, in the wake of the Catholic Reformation, carefully regulated by clergy. The wide range of outlets for female devotion meant that women's religious activity was much more independent than historians have traditionally recognized. Yet at the same time, the dictates of local custom and class were determining factors in the types of religious expression that they chose.

Lay religious culture expected both communal and personal expressions of religiosity from women of all social classes. In terms of corporate, clerically regulated activity, laywomen throughout Spain devoted considerable time and energy to their work with parish confraternities. Confraternities were clerically sponsored, lay organizations around which most of the parish's charitable and festival activities revolved.[4] During the early modern period many laywomen belonged to at least one parish confraternity and in the urban areas many women belonged to two or more.[5] These groups might be either single-sex or mixed-sex. Unfortunately, the dearth of records makes it difficult to assess the degree to which women were allowed to take leadership roles in mixed-sex confraternities and to understand the role of the priest in all-female confraternities. Gender relations within these groups may have varied considerably from parish to parish and region to region. For instance, while there is evidence that women may have held offices in mixed-sex confraternities in some parts of Spain, in Catalonia they were not normally allowed to vote.[6]

Confraternities were typically centered on communal, charitable activities, like burial of the dead and care of the infirm in hospitals. In small parishes all the women in the town may have belonged to the parish's sole confraternity where they attended to the bodies of the deceased before burial, prepared the food for the extensive festival meals, and marched candle-in-hand in procession to the internment. In such activities women could fulfill their traditionally designated roles as caregivers in the broader community. As signs of both opulence and piety, wealthier laywomen in larger cities often chose to belong to more than one confraternity, each of which specialized in a certain charitable act or pertained to a specific occupation, either their own or that of their husbands. Whatever the case, as each confraternity was dedicated to the veneration of a specific religious doctrine or saint, they sponsored annual festivals and masses in honor of their patron. Thus, confraternal prayer and charity took on additional importance as post-Tridentine Catholic doctrine reasserted the necessity of both faith and good works for salvation. In addition to their role in community charity and group devotion, confraternal membership accrued benefits in both this life and the next. In this life, confraternities provided extensive opportunities for social and religious interaction among women as they probably used the gatherings to expand their commercial and emotional relationships. In the next life, those bonds remained intact, as in their testaments many women called upon the living members of their confraternities to join their funeral processions and say masses on their behalf after their deaths.

The Catholic Church extended its ability to regulate women's piety through its extensive program of lay education; however, the expansion of catechism classes also proved to be particularly beneficial to women. Although Spanish laywomen were largely illiterate, the injunction that women attend catechism classes meant that, for the first time, women had access to the same religious knowledge as men. The results were impressive. Sara Nalle has demonstrated that in Castile, as the result of extensive catechization, women learned their prayers just as well as men did. Moreover, although most of the time they learned from men, at least on occasion women relied on traditional female networks to improve their understanding of doctrine. In 1574 Quiteria Sainz, for example, offered to teach the Ten Commandments to her women friends. According to Nalle, women, both literate and illiterate, made significant gains in their ability to recite basic prayers by the middle of the seventeenth century.[7]

Beyond the expanded world of devotions promulgated by the Catholic Reformation, women found opportunities for religious expression in local culture and tradition. For instance, laywomen also expressed their piety through pilgrimages to the holy sites, *ermitas*, that existed throughout the peninsula. An *ermita* was often the site of a newly discovered image of a saint or the Virgin, or a natural wonder like a spring or odd shaped rock formation that was believed to have miraculous healing power. Some of these sites attracted visitors from throughout Christendom, and thus were ecclesiastically regulated and maintained by religious orders, like the shrine of Our Lady of Guadalupe in Extremadura. However, the Spanish countryside was filled with small, often poorly maintained *ermitas* supported by local confraternities, and still others existed beyond the scope of any official ecclesiastical recognition, cared for only by the regular flow of believers. Women frequented these local *ermitas* because of their accessibility, invoking the aid of the miraculous images for the cure of illness, help in childbearing, protection for loved ones, or to give thanks for saintly intervention. At the *ermita* women prayed, wept, and left offerings. When their requests for holy intervention were granted, they left ex-votos, small pictures of the miracle or replicas of healed body parts, in gratitude. In some cases, women also acted as the caretakers of these shrines, despite official disapproval of such activity.[8]

Although the Church supported and even encouraged female participation in confraternities and pilgrimages to shrines, the Catholic Reformation Church actually put forward contradictory regulations about religious activities as basic as female attendance at mass. On the one hand, the mandates of parish visitations formulaically urged everyone, man, woman, and child, to attend mass weekly. Therefore, even women whose families had preferred to adhere to the Mediterranean tradition of segregating them from society found an outlet in going to church. However, at least on occasion, those same Episcopal visitors exhorted women with small children to stay home, in order to decrease the interruptions of mass.[9] Toddlers running through the nave and babies crying disrupted the solemn atmosphere that the Catholic Reformation Church promoted in the parish church. As a result, many women were temporarily prevented from attaining the spiritual benefits of the Eucharist. Moreover, it was not always in keeping with local custom for women to attend mass regularly. According to Jean-Pierre Dedieu's study of New Castile, in at least one village in La Mancha, women did not attend mass except during Lent.[10]

One reason for ecclesiastical ambivalence about female attendance at religious services might have been that such occasions brought young men and women into regular contact. The parish church offered a prime opportunity for flirtations and even sexual rendezvous. Thus, the clergy felt duty bound to desexualize the site as much as was humanly possible. In reaction, Episcopal legislation demanded that women sit separately from men or sit behind male congregants, despite the fact that it left them situated farther from sacred sites and activities, like the altar and the Eucharist. Similar injunctions sought to thwart sexual interactions during pilgrimages and processions. Bishops attempted to limit the length of processions and the ability of participants to spend the night at the shrines.[11] The fact that those mandates were repeated so frequently indicates that many parishioners failed to respect the stricter sexual mores of the post-Tridentine Church.

The Catholic Reformation Church also attempted to redefine gender relations through renewed prohibitions on nonmarital sexual activity. The Catholic Church promulgated a variety of new or newly enforced regulations that forbade premarital sexual intercourse and the contraction of clandestine marriages. Despite the misogynist tone of the prescriptive literature on female sexuality, both before and during the Catholic Reformation, local toleration of nonmarital and premarital sexual activity varied greatly from region to region. For instance, well before the sixteenth century, the Mediterranean traditions of "honor and shame" frowned upon premarital intercourse, especially in the upper echelons of society. There, the Catholic Reformation injunctions against extramarital sex reinforced local traditions. However, in northern Spain, where local norms had never emphasized premarital virginity, illegitimacy rates remained high throughout the seventeenth century.[12] The effect of the prohibitions against clandestine marriage on Spanish women is also difficult to ascertain. Officially, the regulations were instituted as a means to protect women from seduction; however, these regulations also seriously constrained women's ability to maneuver around parental opposition to preferred marriage partners.

Finally, at the end of their lives, women expressed their piety through pious donations to charitable and religious organizations and sites, and the effect of the Catholic Reformation is evident in their decisions. Spanish women made wills as often as men, and through those records historians can see women making important religious decisions. Wealthy women founded chapels and left large donations to favorite monasteries and convents. Women of lesser means bequeathed cloth, food, and other goods to the poor. Most people also left money to pay for masses to be said on behalf of their souls or for the souls of relatives. Decisions about which church, *ermita*, chapel, or monastery in which to have those masses said and which saint to honor by having the masses said at the altar dedicated to him or her were the last expressions of personal piety that a woman made before leaving this life for the next.

FEMALE MONASTICISM

Entrance into a convent was the most typical expression of religiosity for Spanish women who felt called to a spiritual life that transcended customary lay expressions of piety. The major religious orders were all well represented in Spain. Benedictine and Cistercian foundations had dominated during the medieval period, but by the late Middle Ages the mendicant orders, especially the Franciscans and Dominicans, had also achieved a place of prominence. Fueled by the ethos of the Catholic Reformation, during the sixteenth century Spain saw the rise of various reformed religious orders, including reformed Franciscans and Discalced Carmelites, as well as the rise of new religious congregations like the Jesuits. Convents, like monasteries, had occupied a formidable place in the religious landscape of Spain since the early Middle Ages and provided important spiritual, social, and political services for Spanish society. As spiritual centers, convents performed a wide range of sacred and liturgical activities like the performance of the Divine Office. Nuns were also valued and revered for their proximity to the divine and the prayers that they could offer for those outside of convent walls. Additionally, convents were institutions that honored and protected the culturally esteemed practice of female chastity. To a society that expressed order and control through the regulation of female sexuality, convents were symbolically, as well as spiritually, significant.

Socially, convents were predominantly elite institutions that attracted the daughters and patronage of royalty, nobility, and the upper classes. Prestige and sanctity emanated from convents that could claim royal or noble founders and patrons. Families used endowments and gifts and their connections to religious houses as avenues for displaying their wealth and associating their family name with these revered institutions. These significant ties were reinforced when daughters and female relatives professed as nuns. Such professions reflected well on the piety of families and created for them a living link to the divine. The reformed orders of the sixteenth century sought to create institutions that did not cater exclusively to Spain's socially prominent. In reality, however, the convents of these orders quickly (perhaps out of financial necessity) began demanding dowries that were comparable to those commanded by older, socially prestigious houses.[13]

Despite their spiritual and social power, convents were subjected to intensified ecclesiastical and secular scrutiny and challenges during the early modern period. The call for reform was a constant refrain in the lives of Spain's convents. In the late fifteenth century the Spanish monarchs Ferdinand and Isabel initiated a period of church reform that targeted the abuses and corruption of all ranks of clergy, including convents.[14] The monarchs and their reformers singled out a series of abuses that they believed required immediate correction in female houses: divergence from the standards of communal life, neglect of liturgical duties, and a lack of strict enclosure. Such complaints exposed the reality of life in many late-medieval convents where individual nuns lived surrounded by the luxuries of secular life. They were attended by servants and had private receiving parlors. They dressed extravagantly and dined apart from the rest of the community. Reformers sought to restore communities to a discipline that abolished these differences of wealth and status and to reemphasize the communal nature of meals and other activities. Laxity within the convent walls also led reformers to work to correct the perception that nuns were neglecting their pious duties.

The lack of claustration in many of Spain's convents was the central concern of most early modern monastic reformers. The observance of enclosure as a monastic discipline was quite lax in Spain during the late Middle Ages; however, it was more often required of female than male monastics. Even before the Council of Trent (1545–1563), Ferdinand and Isabel's ecclesiastical visitors traveled throughout the peninsula demanding that nuns comply with basic standards of enclosure to distance themselves from the rest of society. Reformers sought a two-pronged approach to enclosure. First, they wanted to institute active enclosure, which completely prohibited nuns from leaving the cloister. They also sought the enforcement of passive enclosure, which regulated the access of outsiders to the cloister. Frequently, the reforms included instructions that the physical structure of the convent be altered to make the cloister as impenetrable as possible. Reforming clerics ordered doors locked and garden walls constructed. Abbesses were instructed to guard the keys to doors and windows. If male visitors (like confessors and doctors) had to enter the community, they were to be accompanied by a nun at all times. *Escuchaderas*, or listeners, were appointed to monitor conversations between nuns and laypeople in the visiting parlors of convents.

The convents almost uniformly resisted these and other demands of the reformers. Abbesses refused to let the visitors enter and blocked the path of bricklayers sent to make the various structural changes. Frequently they claimed that these demands ran counter to the customs and traditions of their communities. Appealing to the weight of precedent, convent officers argued that their standards of monastic observance were sufficiently rigorous and that their history as self-governing institutions made the imposition of these demands inappropriate. In addition, enclosure would have been a threat to the ability of convents to maintain their ties to secular supporters and to secure their financial stability by maintaining a visible place for themselves in the local economy. In their reactions and resistance to these measures, convents consistently appealed to their right to administer themselves autonomously with as little interference from the male ecclesiastical hierarchy as possible.

Significantly, Ferdinand and Isabel had anticipated the Tridentine Church's position on religious women. In a decree issued in one of its final sessions, the reformers at the Council of Trent demanded enclosure of all solemnly professed women. Yet, as was the case with earlier demands for claustration, the Tridentine decree was limited in its effectiveness. Enclosure was a malleable standard and convents frequently put reformers' definitions to the test, arguing for exceptions and modifications. For example, in 1596 the concerns of a local male ecclesiastic prompted an investigation of the observance of passive claustration at the Franciscan convent of Santa Isabel in Valladolid. An ecclesiastical panel concluded that Santa Isabel had not jeopardized its mission by allowing laypeople to enter its precincts and the community was given the right to allow both men and women to enter the convent buildings.[15]

Overall, the sixteenth-century spirit of church renewal and reform offered little to Spain's female monastics. While male religious companies dedicated to active service, like the Jesuits, flourished in the peninsula, religious women were increasingly defined by the discipline of claustration. For instance, when Isabel Roser, a prominent Barcelona patron of Ignatius of Loyola, approached the reformer and asked to take a vow of obedience to him in the hopes of imitating the Jesuit mission, he rebuffed her overtures and instead instructed her to enter a convent and dedicate herself to the world of contemplative monasticism. In fact, Spain witnessed no incursion of the female-led and active (at least in their inception) religious movements like the Ursulines and the Daughters of the Visitation.

The only female-led monastic movement of the period—that of Teresa of Avila's Discalced Carmelites—was in fact, fairly conservative in the goals it articulated for women dedicated to a religious calling. Though she would distinguish herself as a mystic and spiritually exceptional woman, Teresa's outline for female monasticism was relatively traditional. Emphasizing obedience and structure, her Discalced convents were defined by contemplative endeavors like prayer and the strictures of enclosure. Though aware of the church's active mission in this era, Teresa argued that she and her nuns would use prayer as a tool in the church's fight for spiritual dominance.[16]

Outside of the ecclesiastical hierarchy, Spanish society was much less concerned with issues of monastic discipline. Rather than separate themselves from monastic life, the laity devoted their attention to cultivating particular kinds of relationships with these institutions. The most customary way of expressing support for female monasticism was through patronage. Some patrons founded new convents; others endowed existing communities with generous annuities. Royal and noble families of the Middle Ages had set the precedent for the patronage of female monasticism. Some of Spain's most prestigious convents, like Santa María de las Huelgas in Burgos and Santa Clara de Tordesillas, could trace their inception to royal largesse. In the early modern era the Spanish nobility continued to make convents the beneficiaries of their charitable impulses. As Jodi Bilinkoff has demonstrated, the nobility of Avila, especially its female members, completely expanded the options for female religiosity by creating new houses.[17] This pattern was repeated throughout the peninsula in cities and towns like Barcelona, Toledo, and Valladolid. Though patronage was dependent on a certain amount of wealth, even citizens of more modest means made at least token donations to local convents.

What motivated these individuals in their support of female monasticism? Certainly, the "good work" of supporting a religious house was thought to foster a greater connection to the divine. Patrons could gain additional spiritual aid by requesting special prayers and masses in return for their financial support. However, beyond spiritual concerns, secular motives also informed lay patronage of monastic institutions. Making a foundation or endowing a side chapel in a convent church provided an excellent opportunity to make a statement about familial wealth and status. Founders of a convent might co-opt parts of the building's facade or entrance to display their heraldry. Patrons might request elaborate burials in a side chapel and then display their coat of arms on the sepulchers. At the convent she founded in Avila during the late fifteenth century, Doña María Dávila had her family coat of arms and those of her two husbands displayed on the main entrance and on her tomb sculpture.[18] Such bequests could substantially alter convent life. Diego de la Muela, a royal official during the reign of Isabel and Ferdinand, bequeathed to the nuns of the convent of Santa Isabel in Valladolid 3,000 maravedis for work on their church, 6,000 maravedis for the employment of a chaplain to perform masses in the chapel where he requested burial, and an additional 47,500 maravedis that could be used at the convent's discretion.[19]

In return, it seems that nuns provided important services to their lay benefactors. Although often cited by ecclesiastical authorities as a source of decadence and disruption, laypeople frequently relied upon nuns for spiritual solace and guidance. Family, friends, and the spiritually curious visited the nuns of convents to seek advice and comfort. There is also ample evidence to suggest that convents often served as places of retreat for secular women. These women lived in apartments within the cloister and sometimes paid "rent" to the convent. Further, it was customary within some convents for nuns to leave and stay with local laywomen experiencing a crisis like the death of a child. Even Teresa of Avila, though she resented the distraction it posed, was called upon numerous times to visit laywomen in need of spiritual guidance.

Although the demand for claustration pushed convents and nuns to occupy a less publicly visible place in Spanish society, support for female monasticism does not seem to have waned over the course of the early modern period. Despite the pressures of price inflation and a growing tax burden, the Spanish laity continued to found, lend support to, and place their daughters in convents. The prayers and liturgical activities of these women were still efficacious in the eyes of their contemporaries.

Patronage and the dowries of professed members of the religious community created sizable estates for many of these houses. Convents, especially those founded in the Middle Ages, controlled diverse patrimonies and collected a variety of incomes. Landed wealth—much of it devoted to the cultivation of cereal crops and vineyards—was the backbone of most estates. Yet convents might also rent urban property and be entitled to the income from a variety of private and public annuity contracts. Significantly, many older, wealthier convents also held seignorial titles to towns and villages. The convent of Les Puelles in Barcelona counted among its holdings income-producing mills, ovens, and markets. It also held large tracts of land that it cultivated and rented.[20]

It was chiefly the officers of these convents who administered these estates. In cases where convents held seignorial titles to towns, the abbess acted as "lord" and was entitled to the collection of various levies and the right to appoint local municipal officials. Santa María de las Huelgas of Valladolid, for example, had received the privilege of seignorial jurisdiction of the town of Zaratán from King Alfonso XI in 1335. The abbess of the house was thus recognized as the "lord" in both spiritual and temporal matters pertaining to the town. At a temporal level, the foundation was entitled to the collection of various seignorial dues. It also had the power to appoint appellate judicial administrators for cases not overseen by royal justice and the accompanying right to collect the fees levied in these trials. Spiritually, it oversaw the benefices of the Church of Zaratán and the chaplaincies of two additional foundations. In the early fifteenth century the foundation was required, like other feudal lords, to raise soldiers from the town of Zaratán for the king. The community also had the responsibility of collecting royal revenues like the *tercio* and the *millones* and then turning them over to the Crown.[21] In all of these matters the abbess of the house was pivotal—ultimate control rested in her hands. Curiously, these powers, although in the hands of religious women, were rarely challenged by secular contemporaries. Lawsuits erupted frequently between the convents and their lay subjects, but these disputes centered on perceived abuses of power, not the rights of religious women to exercise such authority.

A convent's commercial activities created opportunities for a number of members of the order to maintain regular contacts with the outside world. Officers of the convent oversaw day-to-day transactions and regulated the flow of the community's income. Stewards (*mayordomas*) and others kept account books and monitored finances. In addition, convents frequently gathered their members to witness the sale of property, the payment of money owed to the house, and other types of contracts. The language that the nuns used on these occasions suggests their cognizance of financial affairs as they called these meetings "to settle the estate and property of the monastery."[22] The convent of Santa Clara in

Valladolid followed this practice and expressed a similar ethos when it came together as a community to approve transactions like annuity contracts. Records of routine transactions like the sale of land or collection of an annuity payment stated: "we come together in the place where we usually meet to discuss and settle the matters and business that have relevance for this convent."[23]

In addition to providing the chance for administrative influence, the convent also created a few rare opportunities for female political activity. Due to their significant ties to the laity, women within convents often played critical roles in events that occurred beyond the cloister. For instance, the convent of the Descalzas Reales in Madrid was home to numerous political and diplomatic discussions during the reign of Philip III. A recent study by Magdalena Sánchez has revealed that while Philip's aunt, the Empress María, and her daughter, Margaret of the Cross, resided there, he consulted them on a variety of political and spiritual issues.[24] Philip IV also relied upon a nun, María de Agreda, for both spiritual and political advice. Their status as holy and pious women brought nuns into regular contact with powerful men and women, lent credence to their advice, and created an acceptable context within which to express political opinions.

Thus, despite the calls for reforms that sought to cloister Spanish nuns more strictly, the lives of these women and the institutions that housed them continued to intersect in significant ways with the secular world. While they clearly provided a site for spiritual devotion and protection for female chastity, throughout the sixteenth and seventeenth centuries convents were economically, socially, and politically active institutions. The cloister was, in fact, a permeable boundary.

OTHER FORMS OF SPIRITUAL ACTIVITIES

Some Spanish women felt a call to the religious life but chose to answer with a life of piety and service lived outside a monastic cloister. These holy women, or *beatas*, were similar to the *beguines* of northern Europe and the *pinzochere* of Italy. Though the lifestyle of the *beata* was frequently left to the interpretation of the woman herself, she typically took a vow of chastity and dedicated herself to a pious calling, sometimes purely contemplative, other times involving charitable service. Sometimes *beatas* lived together in small (usually unenclosed) communities and occasionally wore religious habits. They often took vows of celibacy and poverty in imitation of their cloistered counterparts. Their dedication to piety and their greater accessibility when compared to nuns living in convents attracted the attention of their

secular contemporaries who often appealed to them for spiritual guidance and advice. It was not unusual for the spiritual charisma of these
women to attract small, but enormously devoted followings.[25]

The careers of many *beatas* flourished in the first half of the sixteenth century due largely to the interest of Isabel I's former confessor,
Francisco Ximénez de Cisneros (1436–1517). In addition to overseeing
various monastic reform campaigns and founding numerous Franciscan houses for women, Cisneros also encouraged the careers of several
spiritually exceptional women. One of the first of these women to
attract Cisneros' attention was a peasant woman named María de Santo
Domingo from the region around Salamanca.[26] A Dominican tertiary,
she became known as the Beata of Piedrahíta and was renowned for her
mystical experiences and prophetic proclamations. Her followers
included King Ferdinand I of Aragon and the Duke of Alba.

Despite the encouragement of powerful figures like Cisneros, however, her religious career was suspect. To begin with, female visionaries
or mystics were always regarded suspiciously until they had proven the
divine, and not diabolical, origin of their experiences. Additional con-
troversies stemming from her uncloistered lifestyle threatened her
career. Her close contact with male Dominicans aroused particular suspicions of sexual impropriety. This type of charge or intimation was frequently leveled against charismatic holy women.

For a variety of reasons, however, María's appearance in a series of
trials from 1508 to 1510 questioning the validity of her work and
visions went smoothly. Certainly, her own charisma and piety aided
her cause. All three of her powerful patrons—Cisneros, Ferdinand I,
and the Duke of Alba—were drawn to her due to her pious mission
and her proximity to the divine. In addition, her visions were conducive to the designs of these patrons and the general religious and
political atmosphere of Spain during this period. She did not call for
rebellion or prophesy the downfall or ruin of the country and its leaders.[27] She also supported and participated in the reform of the religious
orders in Spain. In short, there was nothing in her visionary career that
threatened the existing order of things. As such, she emerged
unscathed, but was forced to enter a convent rather than continue her
very public career.

Another visionary woman whose career was enhanced by the
attention of Cisneros was the nun Juana de la Cruz (b. 1481). Juana's
profession as a member of the Franciscan order protected her and
provided some authoritative sanction to her mystical activity. In addition, she engaged in mystical activity that, although it attracted
attention, did not threaten the existing religious orthodoxy. She also

wisely distanced herself from those whose admiration might threaten her reputation. A Franciscan friar, for example, wrote her saying he was destined to be the father of a messiah and that he desired Juana to be the mother. She promptly turned him in to the proper authorities.[28] Notably, however, she was author of various written works that treated spiritual and religious subjects.

Certainly the most celebrated female mystic and spiritual figure in early modern Spain was Teresa of Avila. After having spent almost twenty years in a Carmelite convent known for only minimal disciplinary rigor, Teresa suddenly began having extraordinary mystical experiences. Visions, raptures, and spiritual ecstasies came to her more and more frequently. She felt called by these gifts to live a life of greater monastic observance (hence her foundation of a reformed branch of the Carmelite order). She also used these experiences as a platform from which to begin a life of spiritual exploration, which she shared with others by authoring several spiritual treatises. Suspicions about the orthodoxy and inspiration of her mystical life eventually drew the attention of the Inquisition. As such one of her confessors encouraged her to record her experiences. This push to write led to an extraordinary autobiographical testimony, making Teresa significant not only because of her interior life, but also because of her legacy as a female author. Ultimately, her spiritual experiences were judged entirely orthodox and she was canonized in 1622.

While the spiritual gifts of women like María de Santo Domingo, Juana de la Cruz, and Teresa of Avila were subjects of public and widespread renown, Spanish towns and villages customarily supported the careers of *beatas* whose reputation never grew beyond their local community. Women like Marina de Escobar in Valladolid and Juana Correa in Madrid were locally popular holy women whose spiritual works and charitable activity never transcended orthodox boundaries and whose proximity to the divine was valued by their contemporaries.

Despite, or perhaps because of, their relative popularity and even celebrity among their secular followers, *beatas* came under increasing scrutiny during the sixteenth century.[29] This was due, in part, to the exposure of several false *beatas* in this period. In 1546 Magdalena de la Cruz, abbess of a convent in Córdoba, confessed to having faked her spiritual gifts and experiences. This discovery created an atmosphere of greater suspicion. Teresa of Avila herself was mindful of the shadow cast on all visionary women by these "false" *beatas*. Various attempts were made to enclose *beatas* more strictly. By the seventeenth century some had even attracted the attention of the Inquisition as it prosecuted them for heresy and false religious experiences.

A number of pious laywomen were also caught up in the Inquisition's fervor to prosecute the *Alumbrado* heresy of the sixteenth century. The *Alumbrado* movement, or Illuminism, was as much a religious enthusiasm as a heresy. The movement drew its name from its participants who believed that they were "illuminated" by the Holy Spirit. Its origins lay in the circles of Franciscan mysticism and started in the area around Guadalajara in about 1512 under the leadership of a *beata* associated with the Franciscan order, Isabel de la Cruz. The heresy's emphasis on mysticism and other manifestations of intense, internal religiosity attracted followers from the highest levels of the Spanish Church during the early years of the sixteenth century. Isabel de la Cruz and her followers believed and taught the practice of *dejamiento,* or abandonment, in which they surrendered themselves to the love of God and had no need for the ceremonies or sacraments of the Church. They aimed at direct communication with God by means of inner purification. The first sect of *Alumbrados* was detected by the Spanish Inquisition in 1519. Their beliefs not only implied a rejection of key Catholic doctrine, but the group was particularly troublesome as it became associated with the leadership of vibrant, outspoken women who made direct contact with God through visions. According to Christian tradition, women were forbidden from preaching, and the actions of Isabel de la Cruz and other *alumbradas* came dangerously close to preaching.[30]

Another woman whose spirituality and activity brought her to the attention of the Inquisition was María de Cazalla.[31] Through her brothers, she had ties to the University of Alcalá and she had gained exposure to the works of both Erasmus and Luther. Unlike the women previously discussed, however, María was a married wife and mother. It was, in fact, the disapproval of her husband that probably sparked the initial suspicions. Angered at her neglect of household duties, he scolded her and moved the family to a nearby small town.

However, she continued to cultivate a spiritual life that privileged the belief that the performance of good work distorted the pure love that one ought to feel for God. Furthermore, she came to believe (like Erasmus) that marriage was more spiritually worthy than virginity. Her spirituality attracted a diverse following that included local housewives and teachers associated with the University of Alcalá. To all of them, she dispensed spiritual advice and biblical commentary. She was arrested by the Inquisition in 1534 and ultimately denounced for her beliefs and actions.

The Catholic Church distrusted the religious enthusiasm of women like María de Cazalla and Isabel de la Cruz as they defied the traditional gender order by asserting control over their own religious experiences. Moreover, because they interpreted their prophecies and offered spiritual guidance, their critics believed that female mystics subverted the traditional gender hierarchy by assuming spiritual authority over their male followers.

LAYWOMEN AND THE INQUISITION

Although most women's religious activity fell well within the parameters laid out by the Catholic Reformation Church, some women, through adherence to traditional practices or through unconventional expressions of religiosity, came into contract with the Inquisition. Overall, women were by far the minority of those brought before the Inquisition; however, for that reason alone, it must have been a much more frightening experience. The Inquisition, from its judges and jailers to its executioners, was an entirely male institution, and its structures were all premised on masculine notions of law and order. Typically, women came into contact with the Inquisition when charged with four categories of crimes: the *Alumbrado* heresy, heretical or false mystical activity (both of which we have already discussed), as witches, and for Judaizing or perpetuating Islamic beliefs or customs.

Despite its infamy, in terms of its overall prosecutions, the Spanish Inquisition revealed surprising skepticism when it came to witchcraft. Prosecutions for crimes involving superstition and witchcraft accounted for only 7.9 percent of the total number of cases between 1540 and 1700.[32] Moreover, the witchhunts that characterized much of early modern Europe were remarkably rare in Spain. Certainly, the early modern fear of female power manifested itself most assertively in the prosecution of Spanish women for love magic. Love magic is particularly interesting when it comes to gender since women tended to be both the purveyors of the magic and the petitioners. A woman who desired the attentions of a particular man sought out a sorceress whose magical incantations could allow her to manipulate him. Some women wanted fulfillment of unrequited love; others merely wanted to end abuse or adultery by their husbands. Whatever the circumstances, the Church viewed love magic as dangerous not only because of its blasphemous use of the names of saints and God, but also for its invocation of evil spirits and its infringement on the Catholic notion of free will.

When women were accused of Judaizing before Inquisitorial tribunals, the accusations were aimed at *conversas*, Jewish women who had converted to Christianity or who were members of families that had converted and centered on typically female, domestic activity. *Conversas* were regularly accused of cooking "Jewish" foods, trimming or washing meats according to Jewish law, and/or preparing clean clothing and linens for the Sabbath. They were often denounced by their own servants, with whom they had regular contact and who had either observed such activity or reported that they had been compelled to participate in such ceremonies. While many *conversas* confessed to their "crimes" in the hope of avoiding execution, at least one accused Judaizer, María López, argued that she had been falsely accused. She argued that, in fact, her suspicious laundry and food habits had been those of a conscientious, clean housewife, not those of a clandestine Jew.[33] For similar reasons, women were often the targets of the Inquisition's anti-Morisco activity. Custom dictated that Morisco women tended to live more segregated from Christian life, taught Muslim rituals to the children, and kept their households according to Koranic law.[34] Thus, they bore the brunt of anti-Morisco sentiment.[35]

Despite the misogynist tone of the Catholic prohibitions about sexuality and marriage, relatively few women faced charges before the Inquisition for such crimes. On charges of simple fornication (saying that sex between single people was not a sin), men outnumbered women three to one in the Tribunal of Galicia between 1550 and 1700.[36] Similarly, in Galicia male bigamists outnumbered their female counterparts by nearly six to one, and at the most made up one-quarter of the cases brought before the tribunals in the Kingdom of Aragon.[37]

Finally, as female homosexuality was not well understood by the ecclesiastical establishment, lesbians had few encounters with Inquisitors. In one case, in the mid-1650s, two women were denounced as lesbians to the Aragonese tribunal and were convicted. However, the Suprema also told the Saragossa tribunal not to prosecute another pair of accused lesbians, as they had not used an artificial phallus.[38]

In an era famous for its sexual repression, why did so few women face charges of sexual impropriety? The documentation is not clear, but it seems that women frequently received lighter sentences because legal theory consigned to them the status of children and, therefore, held them less accountable for their actions. In addition, despite the powerful rhetoric, at the local level more relaxed local norms about sexual behavior generally prevailed unless that behavior disrupted other social relations.

Conclusion

The range of spiritual expression available to Spanish women was clearly extensive; however, there were significant checks on the manifestations of female religiosity. To begin with, religious participation was frequently predicated on access to wealth. Religious dowries were sizable and probably a formidable obstacle in a woman's struggle to express her piety. Similarly, patronage required the availability of money and other resources like real estate. Though token donations might procure occasional prayers for one's soul, the standard measure of patronage was still a much greater and more generous show of largesse.

As a result of the Church's fiscal demands, expressions of religiosity were also dependent on social standing. Confraternities and pilgrimage to a shrine were options that were more readily available to a greater range of women. Convents remained largely elite institutions in this period. This may have, in fact, fueled the careers of uncloistered holy women. While it is probably safe to argue that some women chose the lifestyle of the *beata*, others were "pushed" into this religious vocation because convent life was not an option for them.

Finally, these women were never far removed from the watchful eye of the institutional Church and its male administrators. Laywomen, although allowed flexibility in their confraternal activity and devotion to *ermitas*, still had to adhere to the Church's definitions of appropriate female behavior at sacred sites. They were also occasionally constrained by the Church's position on legitimate sexual activity and marital unions. Even those women who dedicated themselves to the Church's ideals of piety and chastity were held to demanding standards of behavior. Increasingly strict codes of enclosure regulated nuns' bodies and curtailed their activity beyond the cloister. The Church only tolerated *beatas* as long as they espoused orthodox spirituality and did not presume to teach or preach. Finally, the existence of the Inquisition frequently influenced women's religious activity, as Inquisitors accused women of heterodox, magical, and heretical practices.

In spite of these constraints, religious piety not only reflected spiritual fervor, but also allowed women to engage in a broad range of activities that were unavailable to them in the political or intellectual spheres. It expanded their social, political, and intellectual possibilities. Whether learning their catechism, visiting shrines, taking monastic vows, living a life of uncloistered spiritual devotion, or interpreting mystical experiences, Spanish women took firm control of their piety.

NOTES

1. For more on women and Spanish law, see Eugene H. Korth, S. J. and Della Flusche, "Dowry and Inheritance in Colonial Spanish America: Peninsular Law and Chilean Practice," *The Americas* 43, no. 4 (1987): 395–410.
2. Juan Luis Vives, *The Education of a Christian Woman*, trans. and ed.

Charles Fantazzi (Chicago: University of Chicago Press, 2000).

3. For a thorough discussion of expectations for female behavior in early modern Spain, see Mary Elizabeth Perry, *Gender and Disorder in Early Modern Seville* (Princeton, N.J.: Princeton University Press, 1990).

4. For an extensive discussion of Spanish confraternities, see Maureen Flynn, *Sacred Charity: Confraternities and Social Welfare in Spain, 1400–1700* (Ithaca, N.Y.: Cornell University Press, 1989).

5. Sara T. Nalle, *God in La Mancha: Religious Reform and the People of Cuenca, 1500–1650* (Baltimore, Md.: Johns Hopkins University Press, 1992), 165.

6. Henry Kamen, *The Phoenix and the Flame: Catalonia and the Counter Reformation* (New Haven, Conn.: Yale University Press, 1993), 333.

7. Nalle, *God in La Mancha*, 126.

8. William A. Christian, Jr., *Local Religion in Sixteenth-Century Spain* (Princeton, N.J.: Princeton University Press, 1981), 171.

9. Allyson M. Poska, *Regulating the People: The Catholic Reformation in Seventeenth-Century Spain* (Leiden: E. J. Brill Publishers, 1998), 63.

10. J. P. Dedieu, "Christianization in New Castile. Catechism, Communion, Mass, and Confirmation in the Toledo Archbishopric, 1540–1650," in *Culture and Control in Counter-Reformation Spain*, ed. Anne J. Cruz and Mary Elizabeth Perry, Hispanic Issues, vol. 7 (Minneapolis: University of Minnesota Press, 1992), 21.

11. Christian, *Local Religion*, 164–65.

12. Poska, *Regulating the People*, 104–5.

13. For examinations of early modern female monasticism in Spain, see Elizabeth A. Lehfeldt, "Convents as Litigants: Dowry and Inheritance Disputes in Early Modern Spain," *Journal of Social History* (March 2000): 645–64 and "Discipline, Vocation, and Patronage: Spanish Religious Women in a Tridentine Micro-Climate," *Sixteenth Century Journal* 30, no. 4 (winter 1999): 1009–30; Jodi Bilinkoff, *The Avila of Saint Teresa: Religious Reform in a Sixteenth-Century City* (Ithaca, N.Y.: Cornell University Press, 1989).

14. For a full investigation of this campaign, see José García Oro, *Cisneros y la reforma del clero español en tiempo de los Reyes Católicos* (Madrid, CSIC 1971).

15. Lehfeldt, "Discipline, Vocation, and Patronage," 1017.

16. Jodi Bilinkoff, "Teresa of Jesus and Carmelite Reform," in *Religious Orders of the Catholic Reformation*, ed. Richard L. DeMolen (New York: Fordham University Press, 1994), 164–86. For more on Teresa of Avila, see Alison Weber, *Teresa of Avila and the Rhetoric of Femininity* (Princeton, N.J.: Princeton University Press, 1990), and Gillian T. W. Ahlgren, *Teresa of Avila and the Politics of Sanctity* (Ithaca, N.Y.: Cornell University Press, 1996).

17. Bilinkoff, *The Avila of Saint Teresa*, 15–52.

18. Ibid., 47.

19. Lehfeldt, "Convents as Litigants," 644.

20. Linda A. McMillin, "Sacred and Secular Politics: The Convent of Sant Pere de les Puelles in Thirteenth-Century Barcelona," in *Iberian and the Mediterranean World of the Middle Ages: Studies in Honor of Robert K. Burns, S. J.*, ed. Larry J. Simon (Leiden: E. J. Brill, 1995), 225–38.

21. Elizabeth A. Lehfeldt, "Sacred and Secular Spaces: Religious Women in Golden-Age Valladolid, Spain" (Ph.D. diss., Indiana University, 1996), 59–60.

22. Ibid., 53.

23. Ibid.

24. Magdalena S. Sánchez, *The Empress, the Queen, and the Nun. Women and Power at the Court of Philip III of Spain* (Baltimore, Md.: Johns Hopkins University Press, 1998).

25. A very useful introduction to the careers of several of these holy women is provided by Milagros Ortega Costa, "Spanish Women in the Reformation," in *Women in Reformation and Counter-Reformation Europe*, ed. Sherrin Marshall (Bloomington, Ind.: Indiana University Press, 1989), 89–119.

26. Jodi Bilinkoff, "A Spanish Prophetess and Her Patrons: The Case of María de Santo Domingo," *Sixteenth Century Journal* 23 (1992): 21–34.

27. Some female visionaries did level these types of social and political criticism in their visions. See, for example, the case of Lucrecia de León in Richard Kagan's *Lucrecia's Dreams: Politics and Prophecy in Sixteenth-Century Spain* (Berkeley, Calif.: University of California Press, 1990).

28. For a study of Juana de la Cruz, see Ronald Surtz, *The Guitar of God: Gender, Power, and Authority in the Visions of Mother Juana de la Cruz (1481–1534)* (Philadelphia: University of Pennsylvania Press, 1990).

29. Perry, *Gender*, 97–117.

30. For more on *Alumbrados*, see Alastair Hamilton, *Heresy and Mysticism in Sixteenth-Century Spain: The Alumbrados* (Toronto: University of Toronto Press, 1992).

31. The most comprehensive study of María de Cazalla is Milagros Ortega Costa, *Proceso de la Inquisición contra María de Cazalla* (Madrid: Fundación Universitaria Española, 1978). See also Angel Alcalá, "María de Cazalla: the Grievous Price of Victory," in *Women in the Inquisition: Spain and the New World*, ed. Mary E. Giles (Baltimore, Md.: Johns Hopkins University Press, 1999): 98–118.

32. Jaime Contreras and Gustav Henningsen, "Forty-four Thousand Cases of the Spanish Inquisition (1540–1700): Analysis of a Historical Data Bank," in *The Inquisition in Early Modern Europe*, ed. Gustav Henningsen and John Tedeschi (Dekalb, Ill.: Northern Illinois University Press, 1986), 114.

33. Gretchen Starr-LeBeau, "Marí Sánchez and Inés González: Conflict and

Cooperation among Crypto-Jews," in Giles, *Women in the Inquisition*, 19–41, and Reneé Levine Melammed, "María López. A Convicted Judaizer from Castile," ibid., 58–59.

34. William Monter, *Frontiers of Heresy: The Spanish Inquisition from the Basque Lands to Sicily* (Cambridge: Cambridge University Press, 1990), 227.

35. Mary Elizabeth Perry, "Behind the Veil: Moriscas and the Politics of Resistance and Survival," in *Spanish Women in the Golden Age*, ed. Magdalena Sánchez and Alain Saint-Saëns (Westport, Conn.: Greenwood Press, 1996), 37–53.

36. Jaime Contreras, *El Santo Oficio de la Inquisición en Galicia* (Madrid: Akal, 1982), 631.

37. Ibid., 648, and André Fernández, "The Repression of Sexual Behavior by the Aragonese Inquisition between 1560 and 1700," *Journal of the History of Sexuality* 7, no. 41 (1997), 487.

38. Monter, *Frontiers of Heresy*, 316–17 and 281–82.

Nuns, Kurakas, and Credit

The Spiritual Economy of Seventeenth-Century Cuzco

Kathryn Burns

To WRITE OF THE CONVENTS OF COLONIAL PERU, and eventually get to the question of what defines a colonial convent, I will start where uncloistered people start when approaching convents, with the *locutorio*. There, in the convent visiting parlor, cloistered women and their visitors confront one another before the bars of an obligatory *reja*, or grille, carefully designed to keep them out of touch.[1] I came to know these places well: the three colonial convents of Cuzco—Santa Clara, founded in the 1550s, and Santa Catalina and Santa Teresa, both founded in the 1600s—still exist, and my relationships to the nuns were made in the tenuous light and shadow of Cuzco's *locutorios*. Small, dark, and plain, the *locutorios* are undistinguished rooms save for the grille that is their central feature, and it makes a vivid first impression. Discipline is strikingly visible here, the separateness and discipline of the cloistered, contemplative life cast in strong bars.

Peru had many colonial convents, and a number of them are still running today. Yet the many chroniclers of Peru's colonial past barely mention the world of the *locutorio*. When they do it is to indulge in light speculation about local ways, like the custom among young men of paying visits to particular nuns, *devociones de monjas. Costumbristas* in a later, anticlerical time have sketched these scenes for us as quaint interludes of period skirt-chasing, the mere romancing of pretty young nuns. And historians, likewise rooted in nineteenth-century production values, have followed through by treating these as mere comic relief from the central action of Peru's colonial drama. Even convent elections for abbess or prioress—which might raise a citywide scandal—are handled lightly, as a curious piece of momentary general indulgence of feminine willfulness (or hysteria), devoid of stronger significance.[2]

I want to argue for a different claim about these places and scenes, their participants, and the meanings they enacted, moving convents to the center of the colonial stage. I am convinced the *locutorios* were among the busiest, most heavily trafficked places in the center of colonial Spanish American cities, and in this essay I hope to show why. Cuzco, the former "capital" of the Inca state and one of the Peruvian viceroyalty's largest and most important provincial cities, is a good place for this kind of inquiry: by the seventeenth century its convents and nuns were playing a leading role in the local economy, with cultural ramifications affecting a wide range of Andeans and Spaniards. The better to focus on action and contingency, I will use the notion of "spiritual economy" to organize some fast takes on the complex mutual engagement of spiritual and economic practices as these ran through, and were conjoined by, convents. I hope to show that *locutorios* were crucial sites of articulation of the economic and the spiritual—sites through which power and influence, men, women, and credit circulated at high velocity—and that ultimately this is all about the production and reproduction of a distinctly colonial society.

In short, I am reading the *reja* not as a barrier, but as a vivid representation of the nuns' and their ecclesiastical superiors' desire to separate the cloisters from the world. Certainly their rules mandated that the nuns do what they could to minimize contact with and attachment to the outside world; the Rule of Saint Augustine begins by cautioning the nuns to divest themselves of the kinds of assumptions that were utterly basic to the workings of colonial Cuzco (1677, 1r–1v):

> Do not be holders of property, but possess everything in common, and give to each in accordance with her need for food and clothing. . . . Those who in the world held possessions, on entering the monastery, should be pleased to share with the rest. Those who had nothing, let them not ask in the monastery after that which they could not have outside it. But let their needs be provided for. . . . Let them not be proud because they mingle with those who in the world they would not have dared to accompany.

Yet convents always participated in the world they called *el siglo*, the secular world, where time ran in mundane ways. For all their rules and their best efforts against the encroachment of the world and its concerns on their lives, convent communities reproduced themselves from the outside—by accepting, selectively, girls and women of colonial Cuzco—and so always and inevitably imported the concerns, the informal and formal precepts of *el siglo*. And this action was reciprocal: the nuns in turn shaped and reproduced those around them.

To trace the logic and the long-term consequences of these arrangements, I will begin by attending to the economic ground rules. Who might enter these communities, and on what terms? At the outset, an economic transaction marked each spiritual commitment: when somebody professed in a convent, in Cuzco as elsewhere, she brought a dowry. The dowry was made to sustain a nun in her spiritual marriage to Jesus, and because the holy brides were supposed to be on equal terms, dowry was fixed at a standard amount.[3] In Cuzco the amount required to profess as a *monja de velo negro*—a nun of the black veil, or "choir nun," with full participation in the convent's affairs—had been established by the early seventeenth century at just over 3,300 pesos.[4] While this was significantly lower than the largest temporal dowries, which might run to the tens of thousands of pesos, it was still a sizable amount. Right away we can glimpse an exclusion operating here: the overwhelming majority of Cuzco's women were the daughters of Andean tributaries who had to struggle to make tribute payments of single-digit amounts of pesos a year to their *kuraka*, or ethnic lord. Only someone whose family was well within the expanding Iberian-style market economy, and in a position of some command over land and indigenous labor (part of, or close to, the colonial ruling class), could hope for a dowry in the thousands of pesos. We will see that by the seventeenth century this mainly meant the locally born daughters of Spaniards, *criollas*.

But to stick to the matter at hand: nuns, like other married women, were required to relinquish control over the marriage portions they brought to sustain them in the observance of their chosen form of married life. Just as married women had to turn over the administration of their dowries to their husbands, nuns had to accept that they held no rights of *dominio* over their dowries. The convents did, and the powers of institutional decision making belonged to the abbess or prioress and her circle of advisors, the *madres de consejo*. The monastic rules and constitutions circumscribed these women's powers carefully. They were cautioned never to use the dowry fund to meet day-to-day operating expenses, but to treat it as a permanent fund for investment. Handled in this fashion, clearly the dowry mechanism would tend to make convents wealthier over time as succeeding generations of nuns professed— a trajectory that, as we will see, can be traced in the case of Cuzco's convents during the seventeenth century.

The acceptable forms of payment for the dowry were several, all derived from European precedent.[5] The dowry might be paid in cash, by imposing a lien (*imposición de censo*) on one's property in the amount of the dowry, or by donating a piece of property of sufficient value to cover the dowry amount. Given the notoriously cash-poor condition of the colonial Peruvian economy, which shipped much of its silver to Spain, it is not surprising that many families met the dowry requirement through liens, and some by ceding property to the convents, rather than pay the nuns thousands of pesos. However, cash does seem to have figured in many of these transactions. And in Cuzco, as in Europe, the convents had ready their *cajas de depósitos* with the prescribed three keys—one for the abbess, one for the nun acting as treasurer or *depositaria*, one for the *mayordomo*—to receive the cash that came their way.

These are some of the basic arrangements that underwrote the nuns' sustenance. Archival traces indicate that by the early seventeenth century Cuzco's first convents, Santa Clara and Santa Catalina, had already acquired considerable assets, largely by means of the dowry.[6] These included real property (urban and rural), mostly in and near the city of Cuzco, and money, for which the nuns had a well-defined investment policy. They aimed to place these assets where they would produce *rentas*—a secure annual return proportionate to the assets' value. In the case of real property this usually meant renting or leasing to local people. A few grain-producing *haciendas* and livestock ranches were administered more tightly to provide steady supplies of basics for nuns' sustenance, but the majority were contracted out in long-term arrangements.

As for the cash obtained from dowry payments, it too was to be deployed in the local economy in such a fashion as to generate an annual return. The founders of Santa Clara had specified at the convent's mid-sixteenth-century foundation that the dowries be invested rather than spent.[7] But disposing properly of cash was a matter fraught with difficulty. Thomas de Mercado, in the 1571 Seville edition of his popular manual *Summa de tratos y contratos de mercaderes*, paints a dire picture to forewarn those with money to invest against the most serious danger they are likely to face:

> No vice bears a greater likeness to the devil than this one. What is there more detestable and frightening for men to look upon than the devil? Yet there are few of us who do not usher him into our hearts a hundred times. (79)

The terrible, lurking evil he goes on to describe is one that today is all but forgotten, even by those in the business of forgiving sins. It is usury, which was defined in Mercado's time as lending at interest—any interest whatsoever, according to the most radical interpretations. Taking interest for a loan was considered completely immoral: "No sin is more vile (besides the abominable sin) than that of usury" (79).[8]

So lending at interest was condemned and prohibited in an Iberian-derived economy marked by abhorrence of usury. To be sure, people did lend each other money at interest (*a daño*), despite dire sermons and the risk of denunciation.[9] But this could hardly be the basis of a monastic house's finances. How then was it possible for nuns in Cuzco to become major lenders? The answer turns on a papally approved contractual mechanism called the *censo al quitar* (also known as *censo consignativo*). The key to understanding such *censos*, which abound in colonial notarial records, is to recognize that borrowers and lenders are transformed in a clever piece of scholastic science fiction: the convent figures not as the lender of a certain amount of pesos, but as the "buyer" of an annual income of a percentage of this amount, and the borrower thus figures as the "seller" of this right to an annual pension. To keep a long story short, this *censo* was a fairly recent European development which further allowed for "redemption" or cancellation via eventual repayment, thus making possible a credit system.[10] People did not have to repay at a fixed time, but could repay if they wanted at any time, and the money could then be lent out again to someone else.

Interest rates for these *censo* transactions were determined not by the nuns but by the Spanish crown, which under the terms of the Patronato Real had considerable authority over the church in its domains. During the sixteenth and early seventeenth century the rate set by the crown was 7.14 percent (expressed as *catorce mil el millar*); it was readjusted in the 1620s and throughout the rest of the colonial period remained at 5 percent (*veinte mil el millar*). This was probably a very attractive rate in the seventeenth century, to judge from the sparse evidence concerning prosecutions for usury. Individual lenders might charge upward of twice as much for lending out money.[11]

Not just anyone could participate in this economy; we need to bear in mind some more of its formal limits. Collateral had to be offered, and the acceptable collateral for these *censo* transactions was overwhelmingly of one kind: *bienes raíces*, real estate. The nuns of Cuzco made plain their preference for landowners—especially owners of rural estates—with property free of other obligations. Anyone without title to some piece of property in this economy could not expect to avail himself or herself of the *censo* as a means to credit.[12]

Exit from these credit arrangements was by one of two means. The recipient of credit (the "seller," in *censo* language, of an annual payment of 5 percent of the principal) might at any time repay the principal and cancel the arrangement. But if he or she fell far enough behind on annual payments (*réditos*), the borrower risked facing the messy alternative: the creditor might initiate legal proceedings against the property specified in the original *censo* bargain as collateral. The nuns had the right to do this after those to whom they had extended credit failed to make two years' worth of payments on their obligations. Even if a *censo* had been dutifully paid up for generations—even if the original amount had been repaid in *réditos* several times over—the nuns could still move against their *censuatarios* if they failed to make payments to the convent for a couple of years in a row. Whether the nuns acted or not was another matter. There might be a significant gap between the rules and actual practice, and what the nuns chose to do depended on a variety of factors, including the quality of the relationships they had with individual borrowers.

In Cuzco *censo* transactions were very extensive and the convents were in the thick of them.[13] Money was scarce, and no sooner was one *censo* paid off than a new borrower stepped up to the *locutorio* to ask to take the money out again. Amounts were usually in the 1,000 to 2,000 peso range, but a few of the largest *censos* obtained from convents in the seventeenth century were up in the 6,000 to 8,000 peso range. The bulk of these transactions do not specify how the money was to be used. But a few do, and these indicate that convent credit might be used to improve productive properties. For example, in 1696 Captain Andrés Arias Sotelo and his widowed mother Doña Agustina de la Borda contracted with Santa Clara to receive 8,000 pesos, offering as collateral their sugar-producing estates in the fertile Abancay region to the northwest of Cuzco, and declaring that they would use the money to install cane-crushing equipment and fix irrigation channels.[14] The following month Don Diego Almonasi and his wife Doña Catalina Alvarez arranged a *censo* of 2,000 pesos from Santa Clara in order to expand their *chorrillo* or urban textile-manufacturing workshop.[15] By making credit available, the nuns were assisting the growth of some of the region's leading productive sectors: during the seventeenth century both sugar and cloth were becoming major regional exports to the markets of Potosí.

Convents were not the only lenders in town; there were institutional alternatives. Unfortunately, there is little research to go on, and we will need to know a good deal more before it is possible to establish even roughly the convents' piece of the credit "pie." But it appears from notarial records that in the seventeenth century ecclesiastical lenders became the major source of credit in the regional economy of colonial Cuzco. This provincial city, midway between the coastal empo-rium of Lima and the blasted mining center of Potosí, had no mint, no merchant guild (*consulado*), and by the seventeenth century its *caja de censos de indios* had been tapped out.[16] What it did have in abun-dance was Catholic institutions—convents, monasteries, a cathedral chapter, parishes, confraternities—all of whom relied to some extent on lending funds by means of the *censo* mechanism to generate income. And by the seventeenth century, the convents seem to have had the most to lend. The annual income of Santa Clara increased strikingly in the course of the seventeenth century as successive generations of nuns professed:

YEAR	INCOME	CENSO INCOME
		(*as percentage of total*)
1602	5,191 pesos	2,230 pesos (43%)
1650 (ca.)	31,000 (est.)	
1690	24,000	17,900 (75%)

In the wake of the severe 1650 earthquake Santa Clara's income fell sharply—to only 10,000 pesos a year, by one account—and had not yet recovered by 1690, when it stood at around 24,000 pesos. Still, the nuns were taking in 17,900 pesos' worth of *censo* payments in that year.[17] A 1684 list of contracts payable to the nuns of Santa Catalina—most apparently *censos al quitar*—contains 166 separate entries, totaling over 297,433 pesos in principal; if the nuns managed to collect on these at the standard 5 percent, then they took in over 14,870 pesos that year.[18] By comparison, the monastery of San Agustín, perhaps the richest of the men's monastic houses, was collecting 11,116 pesos' worth of *censo* payments on seventy-eight separate obligations in the year 1676.[19]

Convents also provided what at the expense of some crude anachro-nism might be called spiritual "goods": prayers offered for the salvation of Christians' souls. Christian *cuzqueños* believed not only in heaven and hell, but in that ample middle ground of the afterlife, purgatory, and that the time one's soul spent in purgatory before making its way to heaven could be shortened by means of prayers offered on earth. While prayers did not have an exact price tag, it is possible to see them being purchased by *cuzqueños* through a very common and widespread contractual arrangement known as the *capellanía*—another transplanted Catholic institution with deep roots in medieval European practice. These endowed chaplaincies helped sustain many male clerics of the city. Cuzco's cloistered convents as well as its monasteries managed a certain portion of these funds too, investing them in the local economy to generate income in the same fashion as the dowries, and using the proceeds to pay priests to say the requisite number of masses for the souls of the dead.

The nuns' prayers were not purchased in this relatively direct way. Yet they no doubt played a precious part in this economy of spiritual assistance. Some hint of this may, I think, be gleaned from a Franciscan hagiography written in the mid-seventeenth-century Andes, in which the contrast between an opulent, Babylonian Cuzco of easy riches and the extreme austerity, rigor, and self-abnegation of individual nuns of Santa Clara is sharply, indelibly drawn. One after another, exemplary Clares are portrayed by the Franciscan chronicler Diego de Mendoza as having sought extreme ways of humbling themselves and attaining utter indifference toward the world's riches.[20] And the author's respect and esteem for them obviously increases in direct proportion to the lengths to which they were able to go (often, it seems, to the extreme detriment of their bodily health). The lower, the more humble, detached, and self-abasing a nun became, the higher her spiritual attainments, the purer and more beautiful her spirit. Though none of these women were canonized, their lives call to mind that of their near-contemporary, Santa Rosa de Lima. It is easy to imagine that the prayers of such women would have been valued by Christian *cuzqueños* as among the most efficacious of all.

Hence the set of relations I am glossing as the "spiritual economy," the inextricable engagement of spiritual and economic interests to which I referred at the outset. Credit was essential for economic activity in an Andean regional economy that by the seventeenth century had been made over to suit the designs of Spaniards and criollos. And to members of this hegemonic elite sincere prayers were also essential, for the eternal salvation of their souls and those of their forebearers, and they were willing to go to great expense to be vouchsafed this spiritual remedy, endowing countless chaplaincies for the regular saying of prayers to speed their souls' progress toward heavenly rewards. By frequenting the *locutorios* of Santa Clara, Santa Catalina, and Santa Teresa, propertied *cuzqueños* could satisfy several needs at once. By turning to the convents for credit, they were supporting not only themselves but the nuns whose prayers went up for the good of their souls.

To this point we have been able to trace lines from convents out into the regional economy, via dowry and then the *censo*. Dowry, I have argued, was a crucial resource not only for convents to maintain themselves but for those in their vicinity needing credit. Now I propose to look the other direction, and consider why local families sent their daughters to the convents. As we have noted, this move implied an economic obligation: the dowry paid on behalf of each nun was the sign of her spiritual marriage to Jesus. We know that marriage alliances in general were carefully struck by elites and would-be elites. Convents have often been seen by historians as a kind of fallback option for elites, an honorable way out for families with too many daughters or too little cash for advantageous marriages.[21] But I will argue that we need to turn this around, and to consider that families might actually be seeking (and gaining) something from the spiritual marriage of their daughters.

Without ruling out the role of individual piety and free will in individual women's professions (decisions about which, unfortunately, there are few archival traces), we can still see how, from several angles, it made good sense for elite families, via their daughters, to marry convents. The spiritual benefits were obvious: a daughter or kinswoman in the convent would constantly offer prayers for the salvation of her extended family. And the material benefits might be substantial, too. As we have seen, the convents were in the business of providing credit from their dowry funds, and having one's daughter in the convent no doubt increased one's chances of competing successfully for a portion of the available loans. In addition, should one's daughter gain position among the convents' leaders, as abbess or prioress or member of the advisory council, she might control the distribution of tens or hundreds of thousands of pesos among Cuzco's prospective borrowers. And for those unable to meet *censo* payments she might, in several senses, intercede and obtain grace.

Now we are in a position to see just how much might be at stake in the *locutorio*. Thus far I have been suggesting we adjust our view of colonial Cuzco, and arguably colonial Peru, more generally to see convents and to see *cuzqueños* in and around them busily making careful investments of time, energy, and money in the *locutorios*, where the permeable grille made it possible for the cloistered and the secular to shape and reproduce each other. Yet up to this point we could be describing a European context: the basic mechanisms that enabled the convents to accumulate and control resources, and underwrote the spiritual economy of Cuzco, are recognizably the same ones that sustained the monastic houses of western European nuns.[22] Across sixteenth- and seventeenth-century Iberia, the *censo al quitar* was making rapid headway as the preferred investment strategy of ecclesiastical (and other) lenders, and nuns were placing dowry funds in this fashion. Through such dealings Iberian convents were participating actively in the fusion and reproduction of economic and spiritual interests in much the same way I have described for Cuzco. In a broad sense, then, Cuzco's convents and nuns behaved in the same ways and achieved the same results as nuns in Iberian and other European contexts: they helped to create and perpetuate the power of local elites.

In Cuzco there is more to this picture, however, and by examining in some detail the historical context we can see how, through the workings of the spiritual economy, the nuns of Cuzco played a leading role in the making of a distinctly colonial elite. If we could peer into the seventeenth-century *locutorios*, who would we see at the grille? What sorts of *cuzqueños* could offer the nuns a piece of real estate as collateral in order to receive the principal of a *censo?* What did local property holders use the nuns' money for? And in what ways did these dealings create and reproduce distinctly colonial relations?

Because documentation is scarce the picture must necessarily remain somewhat blurry, but available records indicate that the *cuzqueños* who engaged in conversation and business deals inside the *locutorios* were, on both sides of the grille, mostly Spaniards and their criollo descendents—in other words, people locally considered "Spanish," and also "white."[23] On the cloistered side of the grille, the women who no doubt appeared most frequently were those in high decision-making capacities, the abbesses, prioresses, and *madres de consejo*; and those whose family histories I have been able to trace were overwhelmingly criollas. Every three years the top position (abbess, in the case of Santa Clara; prioress, in Santa Catalina and Santa Teresa) changed hands through convent elections, as prescribed by the monastic rules and constitutions. This meant turnover was a built-in feature of high office. Yet in the archives the same women appear over in over at the highest level of convent affairs, illustrating that turnover was actually very limited. Abbesses and prioresses could not succeed themselves, but could be reelected after three years, and since there was no limit on the number of terms they could serve some nuns held the office several times in their cloistered lives. Because it was customary for nuns to serve as *madres de consejo* after stepping down from the convent's highest position, a former abbess or prioress might remain powerful in convent affairs for decades. In short, the convents' top decision-making body was comprised of a relatively stable cast of women.

Certain family names—Costilla, Peralta, Esquivel, and a handful of others—appear over and over at this level of convent affairs. The Costilla women had an especially durable influence inside Santa Clara, Cuzco's oldest convent and the wealthiest in the seventeenth century. Lucía Costilla de Umarán appears frequently as a *madre de consejo* from 1621 to 1655. While never abbess (as far as I can tell), she was always close to power as a *madre de consejo*, and thus an active participant in loan approvals and other business decisions. In later years her cousin Constanza Viviana Costilla played a similarly prominent role as abbess for at least two terms (1660–63, 1672–75) and a *madre de consejo* for decades. The Costilla hold on high office in Santa Clara lasted well into the subsequent century.[24] But the Costilla influence in the convent's affairs looks almost subtle by comparison with that of the tireless Esquivel sisters. The record-holder for repeat performances as abbess of Santa Clara, Magdalena de Esquivel y Xarava, served five terms between 1740 and 1773. When she was not abbess her sister usually was: Bernarda de Esquivel served three times during the same period. Between them, these two held Santa Clara's highest office for all but nine of these thirty-three years, and when they were not abbesses they were *madres de consejo*.

These women's families prospered remarkably during these decades, receiving generous infusions of convent funds to power their rise to the heights of local wealth and influence. It must have been a fairly common occurence for members of the same criollo extended family to sit down with each other on opposite sides of the grille to work out the terms of a profession or a *censo al quitar*. The elite families' spiritual relations with the nuns are less visible, but we know that the Costillas had a burial chapel in the church of Santa Clara. Going to mass there must have been a regular feature of the Costillas' lives. And they cultivated good relations with the nuns in any number of little ways. For example, Don Pablo Costilla Gallinato lent his sister Doña Constanza, the abbess of Santa Clara, a diamond-encrusted ring so that she might adorn his daughter Doña Juana Rosa resplendently "for a fiesta" inside the convent.[25] Such entertainments were strictly prohibited but clearly went on anyway. It is worth emphasizing that economic and spiritual motivations are indissociable here, blended in this familial gesture. Don Pablo's actions cannot be read simply as one or the other, yet such favors were highly efficacious in both economic and spiritual terms.

Outside the convents, the Costillas, Peraltas, and Esquiveles were every bit as active and authoritative as they were inside. A variety of circumstances facilitated the emergence of this homegrown aristocracy in the Andes (and elsewhere in Spanish America) by the turn of the seventeenth century. Demographic disaster and brutal labor drafts had drastically undermined Andean resistances to colonial exploitation, and would continue to do so for decades. The Spanish crown was in desperate straits, willing to let local elites do almost anything, purchase almost any office, as long as they would pay for it, and Pablo Costilla, Diego de Esquivel, Pedro de Peralta, and others like them took advantage of this conjuncture. Through elaborate strategies of intermarriage

(which required papal dispensations at times, when the degree of kinship was too close), they became each other's blood relatives and godparents. They bought land, and shoved and finagled their way into
more; they bought permanent rights to membership on Cuzco's town
council; they bought enslaved Africans to do much of their business,
from dressing them to pushing people off their land; they endowed
chaplaincies, commissioned colorful religious canvasses, and became
godparents at the drop of a hat. They also took advantage of the crown's
financial plight to buy their way into titled nobility, whereupon the
Costillas became Marqueses de Buenavista, the Esquiveles became Marqueses de Valleumbroso, and the Peraltas became Condes de la Laguna
de Chanchacalle.[26]

Over the years, while building impressive holdings and intimidat-
ing local reputations, these families sent a steady stream of daughters to
Cuzco's convents. They went both to be educated by their cloistered
female relatives and to become nuns of the black veil themselves. Just
after the turn of the eighteenth century, in 1708, the two heirs of Don
Pedro de Peralta, the first Conde de la Laguna de Chanchacalle—a
brother and sister, Don Diego and Doña Petronila de Peralta—made a
contractual division of their inheritance on the occasion of Doña
Petronila's entrance into the cloisters of Santa Catalina.[27] This example
indicates that in the best of times, a well-to-do family might send
daughters to the convent—even an only daughter. The Peralta case suggests a different logic than the one we have been accustomed to see in
elite families' relations with convents. The cloistered life did not merely
represent an absence of better alternatives for their daughters, an escape
hatch when times were hard and marriage dowries high.

Yet the convents were that too. Good relations with the nuns could
lead to a much-needed break on *censo* payment terms in times of hardship. In fact, from the convents' papers it is possible to see just how
thoroughly indebted to Cuzco's convents certain elite local families
became by the close of the seventeenth century. By 1707 the estate of
Don Diego de Esquivel, the second Marqués de Valleumbroso, had
accumulated some 25,000 pesos' worth of principal from Santa Clara
and just over 28,700 pesos from Santa Catalina. The Marqués was not
punctual with his payments: on January 3, 1707, he gave the abbess of
Santa Clara over 8,300 pesos to make up for more than six years of non-
payment.[28] Such irregularity must have made it difficult for the nuns to
arrange their finances, since a year in which the erratic Marqués failed
to pay meant a year in which Santa Clara had to do without 1,255 pesos
of income or find them elsewhere. Yet barely over a year later the Marqués was back in the same *locutorio* taking out an additional 8,500

pesos.[29] As for Santa Catalina, the nuns, after struggling to collect from the heirs of the same Marqués, went so far as to write off 8,000 pesos of unpaid *réditos* in 1733. Five decades later, in the 1780s, the nuns would calculate that the family still owed nearly 83,000 pesos of back payments, an immense sum at that time. The Condes de la Laguna were not any better. Still, the tightly knit web of kinship and local power and influence kept the convents and these families intimately connected; the families' daughters and kin were, after all, overseeing the convents' decisions. And these densely interrelated clans were, after all, the biggest landowners around.

If elite white *cuzqueños* held leading parts in the action inside convents' *locutorios*, they were not the only ones carefully investing their time and energies there. On the way to and from the grille, an Esquivel or a Costilla might have exchanged greetings with someone like Don Andrés Tecse Amau Inca, a master silversmith and *principal*, or leader, of his kinsmen in one of Cuzco's eight "Indian" parishes, San Sebastián. In early 1697 Don Andrés and his wife Doña María Suta Asa learned that someone had just cancelled a *censo* by paying the nuns of Santa Clara the principal of 1,656 pesos 2 reales, and they quickly moved to take the money out themselves, which they did in a *censo* bargain dated March 5, 1697.[30] As collateral they offered the house they possessed in the city's center as well as the house, cornfields, and orchards they owned in San Sebastián. The contract further reflects that this was not the couple's first trip to a *locutorio*. Their properties already bore a previous *censo* obligation in the amount of 2,000 pesos in favor of the nuns of Santa Catalina.

The case of Don Andrés points to a distinctive feature of Cuzco's colonial elite: it was in a crucial sense double, divided, with a special, subordinate role preserved for the descendents of those who had once been the region's elite: the Incas. Under the Inca state, control over Andean resources and labor had been effected through a far-flung network of ethnic lords, or *kurakas*, with local authority over kinship groups. The Spanish colonial regime had from the beginning sought not to eradicate but to control this highly effective structure of indirect rule, the better to gain access to Andean tribute goods and labor power. And *indios nobles*—a combination of elite Incas and *kurakas* (only some of whom were ethnic Incas)—did remain a vital, indispensable part of Cuzco's elite after the Spanish conquest. They were the linchpin of the colonial system, a "double-edged sword," obliged to deliver their communities' labor and tribute resources to local whites, but also in a position to protect their kin (to some extent) from Spaniards' and criollos' spiritual and material demands.[31]

Men like Don Andrés thus spent their lives moving back and forth: between Cuzco's "Spanish" center and the "Indian" parishes that ringed it; between Spanish and Quechua; between the nuns of Santa Clara and the *ayllus*, or kin groups, that gave structure to life in places like San Sebastián. They gained certain privileges under Spanish colonialism even as its workings gradually impoverished their communities. The textures of their hybridized lives and the bargains they struck must necessarily remain somewhat obscure.[32] In any case, it is clear that local criollos like the Costillas, Esquiveles, and Peraltas relied on men like Don Andrés to obtain labor power, cooperation, tribute. And as long as the Don Andréses of Cuzco had enough of a stake in the colonial system to consent to their critical, contradictory role in it, an unsteady, off-center "Spanish" hegemony could survive in the Andean highlands.[33]

By attending to the goings-on in Cuzco's *locutorios*, we can see that the spiritual economy engaged local *kurakas* and *principales* as well as criollos. As long as they were prepared to offer property as collateral, members of the Andean elite might receive convent credit through the *censo* mechanism, and regularly did, although the amounts were usually modest (in the hundreds rather than thousands of pesos). What did they use this credit for? The evidence is very thin, but a notarial record of 1746 offers significant insight into *kurakas'* difficult position under colonial rule. In that year Don Tomás Thopa Orcoguaranca, the *kuraka* of Guayllabamba in nearby Yucay, sought and obtained 500 pesos in a *censo* transaction from the nuns of Santa Teresa to pay back tribute owed to his *corregidor* (the highest local representative of the Spanish state in his province), who had threatened to embargo his and his wife's assets and imprison him if he did not deliver.[34] No further details are provided, but Don Tomás's predicament can be imagined: he might defy the *corregidor* (and land in jail), force his community to come up with the unpaid sum (and risk straining his ties to his kinsmen), or go into debt himself. When pressed too hard, communities might resist their *kurakas*. Under pressure from the colonial authorities, and perhaps afraid of this kind of outcome, Don Tomás approached the *locutorio* instead, and the nuns came through.

The symbiosis of convents and local elites was proved and renewed once again, keeping an elite family afloat and colonial relations working. Just as a Costilla might get out of trouble by special pleading in the *locutorios* of Cuzco, a Thopa Orcoguaranca might, too—and for the same reason: carefully cultivated relations with the nuns sealed by the professions of elite young women. In 1743, three years prior to the run-in of Don Tomás Thopa Orcoguaranca and the *corregidor*, the daughter of

Don Alejo Thopa Orcoguaranca Lan de Bisnay—an *indio principal* of Guayllabamba, and doubtless a close relative of Don Tomás—had been received as a nun in Santa Clara.[35] In all likelihood, the nuns of Cuzco's convents had seen Thopa Orcoguarancas in their visitors' parlors before and felt comfortable helping them out in a pinch.

Many daughters of Cuzco's Andean elite likewise professed and lived out their lives in the cloisters, women with such family names as Atau Yupanqui, Guamán Cusitopa, Quispe Guamán, Sinchi Roca, Guampu Tupa, Tecce, Tamboguaso. The daughters of Cuzco's *kurakas* and *principales* also made deals in the visitors' parlor, transacted in Quechua and duly registered in Spanish by means of an interpreter. They sold land, sold houses, and lent money, frequently to people who appear to have been criollos.[36] And like many of the elite criollas inside the convents, the Andean nuns might even be attended by slaves. This much is indicated by the widow María Panti's 1642 donation to her cloistered granddaughter in Santa Clara of the services of two Afro-Peruvian slaves, one an adolescent tailor named Gaspar, the other his two-and-a-half-year-old sister Isabel (Gaspar to work outside the convent and send the nun his earnings; Isabel to be raised inside Santa Clara to become her personal attendant).[37] Many of the Andean nuns were certainly far from poor.

However, the criolla nuns kept the daughters of Andean elites out of the highest level of convent affairs. The record makes clear that, with very few exceptions, daughters of *kurakas* and *principales* were permitted to profess only as nuns of the white veil (permanent wearers of the veil that marked a novice or servant)—a boundary fixer signifying a kind of second-class status.[38] Since the sixteenth-century foundation of Santa Clara, Cuzco's Spanish and criolla nuns had used the color of nuns' veils to enforce boundaries and construct differences inside the cloisters, originally between "pure-blooded" (and probably legitimate) Spanish women and the illegitimate mestiza daughters of Spanish conquerors and Andean women. In doing so they were both relying on their monastic constitutions and forging a new interpretation of them.[39]

In time, legitimacy was dropped as a requirement for becoming a nun of the highest rank where high-born criollas were concerned. A rift among the nuns of Santa Catalina in 1644 is revealing. In that year Doña Mencía de San Bernardo, the natural daughter of a local nobleman, was elected prioress, to the consternation of runner-up Doña Juana de los Remedios. Doña Juana quickly contested the result, accusing Doña Mencía of wielding family connections to get around the fact that she was an "unqualified and incapable person on account of not being legitimate, born of a legitimate marriage." And Doña Juana and her followers went further, saying that "the majority of the votes Doña Mencía received were likewise those of illegitimate persons who manifested their support with a view to when their turn might come, which is sufficient cause to annul said votes as a form of simony. . . ."[40] They accused Doña Mencía of making bribes and promises to secure votes in the election, and of holding certain entertainments (*músicas y saraos*) in the convent to court the vote. But the ecclesiastical authorities backed Doña Mencía's representatives, who argued that her alleged impediment of illegitimacy was "easily overcome" by her noble lineage. Other records show the convents accepted quite a number of women like Doña Mencía as nuns of the black veil. In the hierarchical world of Cuzco's cloisters illegitimacy was not an impediment for an elite criolla.

Thus by the seventeenth century the veil categories had shifted in content somewhat, but criollas were still on top. Nuns of the black veil paid the full dowry of 3,312 pesos 4 reales, and could participate fully in the convents' spiritual and business affairs, voting and holding high office. Nuns of the white veil paid exactly half as much dowry, or 1,656 pesos 2 reales, and could neither vote nor hold high office. The amount a nun got to eat and drink, what kinds of labors she had to perform, her right to precedence in the order of seating, worship, and so forth— all these intensely significant issues of daily life came to be bound up in the difference between the black and the white veil. Obviously, so were economic and political clout in *el siglo*. No nun of the white veil could be among the decision-making *madres de consejo*, much less prioress or abbess. So while nuns of the white veil increased the dowry fund with their families' resources, they had no say in how credit was apportioned to local borrowers.

In sum, local criollas were monopolizing leadership inside Cuzco's convents just as their relatives were coming into local power and influence outside convent walls. The use of the veil as a criterion of difference would prove extremely durable, outlasting the Spanish colonial regime itself. The lesser veil was not worn exclusively by Andean nuns. Daughters of Cuzco's nonelite criollos and mestizos also turn up in the archival record as nuns of the *velo blanco*. But this rank was as high as a nonwhite Andean woman could expect to get. The daughter of a *kuraka* almost never became a nun of the highest rank in Cuzco, however wealthy and prominent her family might be, and ability to meet the full dowry payment clearly was not what was holding these women back. As for criollas, inability to pay the full dowry did not necessarily keep them out of the highest rank. The nuns might make an exception and grant full status to a poor criolla if she came from what they regarded as a good family. If a criolla was not particularly elite or wealthy, her family could still get her into a black veil by scraping and sacrificing to come up with the dowry, and she might even rise to become a *madre de consejo*, as occurred in 1780 with Agueda Zamora, whose mother, a poor widow, had managed to get all four of her daughters into Santa Clara as nuns of the black veil.[41] In other words, the one seemingly unshakable requirement for full-fledged status in the convent was whiteness.[42] Just about everything else could be gotten around. Colonial convents, like colonial institutions in general, were often surprisingly flexible, bending strategically so as not to break.

Finally, we must note that the production of whiteness enacted by criollos and through convents implies the simultaneous construction of those who were then called "castes," *castas*: the nonwhite, nonpure, non-Spanish. Cuzco's convents had a place for them, too. They did not get to entertain guests in the *locutorio*, and were not allowed a part in the mass, but worked busily in the kitchen, the pantry, the garden, the laundry, and everywhere else manual labor was required for the support of the nuns. They are almost completely invisible in the archival record. But the day-to-day functioning of a colonial convent, like a colonial culture and society, was predicated on their labor.

Perhaps the defining characteristic of the colonial convent is its occupants' willingness to bend their monastic rules, stretching the limits of individuals' and groups' *dominio*, their power over possessions not strictly theirs. The nuns of Cuzco construed their rules and constitutions in ways that furthered the colonial order of things: they kept personal servants and slaves inside their cells to attend them, while making some nuns full-fledged partners in the convent's business and ruling other professed women inferior and out of bounds. By the seventeenth century criollas had succeeded in establishing a monopoly on the black veil and in increasing their families' wealth through careful deployment of convent funds in credit transactions. Put another way, the convents of Cuzco did not merely buttress the emerging criollo-dominated elite of the colonial, hybrid Spanish-Andean society around them. They actively produced it, importing its distinctions and creating their own markers to help inscribe the boundaries between white and *kuraka* elites, the semi-separate-and-unequal lords of seventeenth-century Cuzco.

Understanding fully the material and cultural implications of the spiritual economy I have described will take much more time and scrutiny of archival traces. It would be worth investigating, for example, whether the *censo* mechanism served to redistribute capital from *kurakas* to criollos; the former, lacking representatives in the convents' decision-making bodies, may well have gotten out of convents a good deal less than they put in. The roles of many actors barely touched on here will need to be explored: for example, the important figure of the *mayordomo*, who served as the nuns' go-betweens and financial agents (sometimes ably, sometimes with a hand in the till). And comparative studies will be needed to clarify the way convents reproduced colonial spiritual and economic relations around Spanish America. *Cuzqueñas* were not unique in setting up black/white veil distinctions; these were inscribed in conventual practice in many other places, although the timing and significance of these divisions has yet to be explored. And what about men's monastic orders? Were there gender-inflected dimensions to the spiritual economy? These are but a few of the outstanding questions that invite study.[43]

Some things at least are clear. In the seventeenth-century colonial context we have examined, in which local criollos like the Costillas and Esquiveles were getting a firm grip on the most valuable property, Cuzco's nuns were dealing with—and actively and deliberately reinforcing—the colonial ruling class, the propertied elite with collateral to offer for loans. We can now see that the availability of both credit and salvation in this spiritual economy was related to women's decisions to profess. The colonial agrarian economy of Cuzco depended on a successful "harvest of souls," *agricultura espiritual.*

NOTES

Research for this article was funded primarily by a Fulbright-Hays fellowship and a grant from the University of Florida. A preliminary version appeared in *El Monacato Femenino en el Imperio Español,* ed. Manuel Ramos Medina (Mexico City: Condumex, 1995), 311–18, and a fellowship from the Shelby Cullom Davis Center for Historical Studies at Princeton University enabled me to revise and expand it substantially. Warm thanks to the many friends and colleagues who responded generously to earlier versions, above all to Louise Newman, Kate Raisz, Stephanie Stewart, Anthony Grafton, Stanley Stein, John Womack, Ann Wightman, Brooke Larson, and Holly Hanson. For opportunities to present work in progress, I thank Manuel Ramos Medina of Condumex, William Chester Jordan of the Davis Center, Carrie Alyea and the organizers of Women's History Week at Harvard University, Charles Walker and Ann Zulawski of CLAH's Andean Studies Committee, and Stephanie Sieburth of Duke University. All translations of citations are mine.

1. The grille is actually double, in accordance with the wishes of Clement VIII, who ordered "that at least two strong, thick grilles be placed, one on the interior, the other at least a little over half a *vara* away, and the iron bars should be close enough that a hand cannot reach through, even a slender hand." Antonio Arbiol, *La religiosa instruida* (Madrid: Imprenta Real de la Gazeta, 1776), 474.

2. Unfortunately, the only book-length effort in English to give convents a serious place in the historiography of colonial Peru tends to reinforce their marginality to the historiographical mainstream. Luis Martín notes the economic importance of the role of abbess and local families' interest in election outcomes, but does not explain or explore these things, and chalks up nuns' efforts to be elected and reelected to office to their personal taste for power. Luis Martín, *Daughters of the Conquistadores: Women of the Viceroyalty of Peru* (Albuquerque: University of New Mexico Press, 1983), 257–79. However, see Brian R. Hamnett, "Church Wealth in Peru: Estates and Loans in the Archdiocese of Lima in the Seventeenth Century," *Jahrbuch für Geschichte von Staat, Wirtschaft und Gesellschaft Lateinamerikas* 10 (1973): 113–32. By contrast, the importance of convents in colonial Mexico has become the subject of extensive research, thanks largely to the pioneering work of Asunción Lavrin on the economic role of late colonial nunneries. Asunción Lavrin, ed., *Latin American Women: Historical Perspectives* (Westport, Conn.: Greenwood Press, 1978); "Ecclesiastical Reform of Nunneries in New Spain in the Eighteenth Century," *The Americas* 22 (1965): 182–203; "La riqueza de los conventos de monjas en Nueva España: Estructura y evolución durante el siglo XVIII," *Cahiers des Ameriques Latines* (2d semester, 1973): 91–122; "El Capital eclesiástico y las elites sociales en Nueva España a fines del siglo XVIII," *Mexican Studies/Estudios mexicanos* 1 (1985): 1–28. For recent fruits of this scholarship, see Gisela von Wobeser, *El crédito eclesiástico en la Nueva España, siglo XVIII* (Mexico City: Universidad Nacional Autónoma de México, von Wobeser, 1994).

3. Like so many other important matters, dowry practice was changing rapidly during the sixteenth century. Kealy notes that "[t]he institution of the dowry of women religious in the canon law sources did not make its appearance until the sixteenth century." Thomas M. Kealy, *Dowry of Women Religious*, Canon Law Studies 134 (Washington, D.C.: Catholic University of America Press, 1941), 8. Not surprisingly, the question received attention at more or less the same time that strict enclosure was being enforced for women. The issue of how much nuns should pay was left in the hands of local ecclesiastical authorities; dowry was not set by the nuns themselves.

4. In Lima it was slightly lower, around 3,100 pesos. No one has studied the "spiritual dowry" for women in Peru, or for that matter temporal dowry, so it is not yet possible to see changes over time, compare regional variations, establish class differences, etc.

5. A. J. Bauer, "The Church in the economy of Spanish America: *censos* and *depósitos* in the eighteenth and nineteenth centuries," *Hispanic American Historical Review* 63 (1983): 707–33. Kathryn Burns, "Convents, Culture, and Society in Cuzco, Peru, 1550–1865." (Ph.D. diss., Harvard University, 1993). Kathryn Burns, *Colonial Habits: Convents and the Spiritual Economy of Cuzco, Peru* (Durham, N.C.: Duke University Press, 1999).

6. On December 3, 1623, prioress Isabel de Padilla registered a list of Santa Catalina's assets before a Cuzco notary, Archivo Departamental del Cuzco (ADC), Francisco Hurtado, 1623, 1580r–1584v. These included six rural properties near the city. Three had been purchased by the nuns, two had been donated to them in wills, and one had been brought by a nun in dowry. Dowry also accounted for the convent's sole urban property. The remaining assets are mostly *censos*: fifteen are listed, and their principals total 38,690 pesos.

7. "Que de los doctes que trajeren las religiosas que profesaren . . . no se gasten en comer ni otros gastos de casa, ni en hacer edificios, sino que se echen luego en renta, en cosa que sea útil y provechosa para el dho. Monesterio." *Libro original que contiene la fundación del monesterio de monjas de señora sta. Clara desta ciudad del Cuzco . . . Año de 1560.* Transcribed with an introduction by Domingo Angulo. *Revista del Archivo Nacional del Perú* 11 (1939): 75.

8. The "abominable sin" that tops Mercado's list is that of homosexuality (*pecado nefando*).

9. Luis Alfredo Tapia Franco, "Analisis histôrico institucional des censo consignativo en el derecho peruano" (B.A. thesis, Pontificia Universidad Católica del Perú, 1991).

10. This was an important development in the history of the *censo*, and an unsettling one for Iberians. Even though Popes Martin V (in 1428) and Calixtus III (in 1455) had approved the practice, it still looked suspiciously like usury to many contemporary observers. For historical perspectives on various forms of *censos*, see Raymond de Roover in *Business, Banking, and Economic Thought in Late Medieval and Early Modern Europe*, ed. Julius Kirshner (Chicago: University of Chicago Press, 1974), and John Gilchrist, *The Church and Economic Activity in the Middle Ages* (New York: Macmillan, 1969). For Peru, see Alfonso W. Quiroz, "Reassessing the Role of Credit in Late Colonial Peru: *Censos, Escrituras,* and *Imposiciones,*" *Hispanic American Historical Review* 74 (1994): 193–230.

11. Tapia Franco, ch. 2, cites a case that came before the authorities in Lima in the early 1640s. A woman contracted to lend a man 4,400 pesos but only gave him 4,000 pesos, whereupon he denounced her for charging interest (10 percent). Tapia Franco, Luis Alfredo, "Análisis histórico institucional del censo consignativo en el derecho peruano" (B.A. thesis, Pontificia Universidad Católica del Perú, 1991).

12. A 1628 case reveals an interesting misstep by the nuns of Santa Clara. ADC Cristóbal de Luzero 1627–28, 521r–v, December 19, 1628. In 1588 they had lent Bernardo de la Torre four silver ingots valued at 1,500 pesos *ensayados* in a *censo* transaction, allowing as collateral his stake in unspecified mines. When the convent tried in the 1620s to recover unpaid annuities (*réditos*), the miner's heirs put up a vigorous opposition, noting that a *censo* could not be placed on mines "since they all belong to

His Majesty." The case went through appeals and the nuns had to settle out of court for much less than they had sought.

13. Burns, "Apuntes sobre la economía conventual," Convents, culture and society in Cuzco, Peru" and *Colonial Habits.*

14. Archivo Departamental del Cuzco (ADC), Pedro de Cáceres, 397r–432v, December 12–15, 1696.

15. ADC, Pedro de Cáceres, 1697, 58r–61v, January 28, 1697.

16. María de Carmen Martín Rubio, "La Caja de Censos de Indios en el Cuzco." *Revista de Indias* 39 (1979): 187–208.

17. Information for 1602 is drawn from *Libro original que contiene la fundación del monesterio de monjas de señora Sta. Clara desta ciudad del Cuzco . . . Año de 1560.* Transcribed and with an introduction by Domingo Angulo, *Revista del Archivo Nacional del Perú* 11 (1939): 170–76. The rest comes from a report of abbess Gerónima de Villena y Madueño to the King, Archivo del Monasterio de Santa Clara, Cuzco. Archivo del Monasterio de Santa Clara, Cuzco, (ASC) "Volúmen de escrituras que pueden servir de títulos," 466r–67r, July 19, 1690.

18. Archivo del Monasterio de Santa Catalina de Sena, Cuzco (ASCS), "Inventario de las escrituras de este Legajo del mes de Marzo," list entitled "Memoria de las escrituras cobrables, que entregó la señora María de los Remedios, priora que fue, a la señora Catalina de San Ambrosio y Mendoza, priora actual," March 2, 1684. Many items are incomplete; the amount of principal cannot be ascertained for 23 of its 166 entries. Since the average amount of a transaction was over 2,000 pesos, the missing principal might have come to some 46,000 pesos, raising the total to 343,433 pesos in principal—in which case the nuns could have been collecting as much as 17,172 pesos annually.

19. ADC, handwritten list of seventy-eight items entitled "Memoria de los Censos que al presente pagan los censuatarios del Cuzco, que se hizo en 29 de febrero de 1676," inserted into the back of a hand-copied volume from the library of the monastery of San Agustín: Lorenzo de Niebla's *Summa del estilo de escribanos y de herencias y particiones y escripturas y avisos de jueces.*

20. Diego de Mendoza, *Chrónica de la provincia de S. Antonio de los Charcas.* La Paz: Editorial Casa Municipal de la Cultura "Franz Tamayo," 1976: 68–72, 377–474.

21. To take a representative example, Reyna's study of Mexican convent finance states: "En principio, las familias económicamente poderosas procuraban que sus hijas contrajeran matrimonio ventajoso; sin embargo, cuando éstos no se llevaban a cabo, el ingreso al convento era lo mejor para la buena reputación y conservación de la fortuna de la familia." María del Carmen Reyna, *El convento de San Jerónimo: Vida conventual y finanzas* (Mexico City: Instituto Nacional de Antropología e Historia, 1990), 33.

22. Constance Brittain Bouchard, *Holy entrepreneurs: Cistercians, knights, and economic exchange in twelfth-century Burgundy* (Ithaca, N.Y.: Cornell University Press), 1991. William Chester Jordan, *Women and credit in pre-industrial and developing societies* (Philadelphia: University of Pennsylvania Press, 1993).

23. The contemporary coordinates of what we would now call an individual's "race" have yet to be worked out for this period, rich in *mestizaje*. By the seventeenth century color came into play, but the palettes people used in referencing their and others' identity were not the same, and other considerations—language, dress, lineage, and situation vis-à-vis Inca culture and the Spanish colonial state apparatus (tributary, *kuraka*, etc.)—appear saliently. For example, early-seventeenth-century notaries registered many contractual parties as "mestizas/os dressed like Indians" (i.e., they looked like tributaries—people with a special legal standing requiring the presence of a state-sponsored advocate—but were not). Getting at seventeenth-century shades of "criollo" v. "Spanish" identity is particularly difficult, since the Spanish regime was not interested in the differences and notaries did not note them. But their privileged position vis-à-vis everybody else results in their being seen/glossed as "whites." In time it may be possible to tell to what extent such seemingly color-specific identities were about other things; for example, no doubt in Cuzco, as in Brazil, money whitened.

24. These women descended from one of Cuzco's first Spanish settlers, the conquistador and self-styled "General" Gerónimo Costilla. Kathryn Burns, "Convents, Culture, and Society in Cuzco, Peru, 1550–1865" (Ph.D. diss., Harvard University, 1993), 63–77. Notarial records in the ADC reflect that Juana Rosa Costilla was a *madre de consejo* (1710–13) and that Rosa de Venero y Costilla was abbess at least twice (1767–70, 1779–82?). These women were legitimate; a natural daughter of the Costilla clan, María Costilla Gallinato, professed as a nun of the black veil not alongside her relatives but in Santa Catalina. ADC, Gregorio Básquez Serrano, 1708–09, 455r–55v, December 12, 1709.

25. We know this because the ring somehow got away from him, and Don Pablo—one of Cuzco's richest and most powerful men—sued to recover it after it mysteriously reappeared five years later in the possession of another local family. ADC, Cabildo, Justicia Ordinaria, Causas Civiles, legajo 11, 1683–89. Interestingly, Don Pablo never accused the Clares of any misconduct. He indicated only that his ring had been replaced with a cheap substitute inside Santa Clara: "La . . . sortija se me trocó en la ocasion en el d[ic]ho monasterio de Santa Clara con otra de muy poca importansia y aunq[ue] se hizieron varias diligensias en su busca, no tubo efecto el hallarla."

26. Burns, "Convents, culture and society in Cuzco Peru," 125–33 and *Colonial Habits*, 122.

27. ADC, Gregorio Básquez Serrano, 195r–200v, 232v–236r, November 7 and December 29, 1708.

28. ADC, Gregorio Básquez Serrano, 32r, 1707.

29. The money had just come into the nuns' hands from the priest of Asillo, who had bought certain haciendas at auction, paying 23,100 pesos in cash to redeem all the *censos* the property carried. The Marqués took his 8,500-peso loan and imposed a *censo* on his nearby hacienda called Chinicara, which already carried 6,000 pesos' worth of principal in a *censo* paid to the nuns of Santa Catalina. ADC, Gregorio Básquez Serrano, 119r–127v, March 15–17, 1708.

30. ADC, Pedro de Cáceres, 105r, 1697.

31. The work of Karen Spalding has been especially important in clarifying the *kurakas'* crucial role. Karen Spalding, *Huarochirí: An Andean Society under Inca and Colonial Rule* (Stanford, Calif.: Stanford University Press, 1984). The important and strategic role of *indios nobles* in Cuzco, former center of the Inca state, is beginning to receive the kind of attention it deserves; I look forward to the completion of several projects now under way. These will extend John H. Rowe's pioneering work on "Inca nationalism" in late eighteenth-century Cuzco, done in an attempt to explain the shattering revolt in 1780–81 of *kuraka* José Gabriel Túpac Amaru (Thupa Amaro) against the colonial regime. John H. Rowe, "El movimiento nacional inca en el siglo XVIII," *Revista Universitaria* (Cuzco) 43 (1954): 17–47.

32. The discourse of Andean lords is largely unavailable to us; almost no Quechua colonial documents survive, and little research has been done on leading Andeans' activities as recorded by criollo and Spanish notaries. Even the institutional contours of their lives are blurry. No archives have yet turned up from the strategically important Jesuit-run *colegio de caciques* of Cuzco, which operated from the early seventeenth century until the Jesuits' late-eighteenth-century expulsion. But art historian Carolyn S. Dean uses artistic and textual clues to show how a major annual religious process kept alive divisions among Andean elites, which no doubt suited white elites' purposes admirably, perpetuating ethnic conflict within the ranks of the *indios nobles*. Carolyn S. Dean, "Ethnic Conflict and Corpus Christi in Colonial Cuzco," *Colonial Latin American Review* 2 (1993): 93–120.

33. Much of the best work in Andean history in recent years has sought to understand the 1780–81 revolt led by Túpac Amaru (Thupa Amaro), asking why such a massive breakdown in colonial relations occurred. What hasn't yet been adequately explored is *why kurakas consented* for centuries to the positions Spanish indirect rule put them in, and how criollos and *kurakas* negotiated their roles vis-à-vis a corrupt, thin-on-the-ground Spanish regime. Stern's work on Huamanga to 1640 constitutes an especially useful exception and model; however, later decades, and their cultural politics in particular, remain largely unexplored. Seventeenth-century evidence will be crucial to getting a sense of these issues in historical perspective. Steve J. Stern, *Peru's Indian Peoples and the*

Challenge of Spanish Conquest: Huamanga to 1640 (Madison, Wis.: University of Wisconsin Press, 1982).

34. ADC, Alejo González Peñaloza, September 15, 1746.

35. ADC, Pedro Joseph Gamarra, 486r–87v, July 1, 1743.

36. In 1741, for example, Juana Francisca de Jesús, widow of Don Alonso Guampu Tupa, and her daughter Pascuala Magdalena Teresa de Jesús, both cloistered nuns in Santa Teresa, sold a house in the city to a merchant named Don Eusebio de Betancur for 400 pesos. ADC, Pedro Joseph Gamarra, 1741, 357r–59v, February 28, 1741.

37. Despite the convents' rules about holding property in common, nuns could receive such services, as well as manage private funds (*peculio*), as long as they had their abbess's or prioress's approval. This donation by María Panti, identified by the notary as an "yndia," was to last for the duration of her granddaughter's life. ADC, Alonso Beltrán Luzero, 105r–107v, January 13, 1642).

38. I have found only one clear case of an elite Andean nun of the black veil; in December 1600, Don Diego Quispe Guaman, gobernador of Parinacochas, promised to pay the nuns of Santa Catalina the full dowry so that his legitimate daughter Doña Antonia Salinas might profess. Archivo del Monasterio de Santa Catalina de Sena, Cuzco. ASCS, "Inventario de las Escrituras pertenecientes al Mes de Diciembre," document 13, December 16, 1660.

39. According to the *Constituciones generales* of the Clares (1689), some servants were permitted to live alongside the nuns, and might leave the cloisters to carry out the nuns' business: "[pueden] ser recebidas algunas, aunque pocas con nombre de serviciales, o de Hermanas, para que prometen, y guarden esta misma Regla, salvo el articulo del encerramiento, las quales . . . podrán algunas vezes salir a procurar los negocios de el Monasterio" (3r). Cuzco's convents made liberal use of this provision and were well stocked with servants. The constitutions also allowed for some servants to profess as lay sisters (*freylas donadas*), at a third or more of the full dowry, and wear the white veil permanently while performing the most "humble" tasks (58r–60v). In Cuzco the record indicates that some servants did profess as *donadas*; they generally paid around 500 pesos in dowry. In other words, Cuzco's nuns turned the servant/white veil category into a two-tier affair: "nuns of the white veil," who paid dowries of 1,656 pesos 2 reales, and *donadas,* who paid dowries of 500 pesos. These women ranked above the convent's unprofessed servants and slaves. Burns, *Colonial Habits*, 15–40.

40. Archivo Arzobispal de Lima (AAL) Apelaciones de Cuzco, legajo 6, 1644–45.

41. In her will, Doña Melchora Lire de la Borda (herself a natural daughter) proudly states "que a las d[ic]has mis quatro hijas las he Dotado en el Monasterio en que se hallan de Monjas de Belo negro con mi propio peculio, y caudal que adquiri con mi trabajo perzonal en obras de Tiraduria, que corria a mi manejo como es publico, y notorio; y asimesmo les he

costeado todo lo presiso, y nesesario, para sus Bestuarios y gastos de sus ingresos en d[ic]ho Monasterio" (210r). ADC, Miguel de Acuña, 209r–213v, May 26, 1765.

42. The work of David R. Roediger and other historians on the making of whiteness in the United States raises provocative questions for colonial Andean history, and I am trying out his insights in a different historiographical location to stimulate debate about the process by which people created *criollo/a identity* in places like Cuzco. David R. Roediger, *The Wages of Whiteness: Race and the Making of the American Working Class* (New York: Verso, 1991). For an interesting attempt to historicize the category "criollo" in a Mexican context, see Elizabeth Anne Kuznesof, "Ethnic and Gender Influences on 'Spanish' Creole Society in Colonial Spanish America," *Colonial Latin American Review* 4 (1995): 153–76.

43. This paper has been concerned with the seventeenth-century buildup of the spiritual economy. The late colonial crisis and long decline of Cuzco's spiritual economy is explored in my dissertation and book. Kathryn Burns, "Convents, Culture, and Society in Cuzco, Peru, 1550–1865," and *Colonial Habits: Convents and the Spiritual Economy of Cuzco, Peru* (Durham, N.C.: Duke University Press, 1999); and Quiroz, "Reassessing the Role of Credit." At present it is only possible to glimpse the factors responsible for the decline of the *censo*-powered spiritual economy of Cuzco, including "enlightened" anticlericalism, the impact of Túpac Amaru's revolt, and *censo* saturation caused by generations of dealings like those described here. New work on late colonial and early republican Mexico suggests ways of approaching this conjuncture, which promises to repay close, local-level study.

FRANCE AND THE NEW WORLD

Spheres of Female Religious Expression in Early Modern France

Susan E. Dinan

IT IS THE GOAL OF THIS ESSAY to examine the impact of the Catholic Reformation, as expressed by the Council of Trent, on the lives of Catholic women in sixteenth- and seventeenth-century France. The Council of Trent limited the vocational choices available to women with a religious calling, but it also, albeit unintentionally, inspired the creation of active religious communities for laywomen. The Daughters of Charity pioneered this new vocational form and I examine their nascent years in order to illuminate the meaning of the Catholic Reformation for French women. Ultimately, I argue that for women the legacy of the Catholic Reformation was ambiguous, restricting the vocational possibilities for some while prompting the invention of wholly new pursuits by others.

The Council of Trent and Women Religious

The Council of Trent, like earlier church councils, was a meeting of archbishops, bishops, priests, and regulars, called together by the pope. Between 1545 and 1563 the men gathered at Trent formulated the official response of the Catholic Church to the Protestant Reformation, a movement that criticized the theology, education, and behavior of Catholics. A primary goal of Trent was to counter Protestant advances in Catholic Europe by both educating and disciplining the clergy and the laity. To this end, for example, it requested that all dioceses provide a seminary to train priests and catechism classes to instruct parishioners.

The Council of Trent issued its legislation regarding women in religious orders during its last session in 1563. Here, the Council issued directives stipulating that women be sixteen before taking formal religious vows and testify that they were joining religious orders out of their own volition.[1] This was in direct response to the problems caused by families who used convents to house "surplus" daughters—those that they could not afford to dower sufficiently to make a good marriage. From the perspective of religious women, the most important doctrine that the Council of Trent promulgated was the decree "Provision is made for the enclosure of nuns, especially those who reside outside the cities." In it the councilors stated, "the holy council . . . commands all bishops . . . make it their special care that in all monasteries subject to them . . . the enclosure of nuns be restored wherever it has been violated and that it be preserved where it has not been violated."[2] With this statement the Council resurrected older papal decrees requiring members of female religious orders to live within convent walls.[3] In contrast to the multiple vocational options available to women before 1563, this decree sought to limit women religious to one acceptable lifestyle, locked within a convent.

Before Trent some women religious lived in tightly cloistered convents whereas others chose convents that allowed them to see visitors or return home when they were needed, for instance to assist an elderly or sick parent. Still others avoided enclosure altogether, like Third Order Franciscans, the *beatas* of Spain, or the beguines of the Netherlands—groups of women who demonstrated their religious calling by working among the poor in their neighborhoods. The decree "Provision is made for the enclosure of nuns . . ." continued, "no nun shall after her profession be permitted to go out of the monastery, even for a brief period under any pretext whatever, except for a lawful reason to be approved by the bishop."[4] Such reasons were few, and unless the convent was on fire or suffering from an outbreak of contagious disease, nuns were to remain inside. The Council's goal was to remove religious women from public life, and its intention was echoed in 1566 when Pius V issued the papal Bull *Circa pastoralis* suppressing all women's congregations not practicing enclosure.[5] With this Bull the pope attempted to cloister or disband all religious women who still lived outside of enclosure, including members of all tertiary orders.

Unlike the regulations that focused on better religious education, "Provision is made for the enclosure of nuns . . ." dictated behavioral expectations. Ostensibly, the Council was acting to protect unenclosed women from what it called "the rapacity and other crimes of evil men," namely rapists who broke into the convents or homes to assault religious women, but it also strove to protect the women from less dubious characters.[6] Scandals occasionally arose at Renaissance convents with lax enclosure when nuns confessed to having consensual sexual relations with priests, laymen, or other nuns.[7] The Council was clearly concerned about restoring enclosure where it had been "violated." The message to women religious was clear: if they violated the regulations of the church by refusing *clausura*, they themselves were vulnerable to violation. This conciliar and papal legislation was indisputably sexual, and points to the fact that there was considerable concern about sexually active nuns who would bring shame and dishonor to the convent, the church, and their families (who, commonly, were important convent benefactors). Church officials, however, sought to control more than just the sexuality of nuns. Enclosed women were more easily watched that those living in society; all aspects of their daily behavior, private and communal, could be better disciplined within the convent walls.

The Council of Trent and Pius V attempted to restrict the vocational choices available to religious women by enclosing convents that had previously interacted with the outside community. After Trent, women interested in spiritual pursuits had only two avenues permitted to them: a *dévote* life within marriage or a religious life in a convent.[8] The first option involved pursuing a religious life in the secular world. Women who did so could adopt the teachings of François de Sales and lead a secular life centered on religious devotion.[9] De Sales encouraged *dévotes* to visit the poor and serve them by cooking their meals and sitting at their bedsides during times of illness. The *dévote* women who joined Vincent de Paul's Confraternities of Charity chose this path of direct service to the poor as a demonstration of their piety.

Early modern women who sought a more intense commitment to religious practice could enter a convent. Unlike *dévotes,* women who entered religious orders lived communally and promised to follow the order's rule by taking solemn vows of poverty, chastity, and obedience. There were two forms of religious vows. Nuns professed solemn vows before the church and the "world" to announce that they had adopted a religious life and were therefore "dead to the world." Simple vows, on the other hand, were nonsacramental and taken by persons not affiliated with formal religious orders.[10] Becoming choir sisters, as full-fledged nuns were called, required a dowry paid by the entrants' families to the convent. Although convent dowries were not as large as those needed to make a good marriage, they could be considerable. Therefore, women from more modest families rarely entered convents or did so as lower-status lay sisters who labored as the servants of the choir sisters within the convent. The hierarchical structure within convents with wealthy choir sisters served by poor lay sisters mimicked the social hierarchies of the outside world in which the poor were the servants of the elites. Convent life, with its solemn vow of poverty, was a life choice available almost exclusively to wealthy women.

The boundary between the active secular life and the contemplative religious life that the authorities at Trent attempted to erect, however, was never achieved. Church authorities were often unable or unwilling to impose the decrees on the diocesan level and the Catholic states of Europe did not uniformly accept or enforce the decrees of Trent. Not only did nations adopt Tridentine reforms at different times, some adopted them only partially, and some not at all. The French crown, for example, never published the Tridentine decrees,[11] while the French church only ratified the promulgations of Trent in 1615 following the cessation of the religious wars that had plagued the sixteenth century.[12] The French bishops who implemented Tridentine accords were those interested in more closely regulating the Catholic populations of their dioceses. They used the council's ordinances to require parishioners to attend catechism classes to improve their religious knowledge; additionally, the decrees allowed church officials to monitor more easily their behavior. Some bishops elected to impose the Tridentine decrees in their dioceses before their national churches or governments accepted them. Reform, therefore, occurred at different times in different locations, and ultimately all reforms were negotiated at the local level. Because of uneven enforcement, the demands that Trent made about women's enclosure were never universally realized.

FROM ACTIVE SERVICE TO ENCLOSURE: THE URSULINES AND THE VISITATION

Church leaders at Trent were not the only Catholics seeking reform. The sixteenth century was a period of general spiritual renewal for Catholics faced with the new threat of rival Christian faiths in Western Europe. Many individual religious orders initiated internal reforms and re-created themselves as more dynamic and spiritually rigorous institutions, most notably the Discalced Carmelites. Across Europe there was a dramatic increase in the number of women entering contemplative convents in the sixteenth and seventeenth centuries.[13] In early-seventeenth-century France a new generation of nuns revitalized existing orders and entered new ones; the increase in the number of women religious was considerable.[14] In Saint-Denis, for instance, enclosed religious orders built three new convents between 1625 and 1629, the largest of which had seventy-four members.[15] Some women were attracted to the reformed monastic houses, like the Capuchins and St. Teresa of Avila's Discalced Carmelites, which had entered France from Italy and Spain. These were austere orders that demanded extreme asceticism and were models of Catholic-Reformation piety. Reformed convents practiced enclosure. Other religious communities emerged with the intention of practicing an active and noncloistered vocation. Few or none succeeded however as church authorities ultimately cloistered them. The Ursulines of Italy and the Visitation nuns of Savoy both began as communities with an active vocation of service to the needy but underwent the transformation into formal religious orders with *clausura* at the hands of local bishops who imposed the rules of Trent in an effort to better control the women religious in their diocese.

Angela Merici, a laywoman, founded the Ursulines in 1535 when she brought together twenty-eight young women in Brescia, Italy. The women promised to live in the world and serve God as consecrated virgins and brides of Christ.[16] In 1544 Paul III confirmed the congregation as a confraternity with some of the privileges of a religious order. Historian Christopher Black defines confraternities in early modern Europe as "groups of people who [came] together in conformity with certain rules to promote their religious life in common, who [did] not take the vows of an order and generally live[d] in the secular world."[17] Confraternities were generally organizations of the laity that united for penitential ceremonies and/or charitable works, such as gathering for prayer or communion, maintaining an altar, or aiding the poor.[18] As members of a confraternity, the Ursulines resided with their families, not in a convent, and performed good works in the community. They also met regularly to participate in confession and to share the Eucharist.[19]

Five years later the community's foundation Merici died, and gradually the nature of her company changed. The mother superior appointed by Merici before her death implemented changes that contradicted Merici's original vision when she required the Ursulines to wear a habit and adopt public vows upon entrance.[20] Eventually, the community came to the attention of Carlo Borromeo, the reforming archbishop of Milan, who saw a way to employ the Ursulines in his diocese. He brought twelve Ursulines to Milan where they taught young girls catechism and lived with local families.[21] He was impressed with their work and by 1576 Borromeo had made it the duty of bishops in his archdiocese to found a Company of St. Ursula to teach girls and young women catechism on Sundays and feast days.[22] For Borromeo the Ursulines were an ideal vehicle through which to teach women and girls the Catholic-Reformation theology and piety that Trent insisted all Catholics learn. Borromeo turned the Ursulines into teachers of Christian doctrine and legitimized the congregation by placing it under clerical controls. He transformed the community's structure when he put the Ursulines of Milan under the leadership of a male prior-general—something Merici had avoided doing.[23] Female control of the congregation shrunk as local bishops and the prior-general increasingly controlled the Ursulines. In the early 1580s Borromeo further transformed the companies by writing a new rule, which dictated not only simple vows, an induction ceremony, and a habit, but also communal living.[24] Borromeo's rule stressed hierarchical governance and obedience, whereas Merici's original rule had encouraged the Ursulines to listen to the Holy Spirit.[25] The archbishop did not trust the flexibility of Merici's rule and insisted that catechists be under the discipline of male church leaders. Within fifty years of their foundation the Ursulines had become much more of a religious order than Merici had originally intended. As the Ursulines grew, both models endured, with some companies in Italy adopting the Brescian model and others adopting the Milanese model.[26]

By the end of the sixteenth century communities of Ursulines had spread to all major Italian cities and into France, and by the mid-seventeenth century, many French towns had a school maintained by the Ursulines.[27] The early French Ursuline communities were based on the Milanese model having both the oversight of the local bishop and a communal life without *clausura*. They served their towns by catechizing girls of all social classes.[28] Over time however, Ursuline communities adopted *clausura*.[29] For instance, in Paris the women who brought the Ursulines to the city, Madame Acarie and Madame de Sainte-Beauve, went beyond the structure imposed by Borromeo and insisted that entrants pronounce solemn vows and accept enclosure.[30] The Ursulines in Paris were no longer a confraternity; they were a formal religious order taking solemn vows, living a communal life organized around a rule, and residing in a convent.

In other cities, including Lyon, church authorities cloistered the Ursulines.[31] Enclosure dramatically changed the order in France. The cloistered French Ursulines recruited wealthy women who could afford the cost of a dowry to support their lives in convents and thus the order became more aristocratic, whereas in Italy unenclosed Ursulines retained more modest congregations.[32] The Ursulines maintained their original purpose of teaching girls albeit in a very different environment. Instead of teaching in charity schools for poor girls, they now instructed wealthy girls who boarded in their convents and accepted only a few poor day students for lessons.[33] The nature of the order's social mission changed and the Ursulines became the prominent teachers of noble and other wealthy girls in France.

A second community with a mission of service that church authorities enclosed was the Visitation. In 1607 François de Sales, bishop of Geneva, and Jeanne de Chantal founded the Visitation nuns in Annecy, a community in which laywomen practiced the virtues of the Virgin Mary: humility, piety, and benevolence toward the sick and poor.[34] The Visitation nuns desired a largely contemplative life of prayer enhanced by occasional acts of charity. Although de Chantal and de Sales placed the Visitation nuns within a cloister, their notion of *clausura* was very flexible in an effort to permit a variety of women access to the community. The nuns lived under mitigated enclosure that allowed the doors to their convent to remain open, permitting laywomen to come into their community on retreats. The Visitation was also a community designed for women of poor health who could not endure the traditional monastic rigors of fasting and discipline. However, when the order established a house in Lyon in 1610, the archbishop insisted that the Visitation nuns comply with the decrees of the Council of Trent, obey a formal rule, and move into a convent to withdraw from the world.[35] In response, de Sales enclosed this community because he respected the fact that the local bishop was the director of the Visitation nuns in his diocese.[36] This transformation made the Visitation's initial mission of providing charity to the poor impossible, and the order became contemplative.[37] As in the case of the Ursulines, it was this cloistered form of the Visitation order that spread across Catholic-Reformation France.

Enclosure re-created the vocations of the Ursulines and Visitation nuns transforming them from flexible communities into formal religious orders and from providers of neighborhood charity into contemplatives who served elite boarders. Cloistered status made the religious orders more appealing to many wealthy families who sought to place their daughters in convents that would leave them "dead to the world" and exclude them from future family inheritance. Enclosed orders were more prestigious in part because entrants presented substantial dowries assuring that they would live with women of similar social and economic backgrounds. Unenclosed communities for women religious did not demand dowries and the organizations relied upon alms, which placed them in a precarious situation. If donations were insufficient, communities might disband or become dependent upon local church officials. Whereas mother superiors commonly invested convent dowries to increases the nuns' collective wealth, this capital provided the orders with stability and could make convents important local financial institutions. A cloistered existence was also a safer one for unmarried women as it removed them from the public world that they would have experienced as unenclosed women visiting the poor or collecting alms. Enclosure changed the nature of the vocation of the Ursulines and Visitation nuns, who became institutions for upper-class women seeking a cloistered life away from the world. No longer were members able to move about their towns serving those in need; instead, members lived in convents and assisted their neighbors in less direct ways. When French bishops embraced the discipline of Trent as it applied to the enclosure of religious women, they forced noncloistered communities to adopt *clausura*. Although this did not reduce the popularity or importance of the communities, it undermined their initial missions and transformed their vocations.

Catholic-Reformation religious communities were the creations of their founders. However, these founders' original visions could be adulterated in the process of making the new communities fit within the more rigid boundaries of the Tridentine Church. In the case of the Ursulines and Visitation nuns, reform-minded bishops and others enclosed communities and undermined the original structure that had permitted their interaction with the outside world. Nevertheless, the Catholic Reformation was not characterized by women seeking a religious vocation in the world and men confining them to cloisters. Many members of the French Ursulines and Visitation nuns supported the move to enclosure.[38] Whether initiated by women founding orders or by men trying to control them, there was a definite move toward female *clausura* in the late sixteenth and early seventeenth century.

AN ACTIVE VOCATION: THE DAUGHTERS OF CHARITY

The Daughters of Charity, however, defied the Council of Trent and retained their active, unenclosed vocation within a centralized and highly organized religious community for laywomen. In the early seventeenth century Vincent de Paul, a member of Louis XIII's Council of Conscience, and Louise de Marillac formed the Company of the Daughters of Charity as a noncloistered community of laywomen dedicated to serving the poor in Paris. The Daughters of Charity became renowned nurses, teachers, and social workers in France and they were never cloistered, although the community was briefly disbanded during the French Revolution. To understand how the Daughters of

Charity escaped enclosure when similar religious communities were cloistered, I will first briefly review the Daughters' development. Second, I will point to three major features of the company that combined to permit their active vocation: the two-tiered structure of the organization, the founders' close ties with the French court, and their successful negotiations with the French church. Finally, I will evaluate what the history of the Daughters of Charity tells us about the Catholic Reformation in France.

The Daughters of Charity's mission to assist the sick and poor of France was a timely one. Historians commonly refer to the sixteenth and seventeenth centuries as a period of crisis, during which Europeans suffered severe weather, recurrent bad harvests, and virulent epidemics.[39] These conditions resulted in large quantities of displaced persons and a rise in the number of vagabonds because traditional local charities could not cope with the expanding population of impoverished families and individuals. Moreover, as the number of poor people increased, so did societal fear because individuals and governments recognized the poor as a threat to the maintenance of social order. To address the increased problem of aiding the poor, the French church and state erected new institutions of charity. King Francis I reformed French poor relief in 1536 with an ordinance that prohibited begging and commanded municipalities to put the able-bodied poor to work.[40] Public assistance in France was highly centralized and came from two institutions, local *bureaux de charité*, through which alms were converted into general relief for the deserving poor, and *hôpitaux-généraux*, which were places to help the deserving poor and confine the undeserving and dangerous poor, such as vagabonds and beggars.[41] The *hôpitaux-généraux* played a larger role in poor relief after 1673 when Louis XIV asked all the major cities in France to establish them.[42] Along with the state's efforts to aid and discipline the poor, Catholic-Reformation piety boosted memberships in private charities and many men and women joined religious confraternities to aid their neighbors. Catholics saw the deserving poor as representatives of Christ, and to perform good works on behalf of them not only benefited the less fortunate, but also helped wealthier individuals reduce their time in purgatory.[43] The Confraternities of Charity, founded by de Paul and de Marillac, were such organizations.

In 1617 Vincent de Paul began creating Confraternities of Charity by bringing together elite women into small, locally directed institutions in order to serve their poorer neighbors. Like Merici, de Paul and de Marillac found the title of confraternity to be an important indicator of the secular nature of their organization; members were not nuns and did not require enclosure. Women in the Confraternity of Charity were responsible for bringing food and medicine to the sick and poor in their parishes. Initially, these Ladies of Charity were zealous in their provision of aid, but over time they became less diligent in their service to the needy. In 1629 de Paul appointed Louise de Marillac, a Lady of Charity who had been performing benevolent works under his direction for four years, as supervisor of the confraternities of Charity. De Paul requested that she visit the confraternities regularly and assure that their members were adhering to the Confraternity of Charity's rules. De Marillac discovered that the Ladies were not conforming to the rules, particularly as they were having their servants perform the charitable works on their behalves. Since spiritual ideals did not motivate the servants, the charitable nature of the service disintegrated. Such behavior was unacceptable because it confounded de Paul's ideal of piety as Christ-like service to the poor. The confraternity was one of charity because each member was to serve God through serving the poor; anything less than this denied the confraternity's mission.

De Marillac confronted a serious dilemma: how to preserve the role of the Ladies in the Confraternities of Charity—who were essential because they provided the financial resources—without losing the community's direct religious devotion to the poor. To address this problem, de Paul and de Marillac began permitting women from artisan and peasant families to aid the Ladies of Charity. In 1630 Marguerite Naseau, a shepherdess, asked de Paul if she could volunteer to serve a Parisian Confraternity of Charity. She had nursed and instructed the poor in her village and hoped to do the same in Paris. De Paul and de Marillac encouraged her to serve the poor because she possessed a wide array of practical skills, including cooking, teaching, and healing, that the wealthy Ladies did not. Naseau died while working among the plague-stricken in 1633, and after her "martyrdom" she became the model for all subsequent Daughters of Charity.[44] Following her example, many other young women, mostly from artisan and middling families, offered themselves as Daughters of Charity, ready to tend to the needs of the poor.

November 29, 1633, is the official founding date of the Daughters of Charity—the title given to the women who assisted the Ladies—and by this year the composition of the confraternities had altered dramatically. No longer was the Confraternity of Charity just an organization of the wealthy serving the poor. Rather, it became an alliance of elite administrators, typically married or widowed older Ladies from wealthy, often noble, families who directed unmarried, younger Daughters in the performance of charitable works.[45] Although Ladies had earlier used their servants to perform their good works, their relationships with the Daughters were different. The Daughters who came to Paris lived in a house with de Marillac or together in small houses in Parisian parishes, not with the Ladies. Although the Ladies supported the community financially, they did not directly pay the Daughters; rather, the company provided its Daughters with the material necessities while they did their religious and charitable works. The connections between Ladies and Daughters grew more distant over time with the first Daughters working directly under the guidance of Ladies in some Parisian parishes.[46] Later, the Ladies' control over the community was diffused because they acted more as a board of directors and had less interaction with the Daughters who followed the directives of de Marillac. The formula of Ladies as administrators and Daughters as workers made the Confraternity of Charity a much more efficient organization than it had been before 1633 because the elites no longer directly performed charitable services.[47] The Ladies proved more competent fundraisers and directors than they were cooks and nurses.

Within a decade the Daughters of Charity were not only serving the sick and poor in Parisian parishes, they were staffing hospitals, hospices, insane asylums, and prisons across northern France, including a huge orphanage outside of Paris largely funded by the Ladies.[48] However, the expansion of the confraternity also endangered its very existence. By the mid-1630s the Daughters of Charity were visible in many of Paris's parishes. As young, single women came to Paris to live with de Marillac and work under her direction, the confraternity began to resemble a religious order, and de Marillac a mother superior.[49] Anything more ambiguous than a direct assertion of lay status could have led to *clausura*. The founders were sensitive to this danger. According to de Paul, "It cannot be maintained that the Daughters of Charity are 'religious,' because they could not be Daughters of Charity if they were, for to be a 'religious,' one must be cloistered."[50] Despite this circular reasoning, de Marillac and de Paul knew from the Visitation's example that they could not retain the confraternity's noncloistered status if they defined themselves as a religious order. The language that the Daughters of Charity used to define themselves indicates their liminal status. For example, the Daughters always asserted that they were a confraternity, a company or a community of laywomen called to service the sick and poor. Additionally, the Daughters never referred to themselves as nuns, for they did not take solemn vows. Instead, they were Daughters or Sisters who shared simple vows that they renewed yearly in a private ceremony on 25 March. The Daughters of Charity created a novel religious community that transcended borders between religious and secular life and granted its members an unusual degree of freedom in early modern France. In order to accomplish the works that comprised their vocation, the Daughters of Charity, of course, had to remain unenclosed. They faced surmountable obstacles to their active vocation as is evident from the fate of the Ursulines and Visitation nuns in France, yet the Daughters of Charity managed to retain their noncloistered status.

There are three main reasons for the Daughters' successful avoidance of enclosure at the hands of reforming bishops. First, the two-tiered structure of Ladies and Daughters of Charity helped to make the company viable despite its innovative mission and noncloistered status. The community's composition of wealthy Ladies and Daughters from artisan and farming families meant that both groups could perform tasks deemed appropriate to women of their social background and marital status. Had the Confraternities of Charity restricted their membership to elite women, the work of helping the sick and poor would not have been regularly accomplished. Moreover, if the company had been composed only of Daughters, the community would not have had the funds to support itself nor the social connections to avoid enclosure. By the early 1630s the value of this structure became obvious to de Marillac and de Paul. They were both aware of the substantial role that the Ladies played as patrons to the Daughters and as the company's link to social and political power and protection.[51] It was also clear that the Ladies were not reliable providers to the needy because they did not possess a knowledge of, or a sustained interest in, the hands-on labor of cooking and nursing. Thus, de Marillac and de Paul were keenly aware that without the Daughters the company could not exist. Both Ladies and Daughters were essential for the company's success.

The close relationship between Ladies and Daughters of Charity did not challenge the social hierarchy of early modern France. Despite their active vocation, the company of the Daughters of Charity was an inherently conservative institution. Like a religious order, it used the model of a family to delineate relationships with de Marillac and the other Ladies in a position of greater authority than their Daughters. With few exceptions, the Ladies of Charity performed tasks suited to women of their social background.[52] Although the Daughters' work varied, they primarily provided food, medicine, and instruction to the poor—some of the same tasks that they would have performed as wives of artisans. However, the company did provide its Daughters with a more comprehensive education and a more vocationally diverse life then they would have experienced if they had remained in their villages and married. However, the Daughters were never to assume that this enhanced their status, and the company expected that the Daughters would remain the humble servants of the poor as well as of the Ladies and never become social climbers. De Marillac demanded that social distinctions remain intact and she did not expect or desire that the Daughters would emulate the social manners of the elites for whom they worked. Neither the Ladies nor the Daughters were to use the company as a means to abandon their proper social station. De Marillac encouraged Ladies to fund and direct the company, and she obliged the Daughters to remain pious servants of the poor.

Second, de Marillac and de Paul cultivated their ties with the Ladies while simultaneously building a relationship with the royal family. De Paul was popular at the court of Louis XIII and the Ladies at court respected de Marillac for her charitable work. The pair was able to use their allies at court to support, politically and financially, their new religious community.[53] For example, Cardinal Richelieu's niece, the Duchess of Aiguillon, was a close friend of the queen and a generous contributor to the company of the Daughters of Charity. She directed the Ladies of Charity until 1652.[54] The royal family was also an important supporter of the Daughters of Charity. The queen provided the company with an annual endowment, and after her death the Daughters petitioned the king to continue this funding, which he did.[55] In addition, the royal family made smaller grants to the company for particular works of charity. For example, in 1665 they provided funds for the establishment of primary schools administered by the Daughters.[56] The monarch's direct and continued support of the company granted it legitimacy and made it less vulnerable to interference from church officials.

The support of the royal family and the court was critical during the company's early years. Once the Company of the Daughters of Charity had changed from a confraternity for married Ladies to a company of unmarried Daughters under de Marillac's supervision, it began to resemble a religious order. It is possible that French bishops could have forced the company to adopt enclosure at this point. The protection of the Ladies at court and the royal family was essential for giving the company time to establish itself before coming under scrutiny for violating the Tridentine accords.

The final ingredient that contributed to the success of the Company of the Daughters of Charity was de Marillac's skill at courting the French Church. In the 1630s the company simultaneously developed relationships with local *curés* and prominent Church officials. In their parish work the Daughters had to balance their demands for independence with the need to work agreeably with the local priest. De Marillac instructed the Daughters to behave in an obedient and humble fashion toward the *curés*; however, she offset the Daughters' deferential demeanor with her own assertiveness. For instance, she insisted that local priests not formally direct the Daughters; instead, she supervised the Daughters from the motherhouse and she and de Paul were the company's ultimate authorities.[57] De Marillac's strategy was to maintain direct control over all of her Daughters while allowing them to work closely with their parish priests. Therefore, she could avoid the fate of the Ursulines who came under the direction of local bishops and lost their autonomy. She told Daughters to defer to the authority of the *curés,* unless they contradicted hers, in which case their allegiance should be to the motherhouse. In most parishes this arrangement worked well and the Daughters became an integral part of the local charitable relief system without becoming dependent upon the parish priests.

De Paul and de Marillac were as successful in their negotiations with high-ranking church officials as they were with local *curés*. By placing the Daughters under the direction of the motherhouse and de Paul's male order, the Congregation of the Mission, the founders circumvented the control of local bishops. This maneuver was critical because it was typically reform-minded bishops who enclosed communities of women religious. The founders were fortunate that de Paul had been the archbishop of Paris's tutor when the man was a boy, and that the archbishop had a personal affinity for de Paul.[58] He agreed with the mission of his new community and granted the company of the Daughters of Charity official approbation in 1646.[59] In 1668 Pope Clement IX recognized the Company of the Daughters of Charity as a confraternity and did not define them as a religious order. The Daughters of Charity, a community that strongly resembled the enclosed Visitation order, had managed to escape the cloister with papal approval. By the time the Daughters approached the pope for recognition, they had the support of the king of France and the archbishop of Paris and they had proved themselves skilled social and spiritual servants to the poor. With Clement's recognition of the Daughters of Charity, the Tridentine decrees restricting religious women to convent life began to unravel. The Daughters of Charity were the largest of several communities of unenclosed women who won the acceptance of the church and the state in seventeenth-century France.

In their role as active women religious the Daughters were critical providers of social services for the church, and cloistering them would have proven detrimental to the church. If church authorities had placed all women with a religious vocation within convents and had restricted their access to their families and communities, who would have established schools and taught girls how to become Catholic mothers? Who would have provided poor women with the knowledge of reformed Catholicism? Who would have cared for the sick and poor in France's hospitals, hospices, and orphanages? Daughters of Charity entered the world of the poor and offered themselves as a model of pious Catholic life. They were also missionaries of Tridentine Catholicism who stressed the importance of confession and communion as well as understanding the basic tenets of the faith. They instructed girls in religious education so that they would make their First Communion and regularly confess and commune in their parishes. They also catechized the sick in their homes and in hospitals preparing the terminally ill to die in a state of grace and the curable to live a more pious life. Enclosure was also not in the state's best interest. The Daughters provided France with an inexpensive corps of social workers. They administered and staffed many municipal hospitals as well as Paris's main orphanage, insane asylum, and hospice. In Paris the Daughters' freedom from enclosure did undermine the goals of Trent, but it also supported the spirit of Trent because the Daughters brought the message of the Catholic Reformation to the poor.

THE GROWTH OF ACTIVE COMMUNITIES FOR WOMEN

Early-seventeenth-century France saw the development of numerous small active religious communities for women, and the organizational structure of the company of the Daughters of Charity, with Ladies directing and financially supporting Daughters, was not unique. For example, in 1630 Madame Pollalion had built *La Pitié* to shelter penitent prostitutes, and she recruited unmarried pious young women, whom she called the Daughters of Providence, to staff the institution.[60] Moreover, Pollalion maintained the company with her personal wealth, much like the Ladies of Charity did. Numerous other religious communities resembled the Daughters of Charity, but were also smaller in scale. What was unusual about the company of the Daughters of Charity was its size and breadth of support. In communities in which one woman was a sponsor, as in the case of Madame Pollalion, the organization generally disintegrated upon her death. The larger scale of the Daughters of Charity meant that there were many patrons and workers and that the death of any of them, even Marguerite Naseau or Louise de Marillac, was not fatal to the company.

The Daughters of Charity also served as a model for subsequent communities of active women religious, many of which devoted themselves to teaching or other social services. For example, in Rouen the *Soeurs du Saint-Enfant Jésus* educated daughters of the working poor by teaching catechism.[61] In addition, in 1685 Louis XIV employed the

Dames de Saint-Maur in the Midi to educate converted Protestants and established communities of the *Dames de Saint-Maur* in Montpellier and Montauban.[62] Additionally, in Paris, the *Filles de la Croix* offered poor women the education that they would need to obtain salvation, and domestic servants often went to study with them during their free time.[63] All of these communities shared the active vocation and non-cloistered status of the Daughters of Charity. According to Elizabeth Rapley, "the[se] active congregations became an integral part of modern France. The vast majority of schoolgirls in the Old Regime were educated by them. The hospitals depended on them absolutely. Society grew up around them, to the degree that it developed no alternative sources for the services which they provided."[64]

The Daughters of Charity and their contemporaries who formed similar active communities for religious women manipulated the spirit of the Catholic Reformation to expand the opportunities available to women of different social backgrounds. The example of the Daughters of Charity demonstrates how the Catholic Reformation actually increased the opportunities available to women of different social classes in France, despite the Tridentine promulgations that sought to restrict women's vocational options. Wealthy women used the spiritual message of the Catholic Reformation to gain physical mobility when they went to visit the sick and poor on behalf of their confraternities. The Daughters of Charity also offered a unique opportunity to women of middling families who experienced even greater freedoms than their wealthy counterparts. Unlike the wealthy, poorer women could rarely enter religious orders because they could not afford the dowries that the orders required. Some did manage to join orders as "lay sisters" without paying a dowry, but in these circumstances they never became fully professed nuns and remained the servants of the "choir sisters." With the advent of active religious communities, like the Daughters of Charity, the opportunities available to women of artisan and middling families increased when they became full participants in these communities. The Daughters of Charity did not require novices to bring dowries to the community, but merely enough funds to pay for their first habit or their fare home if they were found to be unsuited for life in the community. Women from middling and poorer homes could thus afford a vocation within a religious community—an option that provided them with a choice other than marriage or spinsterhood.

Ultimately, the Catholic Reformation proved more flexible than the promulgations of the Council of Trent would indicate. The Catholic Church was never able to enclose all women religious as it had planned.

Tellingly, parish priests and the French government recognized the value of the Daughters of Charity's professional work as nurses, teachers, social workers, and hospital directors.[65] Not only did the Daughters of Charity and other French religious communities defy the prescriptions of Trent, they used their freedom from enclosure to perform a variety of works that the Council could not have anticipated and became important missionaries who brought the message of the Catholic Reformation to the poor and sick of France.

NOTES

My thanks to Jeanie Attie and Benson Hawk and Merry Wiesner-Hanks.

1. H. J. Schroeder, *The Canons and Decrees of the Council of Trent* (Rockford, Ill.: Tan Books and Publishers, Inc., 1978), 226 and 228. See also Elizabeth Rapley, *The Dévotes: Women and Church in Seventeenth-Century France* (Buffalo, N.Y.: McGill-Queen's University Press, 1990), 186.

2. Schroeder, *Council of Trent*, 220–21.

3. The Council of Trent referred to the Bull *Periculoso* of Boniface VIII issued in the early thirteenth century.

4. Schroeder, *Council of Trent*, 220–21. Legitimate excuses for leaving the convent were fire, leprosy, and contagious disease. See also Rapley, *Dévotes*, 27.

5. William Monter, "Protestant Wives, Catholic Saints, and the Devil's Handmaid: Women in the Age of the Reformations," in *Becoming Visible: Women in European History*, ed. Renate Bridenthal, Claudia Koonz, and Susan Stuard (Boston, Mass.: Houghton Mifflin Company, 1987), 209.

6. Schroeder, *Council of Trent*, 221.

7. Particularly in times of severe inflation families would choose to dower one of a few daughters generously in order to provide them with the best marriage options and provide their sisters with more modest convent dowries. Gabriella Zarri, "Gender, Religious Institutions and Social Discipline: The Reform of Regulars," in *Gender and Society in Renaissance Italy*, ed. Judith C. Brown and Robert C. Davis (New York: Longman, 1998). Zarri argues that in the fifteenth and sixteenth centuries "monasteries had not yet been defined as placed separate from the social body and the urban context, and their perimeters could be traversed in both directions." For the less documented issue of love affairs between nuns, see Judith Brown, *Immodest Acts: The Life of a Lesbian Nun in Renaissance Italy* (New York: Oxford University Press, 1986).

8. M. C. Gueudré, "La femme et la vie spirituelle," *XVIIe Siècle* 62–63 (1964): 50.

9. Roger Devos, *L'origine sociale des Visitandines d'Annecy aux XVIIe et XVIIIe siècles* (Annecy: Académie Salésienne, 1973), 25.

10. Rapley, *Dévotes*, 25.

11. J. A. Bergin, "The Crown, the Papacy and the Reform of the Old Orders in Early Seventeenth-Century France," *Journal of Ecclesiastical History* 33/2 (April 1982): 245.

12. Hubert Jedin and John Dolan, eds., *History of the Church. Volume V. Reformation and Counter Reformation*, trans. Alselm Briggs and Peter W. Becker (London: Burns and Oates, 1980), 516. Victor Martin, *Le Gallicanisme et la Réforme Catholique: Essai Historique sur l'Introduction en France des Décrets du Concile de Trente (1563–1615)* (Paris: Auguste Picard Editor, 1919), 385.

13. Pierre Chaunu, *L'église, culture et société: essaies sur Réforme et Contre-Réforme* (1517–1620) (Paris: Société d'Édition d'Enseignement Supérieur, 1981), 401. See also Rapley, *Dévotes*, 20. Dowry inflation of the sixteenth century certainly played a central role in increased vocations; however, reduced dowry inflation and increased demands made upon novices made this less of an issue in the seventeenth century.

14. Rapley, *Dévotes*, 20. See also Bergin, "Crown," 234–55.

15. Rapley, *Dévotes*, 20.

16. Charmarie J. Blaisdell, "Angela Merici and the Ursulines," in *Religious Orders of the Catholic Reformation*, ed. Richard DeMolen (New York: Fordham University Press, 1994), 99.

17. Christopher H. Black, *Italian Confraternities in the Sixteenth Century* (New York: Cambridge University Press, 1989), 23. See also Nicholas Terpstra, "Death and Dying in Renaissance Confraternities," in *Crossing the Boundaries: Christian Piety and the Arts in Italian Medieval and Renaissance Confraternities*, ed. Konrad Eisenbichler (Kalamazoo, Mich.: Medieval Institute Publications, 1991), 194.

18. Black, *Italian Confraternities*, 25. See also Gabriel Le Bras, *Etudes de Sociologie Religieuse* (Paris: Presses Universitaires de France, 1955–1956), 454, and D. Henry Dieterich, "Confraternities and Lay Leadership in Sixteenth-Century Liège," *Renaissance and Reformation* 25, no. 1 (1989).

19. Blaisdell, "Angela Merici," 107.

20. Ibid., 115.

21. Judith Combes Taylor, "From Proselytizing to Social Reform: Three Generations of French Female Teaching Congregations, 1600–1720" (Ph.D. diss., Arizona State University, 1980), 55.

22. Teresa Ledochowska, *Angela Merici and the Company of St. Ursula According to the Historical Documents*, trans. Mary Teresa Neylan (Milan: Ancora, 1968), 85–86.

23. Marie Andrée Jégou, O.S.U., *Les Ursulines du Faubourg Saint-Jacques à Paris (1607–1662)* (Paris: Presses Universitaires de France, 1981), 22.

24. Blaisdell, "Angela Merici," 119.

25. Ibid.

26. Taylor, "From Proselytizing to Social Reform," 51.

27. Ibid., 96.

28. Ibid., 120.

29. Blaisdell, "Angela Merici," 121. See also Marie-Elisabeth Aubry, "La Congrégation de Notre-Dame à Nancy et l'éducation des filles aux XVIIe et XVIIIe siècles," *Annales de l'Este* 26 (1974): 76–96. Aubry details the enclosure of an Ursuline community in Nancy in 1616 and the impact of *clausura* on the community's educational mission.

30. Jégou, *Les Ursulines*, 27.

31. Ibid., 28.

32. Anne Bertout, *Les Ursulines de Paris sous l'ancien régime* (Paris: Typographie Pirmin-Didot, 1935), 81. See also Olwen Hufton and Frank Tallett, "Communities of Women, the Religious Life, and Public Service in Eighteenth-Century France," in *Connecting Spheres: Women in the Western World, 1500 to the Present*, ed. Marilyn J. Boxer and Jean H. Quataert (New York: Oxford University Press, 1987). The French Ursulines also made a distinction between choir and lay sisters based upon the number of vows the women took.

33. Marie de Chantal Gueudré, *Histoire de l'ordre des Ursulines en France* (Paris: Editions Saint-Paul, 1957), I:242. See also Jégou, *Les Ursulines*, 148.

34. *New Catholic Encyclopedia*, 1967 ed., s.v. "Francis de Sales, Saint," 34–36.

35. Devos, *Visitandines d'Annecy*, 29–33.

36. Ibid., 39.

37. In 1618 Paul V made the Visitation order an official religious order. John Patrick Donnelly, "The New Religious Orders, 1517–1648," in *Handbook of European History, 1400–1600*, ed. Thomas A. Brady, Heiko A. Obermann, and James D. Tracy (Grand Rapids, Mich.: William B. Eerdmans Publishing Company, 1995), 303.

38. Linda Lierheimer points out that many Ursuline communities divided over the issue of enclosure, with younger sisters wanting *clausura* and older sisters opposing it. Linda Lierheimer, "Redefining Convent Space: Ideals of Female Community among Seventeenth-Century Ursuline Nuns," *Proceedings of the Western Society for French History* 24 (1997): 211–20.

39. Robin Briggs, *Early Modern France 1560–1715* (New York: Oxford University Press, 1998), 36.

40. Robert Jütte, *Poverty and Deviance in Early Modern Europe* (New York: Cambridge University Press, 1994), 117.

41. Ibid., 119. See also Colin Jones, *The Charitable Imperative: Hospitals and Nursing in Ancien Regime and Revolutionary France* (New York: Routledge, 1989), 4.

42. Daniel Hickey, *Local Hospitals in Ancien Régime France: Rationalization, Resistance, Renewal, 1530–1789* (Buffalo, N.Y.: McGill-Queen's University Press, 1997), xvi.

43. Colin Jones, *Charity and Bienfaisance: The Treatment of the Poor in the Montpelier Region 1740s-1815* (New York: Cambridge University Press, 1982), 76.

44. Illness was a chronic problem for the Company. For example, see Archive de la Maison Mère des Filles de la Charité (hereafter A.M.M.F.C.) 1033/78.

45. Despite de Paul's claims that the Daughters of Charity were "peasant girls," my studies of enrollment records for the company's seminary show otherwise. De Paul saw the Daughters in light of Naseau, the first and model Daughter of Charity. However, by later in the seventeenth century most of the Daughters came from families of the middle classes. Fifteen entrants had fathers who were laborers, nine were active in textiles industry, such as cloth weavers, eight were gentlemen, eight were in military service, eight were in construction industries, like carpentry, six were professionals, such as schoolmasters, and five were merchants. Young women who joined the Daughters of Charity to serve the sick poor were of artisan and middling families, a good number of whom entered the community with some formal education and the ability to read and write. Archives Nationales. L. L. 1664. *Registre de la ville d'Eu.* There are no entrance records extant for the time period before 1685. The sample consulted comprised one hundred individual entrant records between 1685 and 1705 from the Eu seminary in Seine-Maritime. Admissions records for sixty-nine of them provide information about the occupations of the novices' fathers.

46. Elisabeth Charpy, *Petite vie de Louise de Marillac* (Paris: Desclée de Brouwer, 1991), 26.

47. The Ladies of Charity also often established communities of the Daughters of Charity; however, they were still directed by de Marillac from the Motherhouse and not directly by the Lady benefactor. A.M.M.F.C. 68/1018, a letter dated 1656 from the Marquise de Souches to de Marillac requesting Daughters to instruct young girls in her parish.

48. Louise de Marillac, *Ecrits spirituels*, ed. Elisabeth Charpy (Paris: Filles de la Charité, 1983), 208.

49. A.M.M.F.C. 187, letter from Monsieur Lambert, a priest of the Congregation of the Mission, to Barbe Angiboust, a Daughter of Charity at Richelieu, dated May 13, 1641. Lambert asks Angiboust if they are still "passing" for a secular community.

50. Vincent de Paul, *Saint Vincent de Paul. Correspondance, Entretiens, Documents,* 14 vol., ed. Pierre Coste (Paris: Librairie Lecoffre, 1920–1926), IX: 662.

51. See Raymond Darricau, "L'action charitable d'une reine de France: Anne d'Autriche," *XVIIe siècle* 90–91 (1971): 111–125.

52. De Marillac, *Ecrits spirituels*, Letter 38. Louise de Marillac and Elizabeth Turgis were the only noble women who performed the work of Daughters for a long duration. Both defined themselves as Daughters of Charity and not Ladies of Charity. Turgis was Sister Servant at Angers in 1640, went to Richelieu in 1646, to Chars in 1647, and Chantilly in 1648, the year of her death.

53. De Marillac, *Ecrits spirituels*, 10. De Marillac's place at court is remarkable considering the intrigues of her extended family. Her uncles were implicated in the Day of the Dupes by Louis XIII. The king imprisoned Louis de Marillac who died two years later while still incarcerated. Louis XIII recalled Michel de Marillac from the Italian front, tried him on exaggerated charges, and had him publicly beheaded in 1632. These events seem to have had little direct impact on Louise de Marillac, and she was not excluded from the court because of her uncle's behavior. See de Paul, *Correspondance*, IV: Letter 1518. De Paul was popular among the people at court, except with Mazarin. De Paul and Mazarin were frequently on opposite sides of debate in the Council of Conscience. Their animosity increased during the Fronde when de Paul unsuccessfully tried to convince the queen to remove Mazarin from office. After the Fronde Mazarin had his revenge by removing de Paul from the council.

54. Pierre Coste, *Monsieur Vincent: le grand saint du grand siècle* (Paris: Desclée de Brouer et cie Editeurs, 1934) I: 324–27. For her extensive involvement in charitable projects, see also Richard Francis Elmore, "The Origins of the Hopital-General of Paris" (Ph.D. diss., Notre Dame University, 1975).

55. A.M.M.F.C. 1099/155. *Copie d'un Placet au Roy and* 1100/155. *Plaise au Roy.* Also see Darricau, "L'action charitable," 119–22.

56. A.M.M.F.C. 147 (October 27, 1665). *Monsieur d'Horgny a Geneviève Fauter.* For a discussion of the protection that the royal family offered to the company, see also de Marillac, *Ecrits spirituels*, 18. In 1638 de Marillac wrote to de Paul stating that a sergeant wanted to billet his troops of soldiers near the company's orphanage at Bicêtre. De Marillac asked de Paul if the sister servant should refuse and whether she should request support from the Duchess d'Aiguillon until de Paul can secure a prohibition from the queen.

57. De Marillac, *Ecrits spirituels*, 11–13. De Marillac tells de Paul that she thinks it is unwise to make the confraternity entirely dependent upon the pastor because they would want no one else to know what is going on in each confraternity. She believes that this would cause fragmentation. Instead, the Daughters should be accountable to the motherhouse.

58. Ibid., 52. Along with the archbishop, de Marillac and de Paul cultivated relationships with other high church officials. In 1641 she requested that the rector of Notre-Dame de Paris allow her to open a school for poor girls. He agreed with the following stipulations: "She may only teach poor girls and accept no others. She should educate them in good morals, grammar and other pious and honest subjects. First she must swear to

faithfully and diligently operate these schools within their statutes and decrees."

59. Ibid., 379–80.

60. Coste, *Monsieur Vincent*, I: 346.

61. Rapley, *Dévotes*, 121.

62. Ibid., 126.

63. Taylor, "From Proselytizing to Social Reform," 258–59.

64. Rapley, *Dévotes*, 8.

65. The Daughters' labors were an extension of sanctioned women's work and generally earned them praise, not censure. According to Merry Wiesner, contemporaries recognized nursing, like instructing girls and caring for orphans, as within the acceptable realm of women's work. Families expected women to provide food, medical services, and basic education to their family members. "Women not only received charity in early modern cities, but they also dispensed it. The hospitals, orphanages, and infirmaries run by the Catholic church were largely staffed by women. . . . There was never any attempt to shelter women from the danger and drudgery of working in these hospitals, however the women cooked, cleaned, and cared for the patients, and also did administrative work and book-keeping, led the patients in prayer, and carried out examinations of admission." Merry Wiesner, *Women and Gender in Early Modern Europe* (New York: Cambridge University Press, 1993), 94. According to Elizabeth Rapley, "if the appearance of the sisters on the street caused some uneasiness, at least their occupation offended no one." Rapley, *Dévotes*, 114.

WOMEN AT THE CENTERS, MEN AT THE MARGINS

*The Wilderness Mission of the Secular Sisters
of Early Montreal Reconsidered*

William Henry Foster III

THE WOMEN'S RELIGIOUS COMMUNITIES of seventeenth-century French Canada functioned not only as schools or hospitals, but also as sites of managed transculturation. These communities took on the challenge of converting an astoundingly diverse group of resident subjects, men as well as women, boys as well as girls, French immigrants, English captives, and local Indians. Within the limits of French Canadian religion, culture, and imagination, any individual could be made suitable to live and survive in the New France colony.

Marguerite Bourgeoys's community of lay missionary teaching sisters embodied all aspects of this mission. The Congrégation Notre-Dame de Montreal began in 1653 when the fur-trading settlement of Ville-Marie consisted of little more than a stockade surrounding a few wooden buildings. As this outpost evolved into the frontier town called Montreal in the decades leading up to the turn of the eighteenth century, Bourgeoys and her compatriots attended to the increasing human and economic diversifications of the colony and the increasing complexities of its social needs. In the process of providing the professional services of teachers, the Congrégation sisters transformed themselves from individuals at the periphery of the French world into women at the center of the French colonial project. But the vision as realized secularly was the inverse of the original religious ideal. Setting out to make the wilderness into a province of the God of France, they soon redefined themselves as agents of turning French women—and men—into the frontier beings called *Canadiens*.

When gender serves as a primary framework of inquiry, the focus is often on women living on the margins of worlds made by men. The life of the Congrégation in the five decades after its beginning, however, forces us to consider the implications of men living at the margins of smaller worlds made by women. The efforts of these religious sisters to expand their mission, which brought it into the center of colonial life, meant that men and boys would live within the community alongside the female students and sisters. These male subjects contributed to the success of the community's mission through their service. But Bourgeoys's efforts to draw the men from the margins into the heart of the nominal women's community would grow increasingly problematic. Her colleagues would in time reject the idea that men, even as subordinates, should have a place in the women's mission. The male servants for their part would conflate a female-controlled religious mission with illegitimate women's authority.

Marguerite Bourgeoys, a young woman rejected as a postulant by the contemplative Carmelites of Troyes, France, refocused her sense of mission when she turned away from the French cloister to face the North American wilderness on her own terms.[1] Bourgeoys certainly sought to emulate those French lay sisters devoted to social service and to sidestepping the severe restrictions on women religious imposed by the Council of Trent.[2] But her unique vision amounted to a specifically New World version of a Marian, wandering, and apostolic life for laywomen. This was the life she called the *vie voyagère*.[3] Bourgeoys intended this wandering to be nothing short of an explicitly female version of the work of the apostles of Jesus:

> The apostles were sent in the name of Our Lord and they worked wonders. The sisters of the Congregation are sent under the protection of the Blessed Virgin to teach school and they instruct girls as though they were very learned. . . . The apostles were unfaithful in abandoning our Lord at the time of His passion. They needed the Holy Spirit to make them strong. The sisters of the Congregation are timid and slow to advance in perfection. They need the help of the Blessed Virgin to obtain the Spirit of God who will give them courage. The apostles went out to all parts of the world. The sisters of the Congregation are ready to go anywhere they are sent in this country.[4]

Bourgeoys created the means to this end through the office of *filles séculières* (secular sisters) who took simple vows of poverty, chastity, and service. Bourgeoys patterned the life after her interpretation of the Virgin Mary's mission in the world—that her apostolic purpose had been carried out free from the authority of her son's apostles and their successors.[5] That her new sisterhood actually realized this ideal continually rankled a series of bishops in Quebec. But the *vie voyagère* was not in any sense a utopian vision. Bourgeoys harbored no illusions regarding the workings of human nature, clothed in monastic robes or not, and its rather limited capacity for improvement.[6]

This unadorned Gallic pragmatism conditioned the *mentalité* necessary to effect her New World innovations for women religious. Unlike the beguines and other earlier groups of itinerant laywomen, who were never faced with the challenges of transracial or transgender inclusion, Bourgeoys held a nonrestrictive vision of the *vie voyagère*. "If you act as an advocate for the church," she wrote, "its own baptised members will be converted, and unbelievers as well."[7] Her actions revealed precisely how wide a net she cast.

Her original conception of service included teaching and catechizing Indian girls, which placed Bourgeoys squarely within the larger missionary guidelines of Maisonneuve's Société de Notre-Dame, which had founded Montreal. It also followed previous missionary forms widely known and admired in France: that of the long-suffering Jesuits and the cloistered Ursuline mission pioneered by Marie de L'Incarnation.[8] But when the local Iroquois proved hostile to the French downriver fur-trading settlements, Bourgeoys's mission by necessity turned inward to her own people. As a mission by and for Canadians, it became essential to the social and cultural survival of the tiny settlement. Bourgeoys began a school for Canadian girls in a converted stable, and in a nearby structure she sheltered and instructed young immigrant women brought to Canada in order to marry men who the government hoped would settle and permanently maintain the French presence 150 miles further inland from Quebec at Montreal.[9]

With these efforts Bourgeoys succeeded in winning young French female immigrants for the colonial project in the Saint Lawrence as she simultaneously drew some of the first generation of Canadian frontier-born women into her growing community of sisters. Her first local recruits originated in the modest artisan class, giving her practical community the hard skills it needed to survive, while providing a place in which the spiritual life of the women religious could be combined with the rigor of the female missionary. The relative lack of class distinctions began to set the Congrégation Notre-Dame apart from their socially elite Ursuline counterparts in Quebec—but proved congruent to the needs of the rough-and-tumble frontier settlement.

That Bourgeoys created her *vie voyagère* on the New World frontier dictated that her community be completely self-sufficient instead of dependent on potentially fickle and controlling patronage from wealthy individuals or—worse—the mercurial and preoccupied French colonial authorities.[10] Dependence could quickly turn fatal in that particularly harsh environment if the tide of benevolent favor suddenly receded. Self-reliance left Bourgeoys with a stark challenge: the colony needed women, but Marguerite Bourgeoys needed men—to physically sustain her community with their labor. From this sprang the genesis of the Congrégation's mission to and for men and boys. Bourgeoys's men not only made it possible for the Congrégation to survive, but their presence as both subjects and objects of the community's mission came to define a significant part of the collective identity of the sisters and female students. And as for the male subjects, the material needs of the community meant ultimately that men and boys could, at least for a time, be offered a chance to walk in the Virgin Mary's footsteps.

Three types of male residents lived among the sisters during the early days of the Congrégation Notre-Dame. Male indentured servants, also called *engagés*, worked alongside others called *donnés*—men who pledged their service in perpetuity to the community in exchange for a guarantee of food, shelter, and religious guidance. The sisters also instructed boys as student-domestics. In the first years of the colony Bourgeoys educated a few young boys in the absence of available priests—but even after the educational opportunities had expanded in Montreal (and Quebec) by the 1670s, parents or guardians of modest social standing continued to indenture their sons to the community with the understanding that they would be both servants and students there.

Bourgeoys and her companions included their servants in the vital life of the community in a way that differed from their French counterparts as well as the principal men's communities present in and around early Montreal—the Sulpitians and Jesuits—even going so far as to blur in some eyes the distinction between sister and servant. Rituals of everyday life suggest the degree of male inclusion in the early community and reveal more explicitly that Marguerite Bourgeoys considered these men to be an integral part of her novel New World mission.[11] Bourgeoys, for example, indicates in her writings that the sisters and servants shared bread.[12] More than an incidental note, this detail reveals that the Congrégation did not engage in the universal and defining act separating employer and servant symbolically, physically, and materially—eating separate food at separate times in separate locations. In the cultural universe surrounding Bourgeoys, breaking bread with servants removed the axiomatic social hierarchy separating the classes.

Bourgeoys thereby included male servants just as she integrated her female students and wards who originated in an inferior class—actions that troubled her fellow sisters of the Congrégation.[13]

Bourgeoys also decided to include servants as coworshipers with the *filles séculières* in the Montreal's tiny stone chapel built into the palisade in 1675. The inclusion of servants in the back pews at mass would not have been so unusual in an isolated French monastery or *seigneurie*, but having men accompany women religious to worship made a public statement about the nature of the mission—unmistakably contrarian in terms of expected class as well as gender distinctions.[14] As we will see, however, these inclusions were not viewed positively by all members within the community itself.

Relations among all types of residents within the community became defined by their common work. In 1662 Bourgeoys acquired land at Pointe-Saint-Charles on the southern shore of Montreal island, about a half-hour walk outside the town palisade. She established there a sustenance farm in order to provide food for the community as well as extra income to support the sisters' teaching activities. This event triggered the need for the first substantial influx of male laborers. The census of 1666 and 1667 reveals the names of four *domestiques engagés* employed by Bourgeoys. Twelve more are listed in the next census of 1681.[15] These men spent much of their time at Pointe-Saint-Charles working alongside and under the direction of the Congrégation's *soeur fermière*, Catherine Crolo.

Crolo, born at Troyes in 1619, called herself the "donkey" of the community, assuming for herself the servant's role. This work of Martha included all forms of housekeeping, maintenance, and even the heavy business of hauling and beating laundry—all so her companions could be freed to focus on the mission of education. Naturally, then, as the community began aquiring servants her position gradually transformed into being the supervisor of those who now performed and extended her original duties.

Upon the purchase of the farm in 1662, Crolo redefined yet again her professional life, taking on the management of its lands and workers. Leaving the direction of the main house in Montreal to younger colleagues, Crolo walked each day with the menservants from town to farm and back again. And when Bourgeoys finally purchased a large house adjacent to the first acreage capable of providing ample living space, Crolo took up year-round residence at Pointe-Saint-Charles. The servants slept wherever their work dictated.[16]

But the purchase of the farmhouse meant far more than the convenience of those who worked there. The house did nothing less than allow the educational outreach of the Congrégation to assume a scope of the kind originally envisioned by Bourgeoys. Although ongoing war with the Iroquois still meant that the goal of wilderness missions continued to be unrealized, the establishment in 1668 of a school called *La Providence* at the house at Pointe-Saint-Charles allowed the Congrégation to escape the confines of their close quarters at the stable school and begin educating and acculturating large numbers of young women.[17]

Although now directed culturally and geographically inward, the educational mission of the Congrégation Notre-Dame proceeded according to the precepts of the *vie voyagère*. Bourgeoys sought out students from all social origins. The taking in of students from merchant, artisan, and *habitant* (farming) families gave *La Providence* its practical and vocational emphasis. By 1684 Bishop Saint-Vallier wrote that approximately twenty "grande-filles" (girls of roughly adolescent age) resided at *La Providence*, joined by at least the same number of younger students.[18] In addition, Bourgeoys made herself famous (then as now) by charging herself with the task of providing temporary haven for the *filles de roi*—voluntary, royally sponsored, unmarried female immigrants, most of whom had been recruited from Paris's principal asylum for young, unsupported women to become the founding mothers of the then predominently male Canadian colony.

In one sense, the acculturation of the female students and *filles de roi* was intended to be parallel to that of the male *engagés* working at Pointe-Saint-Charles. Bourgeoys sought that all her temporary dependents would in time become permanent—and devout—free settlers in the Saint Lawrence valley. But the reality of indenture exposed the true differences between the statuses of young women and young men at *La Providence*, regardless of Bourgeoys's ultimate goals. Though the vocational students, the *filles de roi*, and the male *engagés* of the Congrégation in theory saw their time at Pointe-Saint-Charles as a stop along the path to better their lives, life at *La Providence* proved in actuality a continuation of the relatively advantageous status of women in the colony generally. With the sex ratio in the colony not equalized until about 1698, unmarried female immigrants, royally sponsored or not, enjoyed a choice of husband soon after arrival.[19] Their male counterparts, usually from farming or artisan backgrounds, were required to serve out their full indentures. The usual term was three years, although some normal terms ranged up to nine.

As a result of the sex ratio in the colony, a pattern emerged by which a young woman would embark upon marriage within months—or even weeks or days—after initial arrival. If the woman in question happened to marry into the merchant, seigneurial, or even the artisan castes, she could easily find the male servant or servants engaged by her husband to be of equal or even superior social origins compared to her own. The *engagés*, for their part, could not fail to notice the disadvantageous aspects of these gendered social dynamics. Whether or not self-respecting would-be farmers or artisans resented living under the authority of their rough social counterparts from the Salpêtrière asylum, they could not fail to appreciate the difficulties they would have competing in the marriage maket after they obtained their freedom.[20] If their master had married beneath himself, what chance did they stand?

A particularly exaggerated form of this general pattern was created at *La Providence*. From the perspective of a young female vocational student, or *fille de roi*, her newly found, if temporary, authority extended not to one or a few servants but many. The instruction at *La Providence* featured as its centerpiece the acquisition of the skills of a *maîtresse de maison*—including the ability to directly manage farm and house servants. This instruction helped construct a distinctly novel New World manifestation of Frenchwomen's authority within a family structure. No matter what their social background, the lessons prepared them for the extended responsibilites they would shoulder when their husbands absented themselves, in the distinctive Canadian manner, for voyaging or military missions of a length not typical in France.

The *engagés*, for their part, found themselves literally part of the curriculum of *La Providence*. The increasingly experienced men were continually managed and "re-trained" by each new group of Crolo's students. This process might well have impressed upon the men that neither experience, skill, nor apparent acculturation could overcome the disabilities of their sex within the Congrégation hierarchy.

Numbers suggest the extent and degree of the male alienation at the Congrégation Notre-Dame, which stood in stark contrast to the degree of female acculturation. The Congrégation successfully acculturated all the *filles de roi* who came to them, and the continual growth of the community in terms of sisters and students speaks to the excellent regard that Bourgeoys's mission enjoyed from both young Montreal women and their families. By 1681 the membership of the Congrégation had grown to twenty-four sisters. This membership taught and met the needs of perhaps forty or fifty girl students of all ages. The number of *filles de roi* during their peak arrival years in the 1670s easily exceeded that of the Canada-born students, although the immigrants had largely stopped arriving by the mid-1680s.[21]

The male population of the community also grew. By 1681 thirteen male servants and about fifteen to twenty indentured boys aged twenty or younger resided at the Congrégation. But unlike the women the males did not tend to remain in Canada. Despite the level of inclusion in the life of the community afforded them by Marguerite Bourgeoys, only two of all the indentured servants (one of them a tailor—the only *engagé* with an easily marketable skill) present at the Congrégation in 1667 or 1681 are known to have stayed permanently in Canada.[22] The 10 percent rate of success enjoyed by the sisters in settling their male dependents was a bare fraction of the 50 percent general rate of return for *engagés* before 1690.[23]

Why, despite their concerted efforts, did the sisters fail to win new men for Canada when their private and male religious community counterparts proved to be relatively successful? Clearly, the simple fact that the men lived under indentured servitude among the sisters did not account for the extent of flight. Other masters had far greater success than Bourgeoys.

Servants came to Canada seeking upward mobility, and an indenture contained an expectation of reciprocal advantage. The authority of the patron rested in one sense on being able to secure the interests of the subject. But the sisters possessed no less an ability to provide these advantages than the other masters in the colony. First, relative access to land was not a differential issue—property could be had by freedmen simply by signing a contract with a local seigneur. And though not seigneurs themselves, as were the Sulpicians and many servant-holding families, the sisters of the Congrégation Notre-Dame enjoyed the aid of benefactors such as Jacques Le Ber, the wealthiest man in Montreal, who could provide at the sisters' request a network of patrons at least equal to any in New France.[24] In short, a servant leaving the sisters on good terms would have every advantage as any of his counterparts. The only real difference was the gender of those in authority.

To clarify the alienating dynamics of specifically female authority, it is necessary to examine the detailed inner workings of the community. The first story is told by simple demographics. In 1667 the median age of servants had been twenty-two, while Bourgeoys and Crolo had been in their late forties. This, combined with the superior class origins of the sisters (several of whom, like the aptly named Bourgeoys, were born into well-off merchants castes of the *haute bourgeoisie*), would have caused no upset to expected lines of authority as perceived by the men, irrespective of gender. But during the fourteen years separating the 1667 and 1681 censuses, the number of sisters had increased sixfold, the scope of the community's activities had increased proportionately, and an influx of young, Canadian-born sisters, mostly daughters of artisans, modest tradesmen, and even farmers had slashed the median age of the sisters to only twenty-five. Of course, large numbers of students as well as a small group of associated free servants (known as the sisters of the gray robe) also took an active role in the management of the communal property—so that the median age of all females exercising daily authority over the *engagés* was certainly no more than seventeen. At the same time, the Congrégation, perhaps wanting more experienced help, had selected servants whose median age approached thirty-four.[25]

Further, the gap in class origins was fast closing as well, with many *engagés* in the 1680s originating in precisely the same tradesmen caste as their new female employers in Canada. While women, in France and in Canada, could theoretically expect the loyalty of male servants by virtue of superior class and seniority, independent female authority in the French-speaking world could under certain circumstances be tenuous.[26] The new realities of class and age inversion at the Congrégation put extreme pressure on the third and more fundamental inversion of power—that of gender.

The transformation of the individual identities of sisters joining the Congrégation complicated further the phenomenon of gender power inversion as perceived by male servants. One such transformation created a specific inversion of authority and race. In 1676, twenty-three years after her arrival in Montreal, Marguerite Bourgeoys finally succeeded in opening a tiny wilderness mission at the Jesuit outpost known as the "Mountain Mission" on Montreal island. Three years later the Congrégation welcomed as the first two Iroquoian sisters, Marie-Barbe Attoncion d'Onotais, then aged twenty-three, and Marie-Thérèse Gannensagouas, aged fourteen.[27]

Marie-Thérèse Gannensagouas remained at the Mountain Mission to teach and catechize Indian girls alongside her fellow sisters. By these efforts she achieved a dramatic change in social standing within the Iroquoian settlement. The Huron-born Gannensagouas and her father had been brought among the Iroquois as captives. Even if "adopted" into Iroquoian families, Marie-Thérèse, as well as her father, in all probability remained marginalized at the Mountain Mission.[28] Gannensagouas then became a teacher and catechist of those who had formally been her social superiors.

For her part, Marie-Barbe d'Onotais, a true *Iroquoise*, accompanied her new sisters back to the French cultural realm where she made her new life as a teacher. In the transcultural sense, d'Onotais's transformation proved more radical than that of her younger counterpart. But in another sense, d'Onotais's life as a teaching and farming sister featured a powerful continuation of the female elements of Iroquoian life. For both Iroquoian women and French Canadian monastic women, agricultural knowledge possessed a spiritual as well as a practical dimension when shared among adult women, between mother and daughter, or between student and teacher.

The presence of the male subjects at *La Providence* indicates both the extent and the limitations of this cultural conversion. Whether instructing students, assisting Catherine Crolo, or most likely doing both, d'Onotais would have been in at least occasional supervisory contact with the French indentured servants.

Though the spectacle of monastic sisters doing much of their own fieldwork and directing their own men to perform the rest may or may not have been arresting to French Canadians, to an *Iroquoise* such a scene would have been familiar. Crucially for all participants, the feminine exclusivity of farming in Iroquois settlements was only breached by those of their male captives who had been spared execution in favor of liminal adoption. A captured warrior, or other man or boy, who was deemed by his captors to be without honor was intentionally humiliated by being forced to work in this separate and distinctly inferior women's sphere of activity. His shame then became ritualized and continually reinforced by the requirement that he not only perform women's work but do so under the direction of the females of the village.[29]

Conflicted perspectives resulted. The Canadian sisters regarded the male presence as a legitimate extension of the *vie voyagère*. But for the increasing number of servants beginning their terms at *La Providence* in the 1680s, the sight of Soeur d'Onotais, a "*sauvagesse*," acting as a responsible director of activities within a French institutional structure could not have failed to drive home the state of inverted authority within the Congrégation. The cultural viewpoint of the Iroquois as personified by d'Onotais represented a middle ground. The Iroquois view regarded men working for women in the fields as a gender power inversion—but a deliberate and, above all, legitimate one. Somewhat ironically, d'Onotais may well have shared with her servants the perception that the service of the men possessed a quality of shame—but this factor of alienation to the men proved one of supreme cultural integration to Marie-Barbe Attoncion d'Onotais. In her new role helping to direct the special demographic structure at *La Providence*, she became able to add the familiar cultural forms and practices of her origins into an evolving new identity. D'Onotais in turn gave to her new French sisters the local knowledge they needed to advance their collective mission.[30]

Transformations of this kind were not limited to cultural outsiders in the French colony. The previously mentioned chief *soeur fermière*, Catherine Crolo, had voluntarily sought a new life within a women's monastic community after surviving what is commonly believed to have been a sexual assault experienced as a young teenager in Troyes. This tragic event evidently catalyzed the impoverished Crolo's friendship with Marguerite Bourgeoys as well as influenced her decision to accompany the foundress to the New World.[31]

Crolo's chosen path within the Congrégation and her relationship with its male residents suggest the nature of the transformation possible for a French woman within Canada's unique forms of women's monasticism. While her early years as the community's "donkey" might be considered by some as a penance for the sin that early modern French Catholic ideology was capable of attributing to a female victim of sexual assault, this interpretation becomes problematic given the nature of Crolo's later life. Especially after the purchase of the farm at Pointe-Saint-Charles in 1662, Crolo lived not as a refugee among women, but as a figure of authority living mostly, and sometimes exclusively, among men. Through the opportunities of the frontier sisterhood, she had redefined in the most obvious and graphic manner her relationship with the male sex. She had transformed herself from a penniless and friendless young rape victim to a respected woman religious who not only directed and disciplined men but trained her younger counterparts and female students to do the same.

Bourgeoys's Congrégation was a place devoted to acculturation; it was not designed as a place of refuge nor as a theater where personal retributions would be acted out. But whether Crolo saw the assumption of the direction of the community's men as exclusively one of maternal guidance to a new life in Canada we do not know. For many of the resisting male servants, Catherine Crolo was the feminine face they saw most often, and as such was the embodiment of the community they found so objectionable. Beyond question, however, is that Catherine Crolo forged her new individual identity within the collective on the anvil of the male presence at Pointe-Saint-Charles.

But we glimpse at closest range the overall impact of the male presence at the Congrégation Notre-Dame by considering a special subset of community servants—the *donnés*. Unlike those servants serving fixed terms of indenture, the four known *donnés* signed contracts that obligated them to remain in and work for the community on a permanent basis. The motivations for the extreme act of rendering oneself unfree in perpetuity are in fact possible to ascertain. For at least one young man it was a religiously motivated act of service and devotion. Older men tended to sign such arrangements after working hand-to-mouth over a number of years. A *donné* had ultimate security on an insecure frontier—he would have food, shelter, and a community of faith for as long as he lived. But the work expected of the *donnés* was identical to that of the *engagés*—helping the sisters and students on the farm, in the school, and in the central household.[32] The *donnés* did not take simple vows, but the restrictions that came with their indentures imposed a life of simplicity, poverty, service, and celibacy that served as rough male equivalents of the sisters' own lives of devotion.

Although in theory the *donnés* would never be free to leave the community, they enjoyed a compensatory special status within it. Bourgeoys recorded in her writings the entrance of the first man into her community:

> A young man, a student, also offered himself to serve this house, to give himself to the service of God for his whole life. He followed us on the voyage and took his quarters [on the ship] near ours. But while he was on board, he was attacked by dysentery from which he later died in our house two years after his arrival in Montreal.[33]

Other men followed with offers of perpetual service and came to share a special title. By the name of one twenty-five-year-old man, Jacques Hordequin, on the 1667 census appear the words "*frère donné*"—"*frère*" meaning "brother."[34] Bourgeoys addressed her three fellow *congrégationalistes* as *soeurs*—sisters. And here in Jacques Hordequin she claimed a *frère*, a brother. Thomas Mousnier, another *donné*, appears in Bourgeoys's own writings as "frère Thomas."[35] These were dependent brothers, fictive "little" brothers if you will, but brothers within the sisterhood nonetheless.

It doubtlessly surprised these sisters profoundly that the *donnés*, the men held closest to the center of community, outdid even their indentured counterparts in resistance to women's authority. Certainly one, and very possibly two, took the extreme measure of running away—a criminal act of contract breach. (The anonymous original *donné* previously mentioned died in 1660.) In addition to the heavy penalties that could be potentially administered by master and civil authorities, flight meant above all elimination of one's support and food-supply network. In the brutal Canadian environment—frozen and barren for eight months, hot and humid for four, surrounded by hostile Iroquois year-round—these absences can only be considered genuine acts of desperation.

First, *donné* Jacques Hordequin disappears from the records between 1667 and 1681, and the lack of a record of his death in the meticulous parish record suggests he fled. A certain fugitive was *donné* Pierre Picard, who abandoned his wife and children, settled on Congrégation land at Pointe-Saint-Charles. The sisters did not pursue Picard as was their right but nevertheless honored their commitment to educate his offspring.[36]

The case of *donné* Thomas Mousnier is more complex. Though Bourgeoys could have retained him within the community on a permanent basis under any circumstances, she wrote in 1682 that Mousnier had been "dismissed" after less than three years of service, apparently after demonstrating some sort of recalcitrant behavior. Bourgeoys, who later encountered Mousnier by chance on a Montreal street, reported that he "regretted" his actions and that he "believ[ed] he could return" to the community.[37]

The case of *frère donné* Thomas Mousnier presented Marguerite Bourgeoys with several options. She could have simply accepted him back into the community on the same terms as before. Even had the *donné's* contrition proved fleeting, she would also have been well within her rights to have him apprehended and delivered back to the community in Montreal by force. When the moment came, Bourgeoys chose neither to enforce her contract nor to accept the servant's contrition. Contracts aside, Bourgeoys did not want *frère* Thomas within her mission unless she could be convinced his heart and soul were engaged in the community's mission. For Bourgeoys a heart and soul took precedence over the advantages of the potential labor of bodies. It would have been a simple matter indeed for Bourgeoys from the outset of her mission to simply adopt the Old World practices of separating sisters from servants entirely and leaving the men under the care and direction of foremen hired for the purpose. But the male presence at the Congrégation Notre-Dame shows again not only the nature of the women's mission, but how Bourgeoys and her companions were able to define that mission according to their own conceptions of spiritual involvement.

Yet ultimately, it was perhaps precisely this sort of intimate inclusion within the community itself that served as the wellspring of the acculturation differential. Serving in any religious community was an all-consuming and highly regimented proposition—the residents at *La Providence*, for example, lived their lives to time of ringing bells.[38] Therefore Bourgeoys's insistence on a complete immersion of servants into the life of the community would come to bear most intensely on the pledged-for-life *frère donnés*. It is not difficult to imagine that their situation may well have been a cloying magnification, instead of an amelioration, of an adult male servant's fictive-childhood status—a status continually reinforced in the households and fields of the Congrégation.[39]

As all servants discovered, the uncloistered nature of the Congrégation did not mean a laxity in monastic discipline. The effort to make her sisterhood legitimate in the eyes of the skeptics—especially clerical skeptics—combined with the educational mission of the community perhaps hardened the resolve of the foundress to live by the strictest internal standards. Bourgeoys, for example, advised aspirant sisters of the community that they must "obey promptly in everything and obey everyone who has any jurisdiction over her without murmur or complaint."[40] Less could hardly have been expected of the servant men.

And as a final example of the partially unintended nature of the gendered hierarchy as it came to exist, we turn to the sons indentured by their parents to the Congrégation sisters. In one such case in 1687 a shoemaker named Vivien Magdelaine and his wife Marie Godin contracted the labor of at least three of their four sons aged fifteen, twelve, and six respectively, to work for the Congrégation as residents of *La Providence*, each for a period of nine years.[41] In exchange, the family Magdelaine became relieved of the necessity to directly support their children, and the indenture included the provisions that the sisters educate the boys. Other boys are listed not as *étudiants* but as *engagés en qualité de domestiques*, who apparently lived something of an ambiguous life between being a young student and a young servant.[42] The Magdelaine case also indicates that the frequent assumption among historians and community chroniclers that Canada's women's religious communities only educated preadolescent boys is false. The lengthy terms of indentures of the Magdelaine boys meant that they would leave the community at the minimum ages of twenty-four, twenty-one, and fifteen.

To be a boy student at the Congrégation after the 1660s one was necessarily also a servant legally obligated to remain at the community. While a few of the girl students of unfortunate circumstances also shared the designation of *domestiques*, most girls occupied a superior position in the communal household and attended *La Providence* simply to learn.

The specific experience of Vivien Magdelaine's oldest son, Joseph, demonstrates the limitations of male inclusion in the community. Indentured to the Congrégation at the age of fifteen for a term of nine years, one wonders about the education he actually received or even wished to receive. At the time when he had just begun his term, he had already reached the age at which most of his male peers had completed their educations and had gone on to apprenticeships, the military, or on trading voyages to the West. By the time he completed his term in 1696 at age twenty-four, Joseph was already older than almost half of his "teachers," and was older than the substantial majority of the sisters and female students supervising his work. That he was a "student" in anything but the most rudimentary and occasional sense, then, strains credulity. To the sisters, his nine-year presence among them was defined not by pedagogy or even faith but rather by what could simply be defined as a relationship of the hearth—a common struggle against the literal and metaphorical cold of the frontier.

Limitations on male integration into the community did not solely arise from the resistance and flight of servants. Though her outreach was genuine, the frontier pragmatism of Bourgeoys and her companions never let the women lose sight of why the men had been brought into the community in the first place—to carry out the physical work needed for survival. An undercurrent of coercion acted always at cross-purposes to the ideals Bourgeoys held about the male presence at the Congréga-tion. The institution of indentured servitude unceasingly shaped the actions as well as the perceptions of sisters, students, and servants.

Bourgeoys's complex mission, which produced these dynamics of gender, culture, and caste, did not survive her leadership. The foundress stepped down from the position of *supérieure* in 1692, almost eight years before her death. In her increasingly bitter writings Bourgeoys noted that in the 1690s the humbler-born sisters became more cognizant of their vastly improved social status as sisters of the Congrégation. The sis-ters sought to reestablish the distinction between themselves and those servants who shared similar social backgrounds. Under the new *supérieure*, for example, servants' bread was now of an inferior quality.[43] This general feeling, according to Bourgeoys, was even more generally applied. "I notice," she writes, "that there are sisters who show more esteem for a girl who has social rank than for one who might be more virtuous. Some are also harsh with the poor, both in giving the pleasure or in lending to them even when this can be done without inconve-niencing themselves."[44] At last, Bourgeoys's daughters-in-religion would fully assert the social privileges that accompanied them as monastics unencumbered by the difficult paradoxes wrought by Bourgeoys's prac-tical ideal of acculturating male servants.

These changes, however, took place in concert with larger trans-formations in the community. By the turn of the eighteenth century the era of the French-born indentured servant was fast closing thanks to the wars with the English colonies which diminished both the frequency of sea travel and men willing to hazard the voyage to an increasingly war-torn land. And the mission itself assumed a new form of the *vie voyagère*. The new generation of leadership in the community at long last accepted the clerical imposition of a rule on the community, making the sisters true *religieuses* and bringing it within the control of the church hierarchy for the first time. But somewhat ironically, the benefit accrued from this submission was the long-delayed fulfillment of Bour-geoys's wilderness mission. With the combination of official support and the end of the Iroquois wars in 1701, Congrégation missions to girls finally achieved their foundress's first and fundamental goal by reaching the frontier in force.

For the next generation of French Canadian male servants, their status as free contract laborers meant the loss of their status as intimate parts of the community. Men and boys at long last became pushed to the true margins of the Congrégation. With its physical expansion, the community became what it had nominally been all along—an exclusively and emphatically female site of transculturation and education.

Old conceptions of inclusion when applied to male subjects –always an uncomfortable fit with reality—were now abandoned. Bourgeoys's efforts to create a center for women's voyaging lives on the periphery of the French-speaking world did not fail, but proved, like all intercultural middle grounds, ephemeral and transitory. Like Natalie Zemon Davis's portrait of the Quebec Ursuline Marie de l'Incarnation creating her own center of influence through her paradoxical cloistered missionary work, Marguerite Bourgeoys established a local center by establishing a site of varied kinds of transculturation.[45]

Her troubled efforts to include all in the Marian *vie voyagère* tells us not only about the nature of the small world made by women but also of their unhesitating efforts to define that world. But their struggle with men was not only waged with the bishop of Quebec. Of more importance to all in the community were the entrenched views of male servants—men who perceived themselves not as creating their own centers from margins, but rather pushed ever closer to the sharp edge of earth. Their refusal to accept inclusion into the mission of the Congrégation Notre-Dame proved the first example of a pattern that would recur throughout the history of French Canadian women religious.[46] No matter the possible destination, men would refuse to proceed along a path cut, cleared, and defined by women, even the followers of Mary herself.

NOTES

This article is adapted from chapter 1 of William H. Foster III, "The Captors' Narrative: Catholic Women and Their Puritan Men on the Early North American Frontier, 1653–1760" (Ph.D. diss., Cornell University, 2000). An earlier version was presented at the 1999 American Studies Association conference in Montreal. I would like to thank Patricia Simpson, C.N.D., Bill Youngs, Sheila Skemp, Elaine Forman Crane, Edie Gelles, Jackie Reynier, Mary Beth Norton, and Susan Lynch Foster for their helpful comments.

1. Patricia Simpson, the author of the recent and definitive biography of the early life of Bourgeoys, writes that although it is possible the Carmelites turned Marguerite down because of her relatively modest social status, another explanation may be that the leaders of the convent had already dis-

cerned the implications of the natural leadership Bourgeoys had assumed among the devout girls of Troyes. The Carmelites may have then benevolently rejected the applicant in order to direct her to the more active life for which she was so obviously suited. See Patricia Simpson, *Marguerite Bourgeoys and Montreal, 1640–1665* (Montreal and Kingston: McGill-Queens University Press, 1997), 43–45.

2. The early-seventeenth-century model for the Canadian wilderness missions included St. Vincent de Paul's *Filles de la Charité*. See Leslie Choquette, "Ces Amazones du Grand Dieu: Women and Mission in Seventeenth-Century Canada," *French Historical Studies*, 17, no. 3 (1992), esp. 631–32.

3. "Wandering life." The most comprehensive study of the theological dimensions of the *vie voyagère* is Mary Anne Foley, "Uncloistered Apostolic Life for Women: Marguerite Bourgeoys's Experiment in Ville-Marie" (Ph.D. diss. [Religion], Yale University, 1991). The historical context that helped create Bourgeoys's vision is dealt with most extensively in Simpson, *Marguerite Bourgeoys and Montreal*, especially chapters 1 and 2.

4. Marguerite Bourgeoys, *Writings of Marguerite Bourgeoys* (hereafter *WMB*), (c. 1658–1698), edited and annotated by Sister Saint-Damase-de-Rome, translated by Mary Virginia Cotter (Montréal: Congrégation Notre-Dame, 1976), 81–82.

5. Bourgeoys's reasoning was subtle on this point. She posited first that the apostles of Jesus had also followed Mary, and that the Virgin had in turn acted as a "mistress of novices" to them. In this conception Mary began to regard the apostles as her superiors only after God gave them the power to "remit sins." Nevertheless, according to Bourgeoys, the apostles always continued to regard Mary as "their mother" and continued to take her advice. This rather obvious analogy to Bourgeoys's mission vis-à-vis the clerical hierarchy suggests her thinking on the subject of male authority. Bourgeoys did not wish to deny the technical superiority of the clergy— but she clearly also felt that they ought not interfere with her mission, which functioned outside that hierarchy. Bourgeoys further felt that she and other followers of the Marian apostolate be accorded the respect due to the Virgin Mother. See *WMB*, 48–49; and Foster, "The Captors' Narrative," 88, n. 80.

6. This characteristic in Bourgeoys's behavior emerges from the supremely pragmatic ways she dealt with a wide variety of individuals. Perhaps the writing that best expresses this pragmatism is her critique of ordinary human uses of "love." She writes: "When we learn that a foreign country is pillaged or oppressed, we have compassion for the people, but this touches us only when we know it. We love those who are travelling through because they bring us some profit; we love the poor to whom we give what is superfluous; we love our associates because to lose them would harm us; we love our friends because their conversation pleases and is agreeable to us; we love our parents because we received good things from them or because we fear to be punished." *WMB*, 59.

7. *WMB*, 54.

8. Simpson, *Marguerite Bourgeoys and Montreal*, passim.

9. The best scholarship on the immigration goals of early French and Canadian authorities as they related to immigrants and the indentured servant trade is Peter Moogk, "Reluctant Exiles: Emigrants from France in Canada before 1760," *William and Mary Quarterly*, 3rd ser., 46.3 (1989): 463–505.

10. Patricia Simpson throughout her text reiterates the importance of financial and material self-reliance. See especially *Marguerite Bourgeoys and Montreal*, 161–69.

11. For the work of Crolo, see Marie Morin, *Histoire Simple et Veritable (Les Annales de L'Hôtel-Dieu de Montréal, 1659–1725)* (Montréal, 1979), 74–75, and Simpson, *Marguerite Bourgeoys and Montreal*, 163.

12. *WMB*, 177, 179.

13. On the conflict between Bourgeoys and her fellow sisters regarding the appropriateness of taking in female immigrants, see Simpson, *Marguerite Bourgeoys and Montreal*, 168.

14. Personal conversation with Patricia Simpson, September 1998.

15. *Recensements*, 1666, 1667, 1681, ANQ–M. For clarity I have not counted the three men with whom the Congrégation signed separate *donné* contracts although two of them are also listed on the census as *domestiques engagés*. I discuss the special cases of the *donnés* below.

16. For Crolo, see Emilia Chicoine, *La métarie de Marguerite Bourgeoys à la Pointe-Saint-Charles* (hereafter *MMB*) (Montréal: Fides, 1986), esp. 15–83. This remarkable volume is the single best resource on the history of the farmschool.

17. Ibid., 35–47.

18. Ibid., 38.

19. Moogk, "Reluctant Exiles," 487.

20. There has been considerable research and debate over the precise social origins of the *filles de roi*. Leslie Choquette has recently summarized the available knowledge neatly in her definitive study of French emigration to Canada. Comprehensive breakdowns of class backgrounds are ultimately impossible to reconstruct because of key gaps in the documentary record. However, of those approximately nine hundred female emigrants between 1663 and 1673 who can actually be considered *filles de roi* because of their royal subsidy, most were recruited via the Salpêtrière. Among the ablebodied inmates at this institution, most were of urban origin, and had been born into artisan, peasant, or laborer families. Those relatively few of the upper classes were usually impoverished. What is certain is that the age-old slur that the *filles de roi* had originally been Parisian prostitutes was emphatically not the case. The asylum did not accept those they deemed *"debauchees"* and extra care on the matter of morality was given by authorities when actually choosing the emigrants from among the interested candidates. Therefore the most accurate generalization that can be made is that *filles de roi* and male indentured servants were drawn from

roughly the same social backgrounds in France. See Leslie Choquette, *Frenchmen into Peasants: Modernity and Tradition in the Peopling of French Canada* (Cambridge: Harvard University Press, 1997), 110–12 (esp. table 4–3), and 235–37.

21. Conversations with Patricia Simpson, September 1998; and Foley, "Uncloistered Apostolic Life for Women," appendix B.

22. This conclusion is reached by a comparison of the names of the Congrégation's servants on the 1666, 1667, and 1681 censuses to the genealogical records compiled by René Jetté in the *Dictionnaire Généalogique des Familles de Québec des Origines à 1730* (hereafter *DGFQ*) (Montréal: Presses de l'Universitéde Montréal, 1983).

23. Moogk, "Reluctant Exiles," passim.

24. For the long and intimate involvement of the Le Ber family with the Congrégation Notre-Dame, see Foster, "The Captors' Narrative," chapters 1 and 2.

25. Computed from Foley, "Uncloistered Apostolic Life for Women," appendix B, and *DGFQ*.

26. As discussed in the introduction to "The Captors' Narrative."

27. Figures computed from the list of early Congrégation sisters contained in Foley, "Uncloistered Apostolic Life for Women," appendix B.

28. *DGFQ*, 24. The status of captives within Iroquoian society is a current topic of debate among scholars. The conventional view, based mostly on selective travelers' accounts, holds that male captives not executed according to mourning-war rites could enjoy true adoption and complete acculturation into an Iroquois family. In recent years, however, William A. Starna and Ralph Watkins have produced a challenging and sophisticated revision of this thesis. Using linguistic and other forms of ethnohistorical analysis, Starna and Watkins conclude that "adoptees" remained permanently liminal to Iroquoian society—even going so far as to claim the outsiders' status could be called a form of slavery. Though the word "slavery" might be inappropriate given the very different systems the word will evoke in the minds of some readers, I find the Starna-Watkins argument to be by far the strongest offered on the question. Therefore, although we cannot approach certainty on the matter, a reasonable supposition would be that the Huron father of Marie-Thérèse Gannensagouas remained liminal at the Mountain Mission, and that the marginality reflected as well upon his daughter. See William A. Starna and Ralph Watkins, "Northern Iroquoian Slavery," *Ethnohistory* 38, no. 1 (1991): 34–53.

29. See, for example, the discussion of this phenomenon in Barbara Olexar, *The Enslavement of the American Indian* (Monroe, N.Y.: Library Research Associates, 1982), 2. The aforementioned article by Starna and Watkins also contains details indicating the nature of the treatment of dishonored captives. They discuss, for example, the Iroquoian practice of amputating the fingers of male captives. The removed digits were very often a combination of those necessary for a man to draw a bow or fire a gun. Though Starna and Watkins do not engage in a gendered analysis of these amputa-

tions, it is more than possible that the practice served as a preliminary ritual in the shameful "unmanning" of their captives. The extent of female
control of these captives is also indicated in the case of an Iroquoian
mother's recorded lament of her daughter's untimely death. The mother
notes incidentally that the young woman had been "mistress here and commanded more than twenty slaves." See Starna and Watkins, "Northern Iroquoian Slavery," 44, 51.

30. Unfortunately, d'Onotais died in Montreal in September of 1691 at the
    age of thirty-five. Gannensagouas only lived until 1695, passing away at
    the Mountain Mission at age twenty-eight. See *DGFQ*, 24, 461. These
    were to be the first and the last Native Americans in the sisterhood during
    the *ancien régime*.

31. Simpson, *Marguerite Bourgeoys and Montreal*, 42–43.

32. Chicoine reviews the work of servants in *MMB*, 76–77.

33. *WMB*, 29.

34. *Recensement*, 1667. Examples of these contracts appear frequently in the
    notarial records relating to the religious communities. For one typical ex-
    ample that spells out the terms of becoming a *donné*, see the self-indenture
    of Pierre Picard to the Congrégation, see the *greffe* of Adhémar
    (9–10–1696), ANQ-M.

35. *WMB*, 155.

36. *MMB*, 164.

37. *WMB*, 101. A slightly different interpretation of the Thomas Mousnier
    encounter is put forth by Chicoine in *MMB*, 79.

38. *MMB*, 44.

39. Pierre Picard, the first foreman at Pointe-Saint-Charles, was not hired
    until 1696. Even after that date however, the chief *soeur fermière* remained
    in residence at the farm and served as the principal authority in the fields.

40. *WMB*, 5.

41. For the family of Vivien Magdelaine, see *DGFQ*, 749–50. For the inden-
    ture, see the *greffe* of Adhémar (26–7–1688), ANQ-M; and *MMB*, 82.

42. This finding was originally made by Benjamin Sulte in 1916. Reported
    by Chicoine in *MMB*, 81, 83 n. 28.

43. *WMB*, 177. Bourgeoys goes on to list several aspects of her successors'
    backsliding in laxity. "Now," she wrote in 1698, "we must have mat-
    tresses, sheets, and all sorts of utensils; we want to live in a different fash-
    ion from simple people. We want to have all the comforts that the settlers
    do not have."

44. *WMB*, 171.

45. See Natalie Zemon Davis, *Women on the Margins: Three Seventeenth Century
    Lives* (Cambridge, Mass.: Harvard University Press, 1995), 63–139.

46. See Foster, "The Captors' Narrative," chapters 2–6.

THE NETHERLANDS AND THE NEW WORLD

Women in and out of the Public Church in the Dutch Republic

Marybeth Carlson

THE RELIGIOUS ENVIRONMENT OF THE DUTCH REPUBLIC was characterized by diversity and by freedom of conscience, at least in comparison to that prevailing in other European states in the early modern period. Alongside the Dutch Reformed Church, Mennonites, Lutherans, Socinians, Collegiants, and Remonstrants followed their own consciences, while Catholics practiced their religion quietly in *schuilkerken,* and Jewish communities took root in the larger Dutch cities, welcomed by an elite that was inclined to see parallels between the Egyptian Pharaoh and the Spanish Philip II. Such a religious mosaic offered both men and women a degree of latitude in religious expression that could not be found elsewhere at the time, but it offered women in particular a measure of agency, for women could provide resources both human and financial, which each community needed to prosper. At the same time, in order to make effective use of those resources, church authorities often had to be flexible in applying ecclesiastical regulations. Not so flexible, it must be noted, that women enjoyed anything resembling religious equality in the Republic. Fundamental concepts of gender and religion in which women were enjoined to silence in the church were the same among the Dutch as among other peoples in Europe. But in the pluralistic religious world of the Republic, church authorities often seemed to find it expedient to interpret tradition broadly when women were performing useful services for their coreligionists.[1]

WOMEN'S AGENCY DURING THE PERIOD
OF REFORMATION AND REVOLT

On the eve of the Reformation, the sphere for women's agency in the territory that would become the Republic was broader than might be expected. This was because ecclesiastical organization was inadequate to control religious life there effectively. Only two bishoprics—Utrecht and Liège—existed to serve almost the entire Dutch-speaking population, and parishes were loosely scattered in the southern and western provinces, reflecting the distribution of the population before land reclamation projects made more cultivable land available in the thirteenth century. An indifferently trained and undisciplined clergy, poorly supervised by a hierarchy often absent from the far-flung dioceses, could not counter the anticlerical dissent and doctrinal critiques whose influence was spreading in the late medieval period. Among the areas that reflected this indifference was the declining size of female monastic houses at a time when the overall population was expanding.[2] The convent of Rijnsburg outside Leiden, for example, housed thirty-six sisters in 1453, down to twenty-nine in 1494, and by 1553 only twenty remained.[3]

Weak ecclesiastical control also permitted the survival of a variety of quasi-religious communities for women, notably, the *beguines*. Dating from the late twelfth century, these groups of women offered an opportunity for unmarried women to live as part of a community with the accompanying protection and support. Communities varied in the depth of their religious commitment and the extent of their communal life. Some *begijnhoven* were built as a group of small individual houses arranged around a common courtyard. In others, women earned a collective living through handicrafts or through caring for the sick. Beguinages were common in northern European cities in the medieval period, but because the *beguines* did not take solemn vows and did not cloister themselves apart from the larger community, they were viewed warily. Sometimes accused of heresy and of undercutting the prices set by crafts guilds, pressure grew on the *beguines* to disband from the fourteenth century onward as city magistrates grew increasingly suspicious of women living independently from any direct male supervision.[4] Groups of *beguines* continued to exist in the Low Countries, however, either tolerated by local bishops or able to survive where episcopal supervision was weak.[5]

Beguinages were only part of the complex of semireligious communal lifestyles available in the northern Low Countries, where a variety of houses for women tertiaries provided opportunities for women who wished to lead pious, chaste lives doing charitable work outside cloister walls. Groups referred to as the Hospital Sisters, and later, the Franciscan Grey Sisters, and the Augustinian Black Sisters maintained an "active" spirituality long before the supposed beginnings of this option for women in the early modern period. Some houses may have actually considered themselves to be solemnly vowed, professed nuns, despite the fact that they did not maintain *clausura* while running charitable institutions that cared for outsiders.[6] Adding yet another ingredient to this muddle of religious communities were the Sisters of the Common Life, part of the larger religious movement known as the *Devotio Moderna*. Spreading outward from the IJssel River valley into northwestern Germany as well as the Low Countries, the thirty-four Sisters' houses in the Netherlands outnumbered those of the Brothers of the Common Life.[7] Such a variety of choices testifies to the popularity of quasi-religious communal living for unmarried women in the northern Low Countries, where neither city nor ecclesiastical authorities regulated them out of existence, as had occurred elsewhere, presumably because the useful services performed by the various sisters filled a necessary social function. The range of possible religious lifestyles provided women without families and without means a vehicle for economic survival that further offered companionship and spiritual fulfillment.

The lackadaisical approach of ecclesiastical authorities toward women's religious communities also characterized their approach to popular religious indifference and dissent in the northern Netherlands. It permitted the development of the very distinctive "bottom up" Reformation process there, which in turn was one of the factors in creating the religious pluralism of the Dutch Republic. By the time Calvinism entered the scene, Protestant pamphlets had circulated for decades, Protestant attitudes toward Scripture and the Papacy had already made their impact, and the traditional church had lost its moral authority for much of the population. To combat this, Charles V ordered the establishment of the Inquisition in the Netherlands in 1522.[8]

The testimony of women who appeared before the Inquisition makes it clear that women were taking part in the turmoil. Wendelmoet Claesdochter of Monnikendam, the first woman executed by the tribunal in Holland, used homely metaphors to criticize the beliefs of her examiners. Questioned about her views of transubstantiation, she said she considered the host "as bread and flour and, though you hold it as a God, I tell you it's your devil." She was scornful of their reverence for the oil used for anointing the sick: "oil is good for a salad or for greasing boots."[9] The three inquisitors condemned her to be burned in The Hague, November 1527.

In Gouda one Jannichgen made no secret of her views, telling her maidservant, "you go as well together with pilgrimages and sacraments as a sack in tatters does. God's in Heaven and He stays there. He's not to be found in any sacraments; these [hosts] are baked gods. It's all done for money." She enraged her neighbor by ostentatiously continuing with her housework when a procession carried the host past her door. She fought with her husband over her beliefs, calling him "the Devil" and claiming he beat her for avoiding mass at Easter and on feast days.[10] Another religious uproar occurred in Gouda when a crowd of women and children chased Weyn Brouwers and her daughter through the streets, crying, "Lutheran whore, Lutheran whore! Burn! Burn!"[11]

Of all the Dutch crypto-Protestants, the Anabaptists were the most fervent in their defiance of the government. Women joined the hundreds who left Holland, Friesland, and the Maas River valley to follow the summons of Jan Matthijsz of Haarlem and Jan Beuckelsz of Leiden to Münster. Those who stayed behind were gripped by a conviction that the apocalypse was at hand, a conviction intensified as the siege of Münster began. In Amsterdam one group of seven men and five women ran naked through the streets, proclaiming to the godless that the truth had to appear naked.[12] After a series of more deadly attacks, including one in which militant Anabaptists stormed the town hall in Amsterdam, leaving dozens of casualties, authorities moved to crush the Anabaptists. In Amsterdam, only five days after the attack on the town hall, seven Anabaptist women were executed by drowning. Eventually the city tried 178 individuals as Anabaptists, including 62 women.[13] The prosecutions extended throughout the northern Netherlands, falling on women as well as men. The *Martyr's Mirror* identifies 1,007 people accused of heresy by sex, 28.6 percent of whom were women.[14] The wave of executions ended the revolutionary wing of the Anabaptist movement, but did not destroy the whole movement. Other branches embraced a pacifist theology and survived underground until members of the Mennonite church were able to openly practice their religion in the seventeenth century.

None of the actions taken by ecclesiastical or secular authorities were able to halt the penetration of Protestantism into the Low Countries. The arrival of Calvinism accelerated the crumbling of the official Church. Coming at precisely the moment that tensions between Philip II and local authorities were intensifying, Calvinist hedge-preaching set off a wave of popular violence in the summer of 1566 (the *beeldenstorm*) that triggered a harsh royal crackdown and, ultimately, the Dutch Revolt. Women joined—and sometimes even led—the crowds that stormed the churches and monasteries. Neel Spaens, for example, provided tools used by the rioters to break open church doors and to smash religious images. She was sentenced to death for her actions, but escaped into exile.[15]

WOMEN'S AGENCY IN THE PROTESTANT COMMUNITIES

At the beginning of the seventeenth century, religious allegiances within the northern Netherlands were in a state of flux. Since the Dutch were at war with the Catholic Spanish, anti-Catholic feelings ran high. Catholic worship was suppressed and church property seized wherever the Spanish were driven out. But each province had agreed to prohibit religious persecution at the time it signed the 1579 Union of Utrecht, so a simply private practice of Catholic religion was not criminalized. And the general population was far from committed to the Reformed Church. Due to the erratic manner in which Protestantism had entered the Netherlands, a wide diversity of opinions on matters of belief flourished. Well into the seventeenth century a sizable minority of the population did not belong to any organized church.[16] Among the new republic's officials (the *regenten*, or regents) only a small minority were zealous Calvinists. The majority hoped to see the Protestant faith in the Netherlands organized as a church with a relatively flexible dogma, which would serve to unify the new state. The clergy of the Reformed Church, however, had a stricter view, believing that only those who submitted to church discipline ought to be admitted to membership. As a result, the Dutch Reformed Church, though called the "Public Church," was not an established state church. Membership was voluntary, and church officials did not hold any seats in the States General nor in any of the provincial estates. The position of the Public Church did give the Reformed Church certain privileges. Anyone holding public office was expected to be a member of the Church and it had exclusive use of church buildings confiscated at the time of the Reformation. It also commanded considerable cultural power due to its role in helping instigate the Dutch Revolt against Spain.

Growing tension over the relationship of church and state and over the disputes between Arminianists and orthodox Calvinists came to a head at the National Synod of Dordrecht (Dordt), convened in 1618, which split the Public Church, producing the orthodox *gereformeerde kerk* plus several minority congregations, including the Remonstrant Church and the Collegiants. Within two decades, this split led to a condition of religious plurality in the Republic, as the city governments permitted the minority congregations, as well as Lutherans, Anabaptists, and other Protestant faiths, to build their own churches.

A further outcome of this process was that the Public Church maintained a much clearer distinction than was typical elsewhere between communicants and the "sympathizers" (*liefhebbers*) who came to church services but did not submit to the Reformed Church's discipline.[17] The division becomes particularly significant in looking at the role of women in the church, since a number of local studies have determined that women usually were a majority of the communicants. In Edam, for example, roughly 65 percent of the church members were women, 35 percent men, in the years 1608 to 1650. And in Delft between 1573 and 1621, women made up about 60 percent of the communicants, men about 40 percent.[18] A reluctance to submit to church discipline and the consistory's close supervision of a member's lifestyle which that discipline entailed was the main reason why one might choose to attend church as a *liefhebber* rather than to make a formal profession of faith to become a communicant. It is possible then that there was something about the actual practice of church discipline that made membership particularly attractive to women. In Edam through the mid-seventeenth century, approximately equal numbers of men and women were summoned before the consistory, but since women outnumbered men overall in the congregation, the Edam consistory may have been treating women with greater leniency.[19] If this were true elsewhere, church discipline would have been a lesser barrier for women than for men in formally joining the Church. In cases of family conflicts, consistories in the Dutch Republic used their authority to effect a reconciliation between disagreeing couples. In Edam, this tended to work to the wife's advantage, since the consistory found the husband to be at fault more often than the wife.[20]

In some congregations, formal membership also offered women a vehicle for greater influence and recognition in the community. Technically, there were no church offices open to women in the Public Church. In the earliest years of the Reformed Church in the Low Countries, some congregations established the office of deaconess, according women public responsibilities in administering poor relief. The first congress of delegates from reformed communities of exiled Netherlanders, which met in Wesel in 1568, agreed to establish the office of deaconess, recruiting for it older, pious women with standing in the community, but the National Synod at Middelburg in 1581 ruled that a formal office of deaconess was not advisable.[21] Despite this, it is clear that deaconesses were appointed in Amsterdam and Edam, and that the establishment of the office was debated by the consistories in Purmerend and Monnickendam.[22] Such appointments were always justified by arguments that women were more familiar with social realities in the local community than were men. Local necessity moved consistories to flout the ruling of the synod and name deaconesses, and where they did not, women may have assumed the role of "deaconess-in-fact," if not in name.

During the course of the seventeenth century, the Reformed Church gradually relaxed church discipline somewhat, in keeping with its role as the Public Church. But some Calvinists resisted this trend, calling on their coreligionists to make their beliefs more inwardly meaningful, to adopt a regimen of personal piety, all while avoiding interaction with worldly and sinful people as much as possible. A movement known as the *Nadere Reformatie* (Further Reformation) coalesced around these ideas in the seventeenth century, as its proponents developed a sense of purpose, arguing that the Reformation of the sixteenth century was incomplete. Some of its adherents grew so zealous that they left the church to form their own smaller sects, finding even the pietistic ministers within the church too worldly.[23]

Contemporaries belittled such pietistic sects by overdramatizing the role of women in them.[24] But the visibility of women in the sects results in part from the nature of the available historical sources. Women may have been more active in the Public Church than is apparent in the sources, since that activity was probably more often than not informal, and since when women do appear in church records, it is at moments of conflict. At the same time, women did play significant roles in the pietistic movement, prompted to do so for many of the same reasons that men participated: in autobiographies or other writings, women themselves emphasize an inner spiritual calling. Beyond this, women were active in Dutch pietistic sects for the same reason they were more likely to formally join the Public Church than were men: they sought the community support and sometimes the possibility of a role with at least informal public authority.

Both of these motives can be discerned in the choices made by the Republic's most famous woman scholar of the seventeenth century, Anna Maria van Schurman (1607–1678). After her family moved from Cologne, where she was born, to Utrecht, Van Schurman won admiration as an artist, a linguist (she was especially noted for her command of biblical languages), and as a philosopher and theologian.[25] But it was the publication of a Latin discourse defending women's aptitude for scholarship that established Van Schurman's international reputation for learning. The *Dissertatio, de Ingenii Muliebris ad Doctrinam, & meliores Litteras aptitudine* (1641)[26] argued that any woman with sufficient leisure and an interest in the arts and sciences ought to be able to pursue that interest. Contrary to others who defended the education of women as a device for creating better wives and mothers, Van Schurman believed women should pursue learning for its intrinsic pleasure and as a means of ensuring their salvation. Her claims on behalf of women were ultimately limited, however. She did not question the traditional role of women, nor did she argue more generally on behalf of women's equality.[27]

That very traditionalism set the stage for a series of actions Van Schurman took in her later life that shocked the clergymen and scholars who had endorsed her work while she was young. When her mother died in 1637, Van Schurman assumed various family responsibilities, including the care of two elderly aunts. At about the same time, she seems to have grown disillusioned with the Church, seeing it as a gathering of superficial Christians who were more committed to worldly success than to their religious beliefs. She lost interest in scholarship and the arts. Through her brother, she met the charismatic Walloon preacher, Jean de Labadie, who was beginning to attract a following for his message emphasizing inner redemption over the formalism of institutionalized religion. While De Labadie served as minister of the Walloon congregation of Middelburg in Zeeland, his relations with the leadership of the Walloon Church had grown acrimonious, and in 1669 he broke from it, moved to Amsterdam, and set up a household of followers who lived, worshiped, and prayed together. Aged sixty-two by this time, Van Schurman joined the household, and when they were forced to leave Amsterdam, accompanied them to a refuge she had arranged at Herford in Westphalia. The Labadists remained there only two years, then moved to Altona near Hamburg, and finally to Wieuwerd in Friesland, where Van Schurman died in 1678.[28]

Van Schurman attempted to explain her decision to join the Labadists in an autobiography, written in Latin, *Eukleria seu Melioris Partis Electio* (1673).[29] The Labadist community was, in her eyes, a return to the original, true Christian church, as depicted in the New Testament. Within the household, the saved were able to live pure lives, isolated from the sinful world, directed by the Holy Spirit. Her former friends and admirers found it easier to understand her actions as those of an unstable female mind rather than to accept the spiritual motives she described in *Eukleria*.[30]

But the structure of the Labadist community had a great deal to offer an unmarried woman from the Dutch elite. Individuals' role within the Labadists depended firstly on whether or not they were saved and secondly on their social status before joining the sect. This meant Van Schurman was able to claim a place in the community's inner circle, which made all community decisions. And not only was that true for Van Schurman, but also for the two Van Aerssen van Sommelsdijk sisters who provided the Wieuwerd property where the community finally found a refuge. This is not to say that the Labadists recognized anything like equality of the sexes, but Van Schurman had never demanded equality. What the Labadists did offer her was a degree of respect for her theological ideas that she had not previously known. And that respect carried over to wider pietistic circles, especially among Lutherans.[31] Leaving the Reformed Church and the intellectual life of Utrecht for Jean de Labadie's community permitted Van Schurman to command a role in community governance not available to a single woman in the Republic, yet not challenge traditional ideas of gender inequality—a challenge she had clearly been unwilling to undertake at the time she wrote the *Dissertatio*. Under those circumstances then, Van Schurman took from the Labadists precisely what she needed.

These factors are echoed in the life of Antoinette Bourignon, a contemporary of Van Schurman who left the Spanish Netherlands in 1667 in search of a place from which she could safely preach her message of returning to early Christian ideals. In numerous published works and hundreds of letters (themselves published after her death), she predicted the imminent end of the world and proclaimed herself a prophet, sent by the Holy Spirit to call humankind to redemption.[32]

Bourignon's claim to authority was based neither on Scripture nor on theological expertise, but on divine illumination. This enabled her to challenge traditional norms on women's role in religion as they applied to herself, but at the same time not contest those norms for women in general. It appears that to Bourignon women did not have the strength of will necessary for those who would forsake the world for the path to salvation. By minimizing the role of women in her community, she also reinforced her own leadership of the group, in which she claimed a "spiritual motherhood" over her male followers as "spiritual sons." By using the language of traditional family norms to maintain control over her following, Bourignon was able to demand the attention of contemporary theologians and to hold sway over a circle that included male scientists and philosophers, notably the entomologist Jan Swammerdam and the theologian Pierre Poiret.[33]

Historians are only beginning to study the published work of lesser-known women in pietist circles. These women seem to have constructed active and influential roles for themselves, holding catechism classes, or forming conventicles for prayer and Scripture reading. Their initiative sometimes brought them before the consistories when their leadership began to approach the preacher's function too closely. The nontraditional structure of the pietistic movement, with its extra meetings outside of official services, opened up new possibilities for informal leadership inside the Public Church, as well as outside, where their visibility was often the subject of contemporaries' comments.[34]

Women could also play influential roles in the Republic's minority churches outside the Reformed tradition, such as the Lutheran churches tolerated by civil authorities in the Republic. During the early seventeenth century the Haarlem parish was divided between factions supporting a traditional (among Dutch Lutherans) local-control model of authority and a newer model in which centralized control was vested in a General Council (*Algemeen Consistorie*). But it was a dispute over issues of gender that finally brought the rivalry to a head. In 1618 Haarlemers were circulating gossip about a married couple who had traded blows during an argument. One former elder and partisan of the traditionalist faction criticized the husband of the pair as a wife-beater. Conrad Vietor, the Lutheran pastor, reproved the elder, asserting that the Bible upheld the right of a man to strike his wife. The parish council, however, took the matter to the *Algemeen Consistorie*. While they agreed with Vietor's reading of Scripture, they maintained that it was uncivilized of a man to exercise that right. Besides, they said, women had left the church, estranged by the pastor's stand, and they feared that the congregation's good name would be tarnished by his defense of wife-beating. In this way, differing ideas about gender came to define the two sides in a wider dispute. The *Algemeen Consistorie* arranged a cooling-off period while Vietor left Haarlem for six months to assist another Lutheran minister who was sick. Toward the end of the half-year, both sides began to mobilize, one for, one against Vietor's return. This time, a group of forty-nine women joined the faction who supported him. They forwarded a petition to the *Algemeen Consistorie* declaring their support for Vietor as their lawful pastor, whose ouster was being engineered by only a minority of the congregation. The women ignored the discussions of how to understand scriptural support for wife-beating as a mere distraction from the real issue: control of the Lutheran Church in Haarlem. They emphatically defended their right to participate in this struggle by finding biblical precedents for women who had taken part in church affairs, specifically, Miriam, Priscilla, Judith, and the daughters of Philip. In this case, because the Lutheran Church of the Republic was not an established church, because it was weak, the Haarlem Lutheran women were able to claim an active and public role in decision making.[35] This contrasts to the actions of women in the pietistic sects, who rather than seeking a justification for assuming positions of leadership—a justification that would challenge the standard norms concerning gender and religion—cast themselves as exceptions to those norms.

WOMEN'S AGENCY IN THE CATHOLIC CHURCH

Tensions between prescriptive standards and practical necessity also provided an opening for women in the Roman Catholic Church in the Dutch Republic to extend their institutional influence.[36] Political conditions—particularly local ones—determined how rigorously the laws banning Catholicism were enforced. The Vatican placed most of the territory of the Republic under the authority of the "Dutch Mission" (*Missio Hollandica*) headed by a vicar-general, rather than by a bishop. The Mission was troubled by a chronic shortage of priests, and there were jurisdictional disputes between the vicar-generals and the secular clergy on the one hand and the regular clergy, especially the Jesuits, on the other.[37] Under these conditions the Catholic Church became dependent on the laity. Unmarried, affluent laywomen were especially well placed to provide the quarters for the hidden chapels of the Mission, to shelter the itinerant priests, to teach catechism classes, and to provide charity for the Catholic poor. An example of how far that support could conceivably go was described by Arnoldus Buchelius in 1636, when he wrote that the woman who owned a house where officials had stopped a mass offered 20,000 guilders to them if they would promise not to harm the host.[38] The survival of Dutch Catholicism was heavily indebted to the work of such women.

Elizabeth Strouven, the foundress of a religious community in Maastricht, provides an example of how central women were to the revival of Catholicism in the Republic. Maastricht was under Spanish rule at the time Strouven was born in 1600, then was retaken by the Dutch in 1632, so that she lived at a pivotal time in the city's history. After a difficult childhood, she became a Third Order Franciscan, and in 1628 organized a religious community she named Calvariënberg, to emphasize the importance of the suffering of Christ for the spiritual life of the community.[39]

After the Dutch government took Maastricht in 1639, it demanded that regular clergy take an oath of loyalty to the new, Protestant rulers. When they refused, they were exiled, throwing Catholic ecclesiastical organizations into disarray. Secular priests had remained in Maastricht, since the new government had promised to leave Catholic worship intact, but many had lost their means of support. At this time, two priests asked for permission to join the community, begging Strouven to act as their spiritual leader. The first of these, Walthieu de la Montagne, explained that God had sent him to submit to her since he had mistreated his late wife. The second, Maarten Gielis, believed God called him to regard Strouven as his mother. Strouven hesitated to go along with this departure from canonical practice, however divinely inspired. But ultimately, her confessor approved it. And meanwhile, the new magistrates of Maastricht left the sisters of Calvariënberg alone, since they were proving themselves invaluable to the city. They took over nursing plague victims, struck by the frequent epidemics that descended on Maastricht during the turbulent years of the Thirty Years' War. Strouven's rule for Calvariënberg was recognized by the Vatican shortly before she died in 1661, and the community continued to care for the sick until abolished by the French in 1796.[40]

Strouven's life demonstrates how much one determined and charismatic woman could accomplish, despite membership in a religious minority. Of wider significance, however, were the "spiritual virgins" (*geestelijke maagden*) of the Dutch Mission. Like the earlier *beguines*, spiritual virgins—informally called *kloppen* in Dutch (singular: *klop*)— were unmarried women who led sober, pious lives in the world, devoting themselves to charity and good works. Instead of the solemn vows of professed nuns, they made formal promises to obey their confessors. For this reason and because they were not secluded in a cloister, their state of life was not recognized by canon law. Nonetheless, they considered themselves "brides of Christ" and were regarded as such by Catholics in the Netherlands.[41]

The *kloppenstaat* as an institution came about after church property— including monasteries and convents—were appropriated by local governments at the time of the Dutch Revolt. Women who believed they had a calling to the religious life could enter a convent outside the Republic if they could provide the required entry fee.[42] Life as a *klop* provided an alternative for those who could not do this, for those who wished to remain nearby their families, and for those who preferred an active apostolate to life behind cloister walls. The Dutch Catholic clergy, needing the physical and financial resources that the spiritual virgins offered, were not eager to see them emigrate to a convent outside the Republic. They published vigorous defenses of the dignity and worthiness of the *kloppenstaat*, defenses that even tried to establish its legitimacy as a religious vocation for women in a post-Tridentine Catholicism that—at best—discouraged women from trying to construct a form of religious life outside cloister walls.[43] Hence, it seems likely that many priests would have urged women considering a religious life toward this domestic alternative. It is, however, difficult to measure the relative popularity of either form of religious life based on the numbers of women who chose one or the other. A lack of sources makes it difficult to estimate the number of *kloppen*; most of them did not live in established communities that would have maintained membership rosters. Only a few such communities existed, notably one founded in Haarlem in 1583, known as "de Hoek." Typically, spiritual virgins lived individually or with family members or in very small groups, and the Dutch Mission did not systematically keep track of their identities or locations. Protestants at the time complained that there were at least twenty thousand but Monteiro places the number around five thousand in the second half of the seventeenth century. This would mean they made up about 1.6 percent of the Catholic population in the Dutch Mission.[44]

The informal religious status of spiritual virgins was a source of anxiety to the Catholic hierarchy in the northern Netherlands. In their own writings, the *kloppen* make it clear that they regarded themselves as something other than laypersons, although canon law defined them as lay. Priests who wrote devout manuals for the *kloppen* (*kloppenboeken*) prescribed standards of conduct that were intended to underscore the distinctiveness of the group by defining proper modes of dress, devotional practices, and charitable works. By following these standards, the spiritual virgins contributed to the missionary effort not only materially, but as models of Catholic piety both for a religious minority group and for the world of potential converts outside the church.[45]

Divisions within the ranks of the Dutch Mission clergy also provided openings for women to exercise a certain degree of influence. There was some rivalry between the secular clergy, most of whom were Dutch and who answered to the authority of the vicar-general, and the regular clergy, chiefly Jesuits, who had come from the southern (Spanish) Netherlands and who were governed by their own provincials. Clergy from each side depended on spiritual virgins for shelter and material assistance, although it was primarily the secular priests who defended the *kloppen* when queries regarding their activities arrived from the Vatican. The tensions were exacerbated as Jansenist theology attracted a number of powerful supporters among the secular clergy of the Dutch Mission, especially during the leadership of Johannes van Neercassel as vicar-general (1661–1686). Van Neercassel made the Leiden home of two *kloppen*, Wenina and Agatha van Heussen, his de facto headquarters in Holland, and the women frequently hosted such Jansenist luminaries as Pasquier Quesnel and Antoine Arnauld.[46]

CONCLUSION

Reformation and revolt coincided in the northern Netherlands; the breakdown of traditional religious structures permitted women to participate in the process of change, and they continued to wield influence in the new religious landscape, even though thrust into the background. The seventeenth century, particularly its first half, was a period of confessionalization, when both the public Reformed Church and the Roman Catholic Church coaxed a largely noncommittal population into allegiance to one faith or the other. The efforts of women were a necessary part of this transition. The philanthropy of Reformed and Catholic women was one of the factors in the success of each church's confessionalization program. From the later seventeenth century onward, elements in both of these churches rejected forms of religious life that they viewed as excessively worldly, and split off into smaller pietistic sects on the one hand, or the Old Catholic Church on the other. In these smaller organizations, the initiative and financial contributions of women had a greater impact, lending women an unexpected religious visibility. Women thus played a dual role in the construction of the religious mosaic that characterized the Dutch Republic. The resources that women could provide were all the more necessary to churches that were in essence competing in a marketplace of ideas. At the same time, in order to effectively make use of women's resources, churches had to become more flexible in applying ecclesiastical regulations—on deaconesses, for example, or on the cloistering of women religious.

NOTES

1. For an overview of women and the churches of the Netherlands, see Sherrin Marshall, "Protestant, Catholic, and Jewish Women in the Early Modern Netherlands," in *Women in Reformation and Counter-Reformation Europe*, ed. Sherrin Marshall (Bloomington, Ind.: Indiana University Press, 1989). Beyond Marshall's survey, there remains a yawning gap in the literature on women and Judaism in the Dutch Republic.
   A general survey of the religious history of the northern Netherlands during the Reformation and the Revolt can be found in "Het politieke en religieuze leven in noord en zuid," *Algemene Geschiedenis der Nederlanden* 6 (1980): 145–343 and 397–412, and in Jonathan Israel, *The Dutch Republic: Its Rise, Greatness, and Fall 1477–1806* (Oxford: Clarendon Press, 1995), 74–105, 361–98, 450–77. On the confessionalization process in the Dutch Republic and the relationships of the various churches with each other and with the state, see M. Th. Uitdenbogaard, "Godsdienstig leven in de 17de eeuw binnen het protestantisme, " and M. G. Spiertz, "Godsdienstig leven van de Katholieken in de 17de eeuw," both in *Algemene Geschiedenis der Nederlanden* (1979) VIII: 322–57, and Israel, 637–76 and 1019–37.
2. R. R. Post, *Kerkelijke verhoudingen in Nederland voor de Reformatie van +/- 1500 tot +/- 1580* (Utrecht, 1954), 149, 165, and "De Roeping tot het Kloosterleven in de 16de eeuw," *Mededelingen der Koninklijke Nederlandse Akademie van Wetenschappen,* Nieuwe Reeks 13 (Amsterdam,

1950): 31–76; I. H. van Eeghen, *Vrouwenkloosters en begijnhof in Amsterdam van de 14e tot het eind der 16e eeuw* (Amsterdam: H. J. Paris, 1941).

3. M. Hüffer, *De adellijke vrouwenabdij van Rijnsburg, 1133–1574* (Nijmegen: Dekker en Van de Vegt, 1922). While growing estrangement from the church was a major factor in this decline, it may not have been the only cause. Koch makes the argument that noble families placed their daughters in the convent because the entry fees were much smaller than marriage dowries. Esther Koch, *De kloosterpoort als sluitpost? Adellijke vrouwen langs Maas en Rijn, tussen huwelijk en convent, 1200–1600* (Leeuwarden: Eisma, 1994). If this were the case, the growing prosperity in the northern Netherlands might have given families the resources to dower their daughters, channeling them away from the convent.

4. Merry E. Wiesner, *Women and Gender in Early Modern Europe* (Cambridge: Cambridge University Press, 1993), 62, 183.

5. Florence Koorn, *Begijnhoven in Holland en Zeeland gedurende de middeleeuwen* (Assen: Van Gorcum, 1981) and "Beguinages in the Netherlands," in *"Zahlreich wie die Sterne des Himmels." Beginen am Niederrhein zwischen Mythos und Wirklichkeit, Bensberger Protokolle*, vol. 70 (Bensberg: Thomas Morus Akademie, 1992), 41–57. For the southern Low Countries, see Walter Simons, "The Beguine Movement in the Southern Low Countries: A Reassessment," *Bulletin de l'Institute historique belge de Rome* LIX (1989): 63–105.

6. Indeed, the entire convention of distinguishing second-order from third-order religious in the early modern period has probably vastly oversimplified an extremely complicated situation, at least in the Low Countries, as Craig Harline points out in "Actives and Contemplatives: The Female Religious of the Low Countries Before and After Trent," *Catholic Historical Review* 81 (1985): 541–67.

7. Florence Koorn, "Women without Vows: The Case of the Beguines and the Sisters of the Common Life in the Northern Netherlands," in ed. *Women and Men in Spiritual Culture XIV–XVII Centuries. A Meeting of South and North*, ed. E. Schulte van Kessel (The Hague: Staatsuitgeverij, 1986), 135–47; "Ongebonden vrouwen. Overeenkomsten en verschillen tussen begijnen en zusters des Gemenen Levens," in *Geert Grote en Moderne Devotie. Voordrachten gehouden tijdens het Geert Grote congres, Nijmegen 27–29 september 1984*, ed. J. Andriessen, P. Bange, and A. G. Weiler, Middeleeuwse Studies Band I (Nijmegen, Katholieke Universiteit, 1985), reprinted in *Ons Geestelijk Erf* 59 (1985): 393–402; "Hollandse nuchterheid? De houding van de Moderne Devoten tegenover vrouwenmystiek en ascese," *Ons Geestelijk Erf* 66 (1992): 97–114; E. Persoons, "Het Dagelijks Leven in de Windesheimse Vrouwenkloosters," *Spiegel Historiael* 15 (1980): 342–49.

8. Israel, *Dutch Republic*, 74–84.

9. Alastair Duke, *Reformation and Revolt in the Low Countries* (London: Hambledon Press, 1990), 45–46. Duke suggests that Claesdochter was drawing here on a tradition of oral dissent for the phrasing of her criticism (24, 69). Claesdochter's testimony can be found in *Corpus documentorum inquisitionis haereticae pravitatis neerlandicae: Verzameling van*

stukken betreffrende de pauselijke en bisshoppelijke inquisitie in de Nederlanden, ed. P. Fredricq (Ghent and The Hague, 1889–1902) V: 280–81. As the "first female Protestant martyr in the Netherlands," Claesdochter has been the subject of several hagiographical works, notably making a defiant speech before her execution in the seventeenth century *Martyr's Mirror* (Thieleman J. van Braght, *The Bloody Theater or Martyr's Mirror of the Defenseless Christians Who Baptized Only upon Confession of Faith, and Who Suffered and Died for the Testimony of Jesus, Their Saviour, from the Time of Christ to the Year A. D. 1660,* trans. Joseph F. Sohm, 13th ed. [Scottsdale, Pa.: Herald Press, 1982], 422–23. In this translation she appears as Weynken Claes.)

10. Duke, *Reformation and Revolt,* 67.

11. Ibid., 35, 78.

12. Marshall, "Protestant, Catholic, and Jewish Women," 126.

13. Duke, *Reformation and Revolt,* 87. See also G. K. Waite, "The Anabaptist Movement in Amsterdam and the Netherlands, 1531–35: An Initial Investigation into Its Genesis and Social Dynamics," *Sixteenth Century Journal* 17 (1987): 249–65.

14. John Klassen, "Women and the Family among Dutch Anabaptist Martyrs," *Mennonite Quarterly Review* 60 (1986): 549. For more on the image of Anabaptist women in the Martyr's Mirror, see Jennifer Hiett Umble, "Women and Choice: An Examination of the *Martyr's Mirror,*" *Mennonite Quarterly Review* 64 (1990): 135–45.

15. Sherrin Marshall Wyntjes, "Women and Religious Choices in the Sixteenth Century Netherlands," *Archive for Reformation History* 75 (1984): 285. Women continued to play important roles in popular religious protest in the Dutch Republic. Political riots often had religious overtones, as rioters celebrated the House of Orange as defenders of Calvinism. See Rudolf Dekker, "Women in Revolt: Popular Protest and Its Social Basis in Holland in the Seventeenth and Eighteenth Centuries," *Theory and Society* 16 (1987): 337–62.

16. A. Th. van Deursen, *Bavianen en slijkgeuzen. Kerk en kerkvolk ten tijde van Maurits en Oldenbarnevelt* (Assen: Van Gorcum, 1974), 131–33, and J. J. Woltjer, "De plaats van de calvinisten in de Nederlandse samenleving," *De zeventiende eeuw* 10 (1994): 3–23. Local Reformation studies have confirmed these estimates. See Joke Spaans, *Haarlem na de Reformatie: Stedelijke cultuur en kerkelijk leven, 1577–1620* ('s-Gravenhage: Stichting Hollandse Historische Reeks, 1989); Herman Roodenburg, *Onder censuur: de kerkelijke tucht in de gereformeerde gemeente van Amsterdam, 1578–1700* (Hilversum: Verloren, 1990); Benjamin J. Kaplan, *Calvinists and Libertines: Confession and Community in Utrecht, 1578–1620* (Oxford: Oxford University Press, 1995); and A. Ph. F. Wouters, *Nieuw en ongezien. Kerk en samenleving in de classis Delft en Delfland, 1572–1621,* vol. 1, *De nieuw kerk* (Delft: Eburen, 1994).

17. James D. Tracy, "The Calvinist Church of The Dutch Republic,

1572–1618/9," in *Reformation Europe: A Guide to Research II*, ed. William S. Maltby (St. Louis: Center for Reformation Research, 1992), 255–64.

18. Liesbeth Geudeke, "Mannenbastion of vrouwenbolwerk? De positie van vrouwen in de gereformeerd kerk, 1566–1650," in *Vrome vrouwen: Betekenissen van geloof voor vrouwen in de geschiedenis*, ed. Mirjam Cornelis, Marjet Derks, Marit Monteiro, and Josian Strous (Hilversum: Verloren, 1996), 72–73. Similar ratios have been uncovered for congregations in Dutch towns outside the province of Holland. See Van Deursen, *Bavianen en slijkgeuzen*, 134–35.

19. Geudeke, "Mannenbastion of vrouwenbolwerk?," 74.

20. Ibid., 75. For Public Church discipline in Amsterdam, see Roodenburg, *Onder censuur*, 362–69.

21. F. L. Rutgers, *Acta van de Nederlandsche synoden der zestiende eeuw* (Dordrecht: Uitgeverij J. P. van den Tol, 1980 reprint of the 1889 edition), 26, 437.

22. Geudeke, "Mannenbastion of vrouwenbolwerk?," 82; for Amsterdam, see Charles H. Parker, *The Reformation of Community: Social Welfare and Calvinist Charity in Holland, 1572–1620* (Cambridge: Cambridge University Press, 1998), 120.

23. A general introduction to the Further Reformation can be found in Fred A. Van Lieburg, "From Pure Church to Pious Culture: The Further Reformation in the Seventeenth Century Dutch Republic," in *Later Calvinism: International Perspectives* (*Sixteenth Century Essays and Studies*, vol. 22), ed. W. Fred Graham (Kirksville, Mo.: Sixteenth Century Journal Publishers, Inc., 1994), 409–29.

24. Natalie Zemon Davis places this approach to women's roles in dissident churches in a larger context in "City Women and Religious Change," in *Society and Culture in Early Modern France* (Stanford, Calif.: Stanford University Press, 1975), 65–96.

25. Mirjam de Baar, Machteld Löwensteyn, Marit Monteiro, and A. Agnes Sneller, eds., *Choosing the Better Part: Anna Maria van Schurman (1607–1678)* (Dordrecht: Kluwer Academic Publishers, 1996).

26. Anna Maria van Schurman, *Whether a Christian Woman Should be Educated and Other Writings from Her Intellectual Circle*, trans. and ed. Joyce L. Irwin (Chicago: University of Chicago Press, 1998).

27. Joyce Irwin, "Anna Maria van Schurman: From Feminism to Pietism," *Church History* 46 (1977): 48–62.

28. T. J. Saxby, *The Quest for the New Jerusalem, Jean de Labadie and the Labadists, 1610–1744* (Dordrecht: Martinus Nijhoff Publishers, 1987).

29. Translated into Dutch as *Eucleria, of Uitkiezing van Het Beste Deel* in 1684, excerpts from which appear in Irwin's English collection of Van Schurman's works, *Whether a Christian Woman Should Be Educated*.

30. A. Agnes Sneller, " 'If She had Been a Man …'. Anna Maria van Schur-

man in the Social and Literary Life of Her Age," in de Baar et al., *Choosing the Better Part*, 133–50.

31. For the Labadist respect for Van Schurman as a theologian, see Mirjam de Baar, " 'En onder 't haantje zoekt te blijven.' De betrokkenheid van vrowen bij het huisgezin van Jean de Labadie (1669–1732)," *Vrouwenlevens 1500–1850. Jaarboek voor Vrouwengeschiedenis* 8 (1987): 35. For her influence among Lutheran Pietists, see Erica Scheenstra, "On Anna Maria van Schurman's 'right choice,' " in de Baar et al., *Choosing the Better Part*, 119–24.

32. Mirjam de Baar, " 'Ik moet spreken.' Het spiritueel leiderschap van Antoinette Bourignon," in *Terra Incognita: Historisch onderzoek naar katholicisme en vrouwelijkheid*, ed. Annelies van Heijst and Marjet Derks (Kampen: Kok Agora, 1994), 87–108. De Baar plans to correct the gaps in the standard bibliographies of Bourignon's work in her forthcoming book. Several of Bourignon's writings have been translated into English, notably *The Light of the World: A Most True Relation of a Pilgrimess Travelling Towards Eternity*, 3 parts (London, 1696; reprinted 1863; also microform, Early English Books, 1641–1700 [1179:1, 1276:13, 2285:6]).

33. Mirjam de Baar, "Transgressing Gender Codes: Anna Maria van Schurman and Antoinette Bourignon as Contrasting Examples," in *Women of the Golden Age: An International Debate on Women in Seventeenth-Century Holland, England and Italy*, ed. Els Kloek et al. (Hilversum, 1994), 144–52, and Joyce Irwin, "Anna Maria van Schurman and Antoinette Bourignon: Contrasting Examples of Seventeenth Century Pietism," *Church History* 60 (1991): 301–15.

34. Dorothée van Paassen en Anke Passenier, *Op zoek naar vrouwen in ketterij en sekte. Een bronnenonderzoek* (Kampen, 1993); Mirjam de Baar, "Van kerk naar sekte: Sara Nevius, Grietje van Dijk en Anna Maria van Schurman," *De Zeventiende eeuw* 7 (1991): 159–70; F. A. van Lieburg, "Vrouwen uit het gereformeerd piëtisme in Nederland," *Documentatieblad Nadere Reformatie* 9 (1985): 78–87, 119–27, and 12 (1988): 116–27; idem, *Levens van vromen. Gereformeerd piëtisme in de achttiende eeuw* (Kampen, 1991); idem, "Vroomheid kent geen sekse: Piëtistes in de achttiende eeuw," in *Vrome vrouwen: Betekenissen van geloof voor vrouwen in de geschiedenis*, ed. Mirjam Cornelis, Marjet Derks, Marit Monteiro, and Josian Strous (Hilversum: Verloren, 1996), 109–28.

35. Joke Spaans, "Negenenveertig Haarlemse Mirjams over het aandeel van vrouwen in de moeilijkheden rondom de Lutherse predikant Conrad Vietor, 1617–1620," *Nederlands archief voor kerkgeschiedenis* 67 (1987): 1–14.

36. For some general thoughts on theoretical approaches to women and Catholicism, see Annelies van Heijst and Marjet Derks, "Godsvrucht en gender: naar een geschiedschrijving in meervoud," in van Heijst and Derks, *Terra Incognita*, 7–38.

37. Israel, *Dutch Republic*, 377–95, 637–53, 1034–37.

38. J. W. van Campen, ed., *Notae quotidianae van Aernout van Buchell*

(Utrecht, 1940), January 15, 1636, quoted in Judith Pollmann, *Religious Choice in the Dutch Republic: The Reformation of Arnoldus Buchelius (1565–1641)* (Manchester: Manchester University Press, 1999), 149.

39. Florence Koorn, "A Life of Pain and Struggle: The Autobiography of Elizabeth Strouven (1600–1661)," in *Autobiographien von Frauen. Beiträge zu ihrer Geschichte,* ed. Magdalene Heuser (Tübingen: Max Niemeyer, 1996), 13–24.

40. Florence Koorn, "Een charismatische anti-helige: Elisabeth Strouven (1600–1661)," in *Vrome vrouwen: Betekenissen van geloof voor vrouwen in de geschiedenis,* ed. Mirjam Cornelis, Marjet Derks, Marit Monteiro and Josian Strous (Hilversum: Verloren, 1996), 87–107.

41. The most authoritative work on the *kloppen* is Marit Monteiro, *Geestelijke maagden: Leven tussen klooster en wereld in Noord-Nederland gedurende de zeventiende eeuw* (Hilversum: Verloren, 1996); see also idem, " 'Ick ben gekomen inde werelt om vuur te brenghen.' Inspiratie, ambitie en strategie van katholieke geestelijke maagden in de vroegmoderne tijd," in van Heijst and Derks, *Terra Incognita.* Earlier important works on the spiritual virgins are Elisja Schulte van Kessel, *Geest en Vlees in Godsdienst en Wetenschap: Vijf Opstellen over Gezagsconflicten in de 17de Eeuw* ('s-Gravenhage: Staatsuitgeverij, 1980), and Eugenie E. A. J. M. Theissing, *Over klopjes en kwezels* (Nijmegen/Utrecht, 1935).

42. Further research will be required in order to determine how popular this alternative was. One researcher has determined that forty-one women from the northern Netherlands (excluding Limburg) entered Carmelite convents in the Spanish Netherlands between 1606 and 1648 (Isabel van de H. Drieëneid, OCD, *Karmelites in den vreemde* [Beek, 1992]).

43. Monteiro, *Geestelijke maagden,* 143–57.

44. Ibid., 55. For Protestant complaints about the effectiveness of the missionary work done by *kloppen,* effectiveness which they explained by overestimating the size of the *kloppen* population, see Theissing, *Over klopjes,* 65–66. In Amsterdam magistrates tried to curtail the success of the *kloppen* by forbidding them to run elementary schools in 1640; the *kloppen* simply took their schools underground. Elsewhere, Protestants were known to send their young children to schools run by the *kloppen* (Schulte van Kessel, Geesten Vlees, 57; Van Deursen, *Bavianen en slijkgeuzen,* 301).

45. Monteiro analyzes the thirty-four *kloppenboeken* she has discovered at length in *Geestelijke maagden,* 122–204, and also in her article "Een maagd zonder regel is als een schip zonder stuurman. Richtlijnen voor geestelijke maagden in de Noordelijke Nederlanden in de zeventiende eeuw," *Trajecta* (1992): 332–51.

46. Schulte van Kessel, "Scandaleuze dienstmaagden in de zielzorg," in *Geest en Vlees,* 91–116.

Recovering the Religious History of Dutch Reformed Women in Colonial New York

Joyce D. Goodfriend

WHEN ANNEKE AND HESTER VAN DEURSEN entered New York City's New Dutch Church in August 1766 with a hatchet and began mutilating the pew assigned to the city's corporation, the *New York Post-Boy* published a detailed account of their actions.[1] Yet the countless other women who for generations had regularly flocked to worship at Dutch Reformed churches in New York never attracted the attention of newspaper editors. Nor, indeed, have they captured the interest of historians, despite a spate of studies dealing with women in colonial New York and a burgeoning literature on women and religion in colonial America.

Dutch colonial women conventionally have been characterized as shrewd traders not above earthy language and abusive behavior. Beneficiaries of laws that enhanced their status, they routinely participated in the marketplace. Moreover, time and time again they demonstrated their independence in the courtroom. This thoroughly secular image of New York's Dutch women has not been challenged by historians who have expounded the consequences of the transition from Dutch to English sovereignty on the legal rights of women.[2] Investigations of inheritance practices and mercantile activities reinforce the impression that worldly matters were uppermost in the minds of Dutch women. Although clues to the spiritual dimensions of Dutch women's lives appear in the work of Alice Morse Earle and Alice Kenney, and recent research has confirmed the significant role played by Dutch Reformed women in congregational life in the seventeenth and eighteenth centuries, the religious beliefs and practices of the women who attended New York's largest denomination have not been the subject of sustained inquiry.[3]

Dutch Reformed women also have been conspicuously absent from the widening stream of scholarship on women and religion in colonial America. An impressive array of studies has delineated cultural assumptions about women's ideal religious qualities, assessed female influence on congregational life, and anatomized the spiritual development of individual women.[4] This pathbreaking scholarship has been centered on Puritan and Quaker women in New England and Pennsylvania— groups that have perennially fascinated historians because of their bold challenges to orthodoxy and their propensity to chronicle their spiritual progress in excruciating detail. Regrettably, the introspective journals that form the underpinning of most research on female churchgoers in the English settlements do not appear to have survived for Dutch colonial culture.

Nevertheless, it is possible to appraise the beliefs and behavior of female adherents of the Dutch Reformed Church in New Netherland and New York by culling pertinent information from a variety of sources, including personal documents, travelers' accounts, church records, and wills and inventories. Linking demographic and church records enables us to reconstruct the religious life cycle of Dutch Reformed women, while some sense of the meaning of religious milestones can be teased out of literary sources.

Dutch Reformed women in colonial New York demonstrated a commitment to their beliefs by participating in family worship, reading the Bible and other devotional works, regularly attending church services and joining the congregation at an early age, and bestowing charitable gifts on their churches.

Religion played a fundamental part in the patterning of a Dutch Reformed woman's life in New Netherland and New York during the seventeenth and eighteenth centuries. From the time after baptism, through the years of parental religious instruction and formal catechism classes, to the date of her becoming a communicant of a congregation, she absorbed the essentials of her faith, practiced its rituals, and cemented ties with its adherents. Marriage, soon followed by childbirth, initiated a new stage in a woman's spiritual development as she focused her attention on bringing her children into the Christian community through baptism and instilling religious values in them. In her adult years, she frequently would stand as a godparent for the offspring of kin and friends and eventually for her own grandchildren. During the latter portion of her life, attending the funerals of close kin and friends may have heightened her consciousness of her own approaching death and intensified her spiritual activity.

Dutch Reformed girls grew up in a setting conducive to learning the ways of God's people. Family worship was fundamental to Calvinism in the Netherlands and in the overseas colonies.[5] Scriptural teachings formed a guide for personal conduct as well as the cornerstone of family life. The presence in numerous Dutch colonial households of folio Bibles printed in the Netherlands attests to the customary nature of Bible reading in New York's Dutch Reformed families. Expensive versions of the *Statenvertaling,* the 1637 translation of the Bible into the Dutch vernacular authorized by the States General, these folio Bibles were "great volumes often illustrated with numerous engravings and ornamented with brass comers and clasps."[6] Cherished possessions handed down from generation to generation in Dutch families, they were used to record vital events and played a central role in family worship.[7] Hearing the contents of the Bible pronounced in the family circle and observing family members in private devotions gradually prepared girls, as well as boys, to enter the community of believers.

Visual representations of biblical themes may also have played an important role in conveying religious precepts. Spending her early years in a home adorned with objects displaying religious motifs conditioned a girl to accept spiritual values as an integral part of her everyday life. Delft tiles decorated with scriptural scenes and texts, installed around the fireplace in Dutch homes both in the Netherlands and in America, have been viewed as a means of instilling religious verities in impressionable children. The educational value of the biblical tiles was undoubtedly enhanced by their pictorial attractiveness. Children learned the stories of the Bible through oft-repeated explanations of the tiles by adult members of the household coupled with family Bible reading.[8]

A variety of other objects in Dutch households—furniture, firebacks, bed warmers, and plates—might also be decorated with religious scenes and inscriptions.[9] Paintings with religious themes done by New York artists were commonplace among the Hudson Valley Dutch in the eighteenth century. These Scripture paintings were based on illustrations in Bibles imported from the Netherlands.[10]

Formal religious instruction in the church or local elementary school began early in a Dutch Reformed girl's life. To judge from the comments of Dominie Henricus Selyns on the accomplishments of his catechism class in 1698, Dutch girls were eager to absorb the tenets of their faith. Of the forty-four boys and twenty-one girls, aged seven to fourteen, who recited "all the Psalms, hymns and prayers in rhyme" in the church on the second day of Easter, Ascension Day, and the second day of Pentecost, "the girls although fewer in number, had learned and recited more in proportion than the boys."[11] The perfect performance of one five-year-old girl brought tears to the eyes of the congregation.[12] Religious education for older girls was available in catechism classes such as the one run by schoolmaster Abraham Delanoy in his New York City home in 1679. "A company of about twenty-five persons, male and female . . . , mostly young people . . . sang some verses from the Psalms, made a prayer, and, answered questions from the catechism, at the conclusion of which they prayed and sang some verses from the Psalms again."[13]

Dutch Reformed women's affinity for religion was manifested in their early attachment to the congregation and their enduring loyalty to the church. Religiosity was a quality Dutch Reformed men valued in their prospective brides. Marrying a godly woman was of great importance to Jeremias van Rensselaer, director of the colony of Rensselaerswijck, who, shortly after he wed Maria van Cortlandt in 1662, informed his mother that "to live together so calmly and peacefully with a wife who has always led a good and moral life and feared the Lord God is the best thing I could wish for here on earth."[14] Maria van Cortlandt married Jeremias van Rensselaer when she was almost seventeen; she had joined the Reformed Church a few months before she was sixteen.

The timetable of church affiliation in women's lives reflected both cultural expectations and personal attitudes toward religion. Female communicants of the Dutch Reformed Church in New York City followed a pattern established in the Netherlands among Calvinists. Church membership was regarded as marking the attainment of maturity and thus was the normal prerequisite for marriage.[15] The fear of dying in childbirth may also have prompted women to join the church at an earlier age than their husbands.

Analysis of the ages at which a sample of women was admitted to the New York City Dutch Reformed Church between 1660 and 1710 reveals that of the 108 women for whom baptismal dates and dates of church admission are available, 69 (64 percent) became communicants before their twentieth birthday, 28 (26 percent) were admitted between the ages of twenty and twenty-five, and only 11 (10 percent) were older than twenty-five when they joined.[16] The median age of the women received into the congregation during these years was eighteen. Not only did Dutch girls join the church at an early age, the overwhelming majority did so prior to marriage. Of the 117 women whose dates of marriage and church admission are known, 94 (80 percent) joined the church before being wed for the first time. A similar pattern was found in the Tappan Reformed Church between 1694 and 1751. Firth Fabend's research disclosed that "two-thirds of [the Haring women] joined before marrying, most at age eighteen to twenty-one."[17]

Gerald Moran's examination of the age and marital status of the female members of a representative group of Puritan churches in Connecticut between 1660 and 1699 uncovered a strikingly different pattern. Only 15 percent of females were under the age of twenty when admitted to the congregation, 29 percent were between twenty and twenty-four, and 57 percent were twenty-five or older. Moreover, admission to the church customarily followed marriage and frequently parenthood. Over three-fourths of the men and women who joined these Connecticut churches did so after they had wed.[18] In contrast to their Dutch neighbors, New England Puritans did not view most young women (or men) as sufficiently mature, in a spiritual sense, before marriage to be received into the church.

Women's religious life during the years following entrance into the community of believers is less susceptible to precise measurement, but no less important to document. Given the religious cast of the colonial Dutch domestic environment, there is little doubt that most women in New York were familiar with the contents of the Scriptures. But, more significantly, the majority of Dutch colonial women, in all likelihood, were sufficiently literate to read the Bible. Because investigators of literacy generally have equated the ability to read with the ability to sign one's name, they concluded that the large numbers of women who signed documents with a mark could not read.[19] However, recent scholarship has convincingly demonstrated that reading and writing were taught as separate skills in early modern Europe and America and that, therefore, women who were unable to sign their names might indeed have been able to read.[20]

Abundant evidence exists to show that reading and writing were taught separately in colonial New York.[21] When Anne Grant described female education in early-eighteenth-century Albany, she specifically noted that girls "were taught . . . to read in Dutch, the Bible and a few Calvinist tracts of the devotional kind . . . few were taught to write."[22]

In letters penned between 1675 and 1688, Maria van Cortlandt van Rensselaer illustrated her knowledge of the Bible's contents. To a troubled Richard van Rensselaer, she offered words of consolation from John 16:33: " The good Lord himself said to His disciples: 'In the world ye shall have tribulation; but be of good cheer, I have overcome the world.' Only let us always keep our leader, Jesus Christ before our eyes and firmly trust that nothing happens without his Will."[23] She did not hesitate to use spiritual teachings to judge the behavior of others. Deeply disturbed by the attempts of Phillip Schuyler's widow to obtain portions of the Van Rensselaer lands, Maria averred that Mrs. Schuyler "thinks as little of God's word and law as is written in Exodus, ch. 22, where God speaks of the widows and orphans, but where there is money, there is power. But God, who will take care of the widows and orphans, will not desert me and my six children."[24]

Maria van Rensselaer's family connections placed her at the apex of New York's social structure, but, in all probability, her life experience did not differ radically from that of other seventeenth-century Dutch women on the frontier. Bible reading was part of that experience. What distinguished Maria van Rensselaer from some of her counterparts was her ability to write, not her knowledge of the Bible. Most of the women with whom she came in contact could read sufficiently well to understand the Bible. That many Dutch women owned Bibles, Testaments, and Psalters is well-documented in wills and inventories. In the years 1664–1730 members of the New York City Dutch Reformed community, from all ranks of the social structure, were much more likely to possess Bibles, Testaments, and Psalters and to include provisions in their wills for passing on these objects than their neighbors of other faiths.[25]

In colonial America the massive Dutch family Bibles usually passed from father to eldest son. Garret Hansen Noorstrandt of Flatbush spelled out this tradition in his 1724 will: "I leave my son Hans, my Great Nether Dutch Bible, as his right as first born desiring that he would bestow the same upon his eldest son Gerritt, when he is of age."[26] Widows who came into possession of these folio Bibles as a rule passed them on to their sons. In 1677 Mary Jansen, the widow of merchant Govert Loockermans, bequeathed the Great Bible to her son Cornelis; more than half a century later the widow Ann van der Spiegel left her large Dutch Bible to her son, Lawrence.[27] On occasion, women kept the family Bible. Margareta de Riemer Steenwijck recorded in her family Bible "on the 21st of Nov. 1684 died (Cor)nelius Steenwijck (58 years 8 months and 5 days old) unto his Lord, and lies buried with his daughter and 6 sons in New York in the church."[28] When there were no male heirs in the family, the folio Dutch Bible was given to the eldest daughter. Evert Van de water, a New York City merchant, bequeathed to his eldest daughter Katharine "my large House Bible and a New Testament with silver clasps." Hybert van der bergh, a carman, also from New York City, specified that his Great Bible was to go to "my eldest daughter Elizabeth for priority of birth," and John van Wickell, of Flatbush, left his Great Bible to his daughter Hyltie.[29]

Daughters in Dutch families customarily received Psalters from their mothers and eventually passed them down to their own daughters. Psalters were "Small portable books containing the New Testament and Psalms [and] were sometimes ornamented with silver comers, monogrammed clasps, and carrying chains and were taken to church for use in services of worship."[30] In 1708 Gertie Jans van Langedyck gave instructions in her will that her daughter's daughter was to receive her two Dutch church books with silver clasps and in 1758 Margaret Gouverneur bequeathed "my Psalm book with gold clasps" to Gertruyd Gouverneur.[31]

An unusual 1655 court case in New Amsterdam furnishes persuasive evidence that ordinary Dutch women treasured their Bibles, which they read over and over. A young girl was captured by Indians, who gave her two inexpensive Bibles, which they had taken from another New Amsterdam home. When the girl was returned to the settlement, she wished to keep the Bibles, which had undoubtedly given her spiritual comfort during her ordeal. Nonetheless, the housewife whose property they were sued for their return and won the case.[32]

Other religious books occasionally were mentioned in Dutch women's wills or inventories. Elizabeth van Corlaer of Albany provided that the eldest son of her deceased eldest son have a "New Large Dutch Bible, as cast in Holland 20 or 22 guilders, Holland money" for his birthright. To another son she bequeathed "my two books, made by Willem a Brakel."[33] Anna van Driesen, whose father was Albany's Dutch Reformed minister, left her niece a book entitled *Milk der Waerheyt* (milk of truth) in her will drafted in 1759, and Mary Leisler Gouverneur mentioned "my Large Book of Martyrs with silver hooks" in her 1740 will.[34] The 1693 inventory of Elizabeth Bancker, the widow of a wealthy Albany merchant, listed a number of titles including "two Catechisms; one Isaac Ambrosius; . . . one Horin's Church History; one Flock of Israel, in French; one Coelman's Christian Interest; three volumes Christ's Way and Works; one DeWitt's Catechism; two Duycker's Church History; [and] one Cudemans on Holiness."[35]

Attending Sunday church services was the high point of a week devoted to household labor. When Benjamin Bullivant, an observant English visitor to New York City in 1697, noted that "the Dutchwomen (of ye younger sort) troop the Streets in morning gowns very long, theyr heads cleane, & well enough set off (for theyr faces) but without shooes & stockings, unless of a Sabath day," he confirmed the sacred character of the Sabbath for Dutch women.[36]

The regular round of attending worship and taking communion four times a year was interrupted only by the rituals surrounding childbirth. More needs to be known about the part Dutch colonial mothers played at the baptism of their children or the custom of "churching" women a few weeks after the delivery of their baby.[37] Though scholars have emphasized the significance of eighteenth-century mothers' efforts to instill spiritual values in their offspring, a great deal remains to be learned about the maternal role in the process of religious education in colonial New York.[38] In 1683 Maria van Rensselaer proudly reported that her eldest son Kiliaen was "a member of God's church. May the Lord let him grow up in virtue and grant His blessing as to soul and body."[39] A generation earlier, Anna van Rensselaer, Maria van Rensselaer's mother-in-law, had expressed deep concern for the spiritual welfare of her son Jeremias. Soon after he left the Netherlands for Rensselaerswijck in 1654, she counseled him: "Above all, fear the Lord God and keep Him constantly before your eyes and pray fervently that His Holy Spirit may guide you in truth. Go diligently to church and practice God's Holy Word, As thereby you may save your soul. In that way you may expect the blessing of the Lord here temporarily and hereafter eternally."[40]

A great deal has yet to be learned also about women's interpretation of the role of godparent. How frequently were women called upon to sponsor children for baptism and what responsibilities did this entail? Did they seek to emulate Margareta Selyns, the widow of New York City's Dutch Reformed minister, who left "to all the children whereof I have been Godmother, the sum of L6 5s, and they are to produce a certificate thereof out of the Church Registry"?[41]

In times of adversity Dutch Reformed women drew solace and courage from their faith. Widowed at the age of twenty-nine with six children, and handicapped by chronic illness, Maria van Rensselaer found herself enmeshed in a complex web of family and political intrigue that prevented her from settling her husband's estate. When Labadist missionary Jasper Danckaerts visited the young widow in 1679, he portrayed her as a woman of deep-seated faith. "This lady was polite, quite well informed, and of good life and disposition. She had experienced several proofs of the Lord. . . . In all these trials, she had borne herself well, and God left not Himself without witness in her. . . . We had several conversations with her about the truth, and practical religion, mutually satisfactory."[42]

Maria struggled unsuccessfully to extricate herself from financial difficulty and to secure a stable economic future for her offspring. Her personal tragedy was compounded in 1684. "It has been a sad summer for me," Maria wrote after the death of both her parents in 1684. "I doubt not but God will again rejoice us with His spirit and grace, for the Lord chastises whom he loves and punishes every son whom He adopts. If this had not been my joy and strength, I should long ago have perished in my sorrow."[43] Nurtured in a devout family (her father died while saying his prayers), Maria harbored strong religious convictions, thereby mirroring her mother, Anna Loockermans van Cortlandt, to whom Dominie Selyns paid tribute in these words: "Here rests who after Cortlandt's death no rest possessed, and sought no other rest than soon to rest beside him. He died. She lived and died. Both now in Abram rest. And there, where Jesus is, true rest and joys abide in. Gods will did Anna serve; God's aid did Hannah pray. In this alone alike, that both have passed away."[44]

Ascertaining the ways in which religious faith shaped Dutch women's lives in colonial New York is only part of the story. The nature and extent of female influence on the colony's Reformed churches also needs to be assessed. Though women enjoyed spiritual equality with their male counterparts in New York's Dutch Reformed Church, this equality did not extend to the temporal realm. Unwritten rules severely restricted women's participation in the administrative affairs of the congregation. Authority in the church was centered on males; the minister and auxiliary church functionaries were men, as were the lay leaders of the congregation.[45] Women's subordinate status was visibly displayed in seating arrangements in the church edifice. Women's pews were not only separate from those of men, but less favorably situated. In some cases the price of women's seats was lower than that of men's. Additionally, children sat with their mother, not their father.[46] A gender-differentiated seating plan was also adopted by New York City's Dutch Lutheran congregation when its new church building was nearing completion in 1729. Church authorities decided to sell the men's seats in the front, but "in the rear part for the women, no seats are to be made, but only chairs are to be placed there, for which everyone has to pay."[47]

Whether clustered together in a separate area of the church or intermingled with their male kin in family pews, as later became the custom in some churches, female churchgoers were far from being an undifferentiated mass. The spatial patterning of the congregation reflected distinctions among female worshipers, whether these stemmed from the worldly status of husbands or their own spiritual standing. In Dutch Reformed churches, a special bench, the *juffrouw bank*, was set aside for ministers' wives.[48] Much can be learned about the sources of gradations among female worshipers from systematic analysis of lists of seating such as those for the Albany Dutch Reformed Church from 1747 to 1764 and the Tappan Reformed Church in 1724.[49]

Barred from the exercise of power in the church, it seems improbable that Dutch women would be called upon to deliberate on matters of doctrine or administration. Did this mean, then, that they were content to acquiesce in the teachings and decisions of males or did they, on occasion, criticize clergymen, question doctrine, or defy ecclesiastical authorities? The dramatic actions of the Van Deursen sisters in hacking away a church pew were clearly exceptional, but the lack of direct evidence should not sway us into believing that Dutch women never articulated their dissatisfaction with the course of church affairs and never sought to place pressure on their congregation to act in ways they deemed appropriate.

Because Dutch colonial women were not free to express their views on religious issues in public does not mean that they kept silent in private. Labadist missionary Jasper Danckaerts was clearly moved by his encounter with a young woman whom he perceived as critical of the Dutch Reformed Church. "Elizabeth van Rodenburgh ... has withdrawn herself much from the idle company of youth, seeking God in quiet and solitude. She professes the Reformed religion, is a member of that church, and searches for the truth which she has found nowhere except in the word and preaching, which she therefore much attended upon and loved, but which never satisfied her, as she felt a want and yearning after something more." Danckaerts sought to further her quest for religious illumination by translating and copying pietist tracts for her. That Dutch women possessed opinions on a variety of religious subjects is also evident from a jotting Dr. Alexander Hamilton made in his diary when he visited Albany on June 29, 1744: "We ... supped at Widow Skuyler's where the conversation turned upon the Moravian enthusiasts and their doctrine."[50]

Dutch women's conception of their religious duty was shaped by their gender. Church discipline cases offer a rare glimpse of the strategies employed by Dutch women to reconcile worldly needs with spiritual values. When in 1663 officers of the Breuckelen Dutch Reformed Church investigated the conduct of a female member who had allegedly become engaged to marry too soon after the death of her husband, they discovered that pragmatic considerations rather than deliberate violation of communal values dictated her behavior. The consistory "reprimanded [Catherine Letie] and asked her what ever moved her to have her banns proclaimed so soon which was indecent (since her previous husband, who had led a Christian life, had just died). [She] apologized and replied that otherwise she would become a burden to the poor and that it would be impossible for her, a woman with a young child, to plant, plow, sow, weed, or use the land, which would lie barren; this second marriage could turn all of this for the better for her and lighten our burdens. And when we said that this was unallowed because she might be pregnant from her deceased husband who died six weeks ago yesterday after a sudden illness, [she] assured us with great emphasis that she was not pregnant, and to that end she mentioned several women, members, who knew this according to her."[51]

Even though women were denied an official voice in church affairs, the fact of their membership cannot be dismissed as insignificant for the simple reason that they formed a numerical majority in many colonial congregations. The "feminization" of churches during the colonial period was originally documented by scholars investigating women's role in New England church life and now the phenomenon has been examined in a broader context by Patricia Bonomi.[52] The trend toward increasing female dominance in Massachusetts and Connecticut congregations that began in the late seventeenth century was paralleled in the New York City Dutch Reformed Church.

In 1686, 344 (62 percent) of the congregation's 556 communicants were female. Of the 882 persons admitted to the church between 1665 and 1695, 517 (59 percent) were women. Women continued to outnumber men among those entering the church between 1696 and 1730 by a ratio of approximately two to one. As the English colonial government chipped away at the egalitarian practices and other legal safeguards of women's rights that had been transplanted from the Netherlands, the Reformed Church came to symbolize those aspects of Dutch experience that elevated the status of women. No wonder women kept the Reformed faith, joining the church in large numbers and early in their lives. Churchgoing reinforced the values that gave meaning to their existence.[53]

Dutch women may have played a decisive role in ensuring the vitality of the Dutch Reformed Church in colonial New York not only through their membership, but also through their material support. Charitable gifts and bequests from women aided congregations in helping the poor and enlarging their buildings.

Married women left legacies to the church in conjunction with their husbands. In a customary joint will made in 1678/9, Sybout Claesen and his wife Susanna Jans bequeathed a sum of money to the deacons of the New York City Dutch Reformed Church for the use of the poor.[54] In January 1656 the deacons of the Albany Dutch Reformed Church recorded the gift of 25 florins "from Goossen Gerritsen, being money which his wife has promised to the poor on her death bed."[55]

Such gifts supplemented ongoing charitable collections in the church and were of critical importance in an era when poor relief was doled out sparingly. Margareta Selyns, the widow of Rev. Henricus Selyns, highlighted this problem in her 1711 will. Singling out the group she felt was most deserving of her charity, she instructed the minister and elders of the Dutch Reformed Church to "distribute the sum of L62, 10 s. among the poor widows of New York City who live piously and have nothing given them out of the city or the Deacons, or any of the churches."[56]

Women constituted about one-fifth (58) of the 299 contributors to a 1688 fund for building a new Reformed church in New York City.[57] Moreover, several of the men who made donations to the building campaign did so on behalf of their wives, who were church members. Englishman Walter Heyer, for example, who was married to Amsterdam-born Tryntie Bickers, pledged 12 florins for the fund. These husbands were influenced to contribute to the church by wives whose religious identity was independent of their male kinfolk.

A few women had visions of a more lasting contribution to their churches. Judith Stuyvesant, the widow of the former director-general of New Netherland, donated the chapel on the family's Bowery farm to the Dutch Reformed Church.[58] On October 3, 1684, "Maria Baddia presented the Church of Breuckelen with a silver cup for the administration of the Lord's Supper."[59] In her 1730 will, Catherine Philipse donated "a large silver beaker, on which my name is engraven and a damask table cloth ... with a long table, In trust for the congregation of the Dutch church, erected and built at Phillipsburg by my late husband, Fredrick Philipse."[60]

Studies of religion in early America traditionally have centered on male ecclesiastical and lay leaders as they confronted issues relating to theology, the clergy, and institutional development. The developing interest in lay piety in recent years, coupled with the growing acceptance of gender as a vital category of analysis, has spurred research on colonial women's religious beliefs and behavior.[61] Inquiry into the religious experience of New York's Dutch Reformed women, however, has been deterred by the tendency of historians to devalue religious activities of a routine nature as well as the reluctance of American historians to use non-English-language documents. But the greatest obstacle to serious consideration of Dutch women as religious beings has been the enduring American perception of the Dutch as a people so avid in pursuit of temporal rewards that they paid only token attention to spiritual concerns. Revising the one-dimensional image of Dutch colonial women as essentially economic beings begins with the insight that business acumen did not preclude religiosity either in the Netherlands or the overseas colonies.[62] Ultimately, a fuller picture of Dutch colonial women will emerge, one that takes into account the multiple and sometimes contradictory roles that these hardworking, faithful wives and mothers played.

NOTES

Since this essay was published in *de Halve Maen* in 1991, I have continued to research the religious history of Dutch women in New Netherland and early New York. Readers interested in this subject should consult "Maria van Cortlandt van Rensselaer" in *American Women Prose Writers to 1820*, ed. Carla Mulford, vol. 200 of the *Dictionary of Literary Biography* (Detroit, Mich.: Gale Research, 1998), 299–303; "Incorporating Women into the History of the Colonial Dutch Reformed Church: Problems and Prospects," in *Patterns and Portraits: Women in the History of the Reformed Church in America*, eds., Renee House and John Coakley (Grand Rapids, Mich.: Eerdmans, 1999), 16–32; and "Writing/Righting Dutch Colonial History," *New York History* 80 (1999): 5–28.

1. I. N. Phelps Stokes, *The Iconography of Manhattan Island, 1498–1909*, 6 vols. (New York: Robert H. Dodd, 1915–1928), 4: 768.

2. Linda Briggs Biemer, *Woman and Property in Colonial New York: The Transition from Dutch to English Law 1643–1727* (Ann Arbor, Mich.: UMI Research Press, 1983); Joan R. Gundersen and Gwen Victor Gampel, "Married Women's Legal Status in Eighteenth-Century New York and Virginia," *William and Mary Quarterly* 39 (1982): 114–34; Sherry Penney and Roberta Willenkin, "Dutch Women in Colonial Albany: Liberation and Retreat," *de Halve Maen* 52, no. 1 (spring 1977): 9–10, 14–15, no. 2 (summer 1977): 7–8, 15; David Evan Narrett, "Patterns of Inheritance in Colonial New York City, 1664–1775: A Study in the History of the Family" (Ph.D. diss., Cornell University, 1981); David E. Narrett, "Dutch Customs of Inheritance, Women, and the Law in Colonial New York City," in *Authority and Resistance in Early New York*, eds., William Pencak and Conrad Edick Wright (New York: New York Historical Society, 1988), 27–55; David E. Narrett, "Men's Wills and Women's Property Rights in Colonial New York," in *Women in the Age of the American Revolution*, eds., Ronald Hoffman and Peter L. Albert (Charlottesville, Va.: University Press of Virginia, 1989), 91–133; Jean P. Jordan, "Women Merchants in Colonial New York," *New York History* 58 (1977): 412–39; Christine H. Tompsett, "A Note on the Economic Status of Widows in Colonial New York," *New York History* 55 (1974): 319–32.

3. Alice Morse Earle, *Colonial Days in Old New York* (New York: Charles Scribner's Sons, 1896); Alice P. Kenney, *The Gansevoorts of Albany: Dutch Patricians in the Upper Hudson Valley* (Syracuse, N.Y.: Syracuse University Press, 1969), 160–87; Joyce D. Goodfriend, "The Social Dimensions of Congregational Life in Colonial New York City," *William and Mary Quarterly* 46 (1989): 252–78. For a review of the literature on the religion of Dutch New Yorkers, see Joyce D. Goodfriend, "The Historiography of the Dutch in Colonial America," in *Colonial Dutch Studies: An Interdisciplinary Approach*, eds., Eric Nooter and Patricia U. Bonomi (New York: New York University Press, 1988), 17–19. On women and religion in the early modern Netherlands, see Sherrin Marshall Wyntjes, "Women and Religious Choices in the Sixteenth

Century Netherlands," *Archive for Reformation History* 75 (1984): 276–89; Sherrin Marshall, "Protestant, Catholic, and Jewish Women in the Early Modern Netherlands," in *Women in Reformation and Counter-Reformation Europe*, ed., Sherrin Marshall (Bloomington, Ind.: Indiana University Press, 1989), 120–39; Sherrin Marshall, *The Dutch Gentry, 1500–1650: Family, Faith, and Fortune* (New York: Greenwood Press, 1987), chapter 5, "'One, No Other': The Place of Religion in the Mentality of Early Modern Dutch Gentry Families." See also A. Th. van Deursen, *Plain Lives in a Golden Age: Popular Culture, Religion and Society in Seventeenth-Century Holland* (Cambridge: Cambridge University Press, 1991).

4. For a sampling of this literature, see Mary Maples Dunn, "Saints and Sisters: Congregational and Quaker Women in the Early Colonial Period," in *Women in American Religion*, ed., Janet Wilson James (Philadelphia: University of Pennsylvania Press, 1980), 27–46; Gerald F. Moran, "Sisters in Christ: Women and the Church in Seventeenth-Century New England," ibid., 47–65; Gerald F. Moran, "The Hidden Ones: Women and Religion in Puritan New England," in *Triumph Over Silence: Women in Protestant History*, ed., Richard L. Greaves (Westport, Conn.: Greenwood Press, 1985), 125–49; Joan R. Gundersen, "The Non-Institutional Church: The Religious Role of Women in Eighteenth-Century Virginia," *Historical Magazine of the Protestant Episcopal Church* 51 (1982): 347–57; Jean Soderlund, "Women's Authority in Pennsylvania and New Jersey Quaker Meetings, 1680–1760," *William and Mary Quarterly* 44 (1987): 722–49. See also the essays in Rosemary Radford Ruether and Rosemary Skinner Keller, *Women and Religion in America. Volume 2: The Colonial and Revolutionary Periods* (San Francisco, Calif.: Harper and Row, 1983).

5. Paul Zumthor, *Daily Life in Rembrandt's Holland* (Stanford, Calif.: Stanford University Press, 1994; first published in France, 1959), 79–94; Wayne Franits, "The Family Saying Grace: A Theme in Dutch Art of the Seventeenth Century," *Simiolus* 16 (1986): 36–49.

6. Alice P. Kenney, "Neglected Heritage: Hudson River Valley Dutch Material Culture," *Winterthur Portfolio* 20 (spring 1985): 67. On Dutch Bibles, see also Alfred Bader, *The Bible Through Dutch Eyes: From Genesis through the Apocrypha* (Milwaukee, Wis.: Milwaukee Art Center, 1976); S. L. Greenslade, ed., *The Cambridge History of the Bible. The West from the Reformation to the Present Day* (Cambridge: Cambridge University Press, 1963), 122–25, 352–53.

7. Esther Singleton, *Dutch New York* (New York: Dood, Mead, 1909), 179–80.

8. Ruth Piwonka has stated that "Dutch Bible illustrations and numerous religious subjects depicted on hearth tiles reinforced [biblical] instruction." Ruth Piwonka, "Recovering the Lost Ark: The Dutch Graphic Tradition in the Hudson Valley," in *A Beautiful and Fruitful Place: Selected Rensselaerswijck Seminar Papers*, ed. Nancy Anne McClure Zeller

(Albany, N.Y.: New Netherland Publishing, 1991), 29. On Dutch biblical tiles, see Earle, *Colonial Days*, 125–26; C. H. de Jonge, *Dutch Tiles* (New York: Praeger, 1971), 46–49; Dingman Korf, *Dutch Tiles* (New York: Universe Books, 1964), 8–9, 24–25, 120–21. For illustrations of Dutch tiles with scriptural scenes, see *Dutch Tiles in the Philadelphia Museum of Art* (Philadelphia: Philadelphia Museum of Art, 1984), 116–21; Joseph T. Butler, *Sleepy Hollow Restorations: A Cross Section of the Collection* (Tarrytown, N.Y.: Sleepy Hollow Press, 1984), color plate of the dining room of Van Cortlandt Manor; and *Holland and Britain* (London, n.d.), 79.

9. T. H. Lunsingh Scheurleer, "The Dutch and Their Homes in the Seventeenth Century," in *Arts of the Anglo-American Community in the Seventeenth Century*, ed., Ian M. G. Quimby (Charlottesville, Va.: Henry Francis du Pont Winterthur Museum, 1975), 13–42. A fireback, a bed-warmer, a plate, and a cupboard, all examples of Dutch colonial household items with religious motifs, are pictured in Butler, *Sleepy Hollow Restorations*, 163, 146, 109, 71. A valuable survey of Dutch colonial material culture is Roderic H. Blackburn and Ruth Piwonka, *Remembrance of Patria: Dutch Arts and Culture in Colonial America 1609–1776* (Albany, N.Y.: Albany Institute of History and Art, 1988).

10. Ruth Piwonka and Roderic H. Blackburn, *A Remnant in the Wilderness: New York Dutch Scripture History Paintings of the Early Eighteenth Century* (Albany, N.Y.: Albany Institute of History and Art, 1980). In 1744 Dr. Alexander Hamilton remarked that the Dutch in Albany "affect pictures much, particularly scripture history, with which they adorn their rooms." Carl Bridenbaugh, ed., *Gentleman's Progress: The Itinerarium of Dr. Alexander Hamilton 1744* (Chapel Hill, N.C.: University of North Carolina Press, 1948), 72.

11. Edward T. Corwin, ed., *Ecclesiastical Records of the State of New York*, 7 vols. (Albany, N.Y.: James B. Lyon, 1901–16), 2:1235.

12. Ibid., 1240.

13. Bartlett Burleigh James and J. Franklin Jameson, eds., *Journal of Jasper Danckaerts 1679–1680* (New York: Charles Scribner's Sons, 1913), 63.

14. Jeremias van Rensselaer to Maria van Rensselaer, Aug. 19, 1662, *Correspondence of Jeremias van Rensselaer, 1651–1674*, ed. A. J. F. van Laer (Albany, N.Y.: The State University of New York, 1932), 301.

15. Zumthor, *Daily Life in Rembrandt's Holland*, 80.

16. Joyce D. Goodfriend, "Dutch Women in Colonial New York" (paper delivered at the American Society for Ethnohistory meeting, 1981).

17. Firth Haring Fabend, *A Dutch Family in the Middle Colonies, 1660–1800* (New Brunswick, N.J.: Rutgers University Press, 1991), 149.

18. Moran, "Sisters in Christ," 56.

19. On literacy in early New York, see William Heard Kilpatrick, *The Dutch Schools of New Netherland and Colonial New York* (Washington, D.C.: Government Printing Office, 1912).

20. For a concise statement of this position, see E. Jennifer Monaghan, "Literacy Instruction and Gender in Colonial New England," *American Quarterly* 40 (1988): 18–41.

21. Kilpatrick, *Dutch Schools,* 67–68, 127, 167–68, 174; Corwin, *Ecclesiastical Records,* 4:2626, 3025, 5:3621.

22. [Anne Grant], *Memoirs of an American Lady: with sketches of Manners and Scenery in America, as they existed previous to the Revolution,* 2 vols. (Freeport, N.Y.: Books for Libraries Press, 1972; originally published 1808) 1:33.

23. Maria van Rensselaer to Richard van Rensselaer, January? 1683, *Correspondence of Maria van Rensselaer, 1669–1689,* ed. A. J. F. van Laer (Albany, N.Y.: University of the State of New York, 1935), 88. See also ibid., 85, where she paraphrases Ps. 121:8.

24. Maria van Rensselaer to Richard van Rensselaer, October? 1683, ibid., 128.

25. Joyce D. Goodfriend, "Probate Records as a Source for Early American Religious History: The Case of Colonial New York City, 1664–1730" (paper delivered at the Dublin Seminar for New England Folklife, 1987). Firth Fabend confirms that great Dutch Bibles were ubiquitous in Dutch colonial homes. "Virtually every will of the period and almost every Haring will discovered refers to 'my great Dutch Bible.'" Fabend, *A Dutch Family in the Middle Colonies,* 155.

26. Will of Garret Noorstrandt, New-York Historical Society *Collections* (hereafter CNYHS), (1894), 385. In his 1730 will, Jurian Probasco, also of Flatbush, stated "I leave to my son Christopher my Great Bible, and L l2 for his birthright." CNYHS (1894), 83.

27. Will of Mary Jansen Loockermans, 1677, Historical Documents Collection, Queens College, New York; Will of Ann Van der Spiegel, CNYHS (1894), 95.

28. The De Riemer Family Bible Record," *New York Genealogical and Biographical Record* 63 (1932): 289.

29. Will of Evert Vandewater, 1710, CNYHS (1893),139–40; Will of Hybert Van der bergh, 1728, CNYHS (1902), 109; Will of John Van Wickell, 1731/2, CNYHS (1894), 61–62.

30. Kenney, "Neglected Heritage," 67; Earle, *Colonial Days in Old New York,* 276–77. See also Alice P. Kenney, "Hudson Valley Psalmody," *The Hymn* 25 (1974): 15–26. A photograph of a woman's Psalter can be found in Maud Esther Dilliard, *An Album of New Netherland* (New York: Twayne Publishers, 1963).

31. Will of Gertie Jans van Langedyck, 1708, CNYHS (1894), 49–50; Will of Margaret Gouverneur, 1758, CNYHS (1897),168–69.

32. Ellis Lawrence Raesly, *Portrait of New Netherland* (New York: Columbia University Press, 1945), 257–58. Among the items Evert van Hook, a New York City cordwainer, reserved to his wife if she remarried after his

death was her Dutch Bible. Will of Evert van Hook, 1711, CNYHS (1893), 72.

33. Will of Elizabeth van Corlaer, 1750, CNYHS (1896), 172–73. Willem a Brakel (1635–1711) was a Dutch theologian.

34. Will of Anna van Driesen, CNYHS (1897), 37–38; Will of Mary Gouverneur, CNYHS (1895) 136–37. Cordwainer Evert van Hook left his "daughter Hendrike, my Great Marturas book for her own use." Will of Evert van Hook, 1711, CNYHS (1893), 72.

35. James Grant Wilson, *The Memorial History of the City of New-York from Its First Settlement to the Year 1892*, 4 vols. (New York: New York History Co., 1892), 2:54.

36. Wayne Andrews, ed., "A Glance at New York in 1697: The Travel Diary of Dr. Benjamin Bullivant," revised from the *New-York Historical Society Quarterly* (January 1956), 15. Daily meals were preceded by grace. See Dr. Alexander Hamilton's description of the distinctive style in which a Dutch woman and her daughters said grace before a meal. Bridenbaugh, *Gentleman's Progress,* 39–40.

37. On "churching," see Singleton, *Dutch New York*, 248. The end of a woman's confinement was "ritually signified by a religious ceremony called 'churching.' Traditionally, a woman paid her first visit upon leaving home to her church." Judith Schneid Lewis, *In the Family Way: Childbearing in the British Aristocracy, 1760–1860* (New Brunswick, N.J.: Rutgers University Press, 1986), 200–201.

38. Patricia U. Bonomi, *Under the Cope of Heaven: Religion, Society, and Politics in Colonial America* (New York: Oxford University Press, 1986), 106.

39. Maria van Rensselaer to Richard van Rensselaer, August 15?, 1683, van Laer, *Correspondence of Maria van Rensselaer,* 114.

40. Anna van Rensselaer to Jeremias van Rensselaer, December 26, 1654, van Laer, *Correspondence of Jeremias van Rensselaer,* 15.

41. Will of Margareta Selyns, 1711, CNYHS (1893), 115–16. On godparenthood among the Dutch, see Jessica Kross, *The Evolution of an American Town: Newtown, New York, 1642–1775* (Philadelphia, Pa.: Temple University Press, 1983), 258–59; and Edward H. Tebbenhoff, "Tacit Rules and Hidden Family Structures: Naming Practices and Godparentage in Schenectady, New York, 1680–1800," *Journal of Social History* 18 (1985): 567–85.

42. James and Jameson, *Journal of Jasper Danckaerts*, 214.

43. Maria van Rensselaer to Richard van Rensselaer, November 12, 1684, van Laer, *Correspondence of Maria van Rensselaer,* 174–75.

44. "On the 5th of April it pleased God suddenly to take out of this world my father, while he was in his prayers and in good health." Ibid., 173; Henricus Selyns, "For Madam Anna Loockermans, Widow of Olof Stephensen Van Cortlandt, Esq., Deceased 14 May 1684," in Henry C.

Murphy, *An Anthology of New Netherland or Translations from the Early Dutch Poets of New York with Memoirs of Their Lives* (Port Washington, N.Y.: Ira J. Friedman, Inc., 1969; originally published 1865). For discussions of Selyns as a poet, see Raesly, *Portrait of New Netherland,* 309–30, and Lynn Haims, "Wills of Two Early New York Poets: Henricus Selyns and Richard Steer," *The New York Genealogical and Biographical Record* 108 (1977): 1–10.

45. In the early seventeenth century, there were deaconesses in the Dutch Reformed Church in Amsterdam. K.H.D. Haley, *The Dutch in the Seventeenth Century* (London: Thames and Hudson, 1972), 90.

46. Gerald F. De Jong, *The Dutch Reformed Church in the American Colonies* (Grand Rapids, Mich.: Eerdmans, 1978), 120, 136–37. According to De Jong, children sat with their mothers. Ibid., 137. On church seating arrangements in other colonies, see Robert J. Dinkin, "Seating the Meeting House in Early Massachusetts," *New England Quarterly* 43 (1970): 450–64; and Dell Upton, *Holy Things and Profane: Anglican Parish Churches in Colonial Virginia* (New York: Architectural History Foundation, 1986), 175–96.

47. "Minutes of the meeting of the Church Council and Congregation, Concerning the New Church Building, June 29, 1729," in *Protocol of the Lutheran Church in New York City, 1702–1750,* eds., Simon Hart and Harry J. Kreider (New York: United Lutheran Synod of New York and New England, 1958), 147–48.

48. Corwin, *Ecclesiastical Records,* 4:2866; Earle, *Colonial Days,* 271; De Jong, *Dutch Reformed Church,* 138.

49. "Seatings of the Dutch Reformed Church 1730 to 1770," in *Collections on the History of Albany, From Its Discovery to the Present Time. With Notices of its Public Institutions, and Biographical Sketches of Citizens Deceased,* 10 vols., ed., Joel Munsell (Albany, N.Y.: J. Munsell, 1865), 1:61–78. On the seating arrangements of the Albany church, see Robert S. Alexander, *Albany's First Church and Its Role in the Growth of the City, 1642–1942* (Albany, N.Y.: First Church, 1988), 106. Fabend, *A Dutch Family in the Middle Colonies,* 151–52, 157–60. Alice Morse Earle noted that "a woman's seats descended to her daughter, daughter-in-law, or sister." Earle, *Colonial Days in Old New York,* 269.

50. James and Jameson, *Journal of Jasper Danckaerts,* 146. Quotation is from Bridenbaugh, *Gentleman's Progress,* 66.

51. A. P. G. Jos van der Linde, ed., *Old Dutch Reformed Church of Brooklyn, New York: First Book of Records, 1660–1752* (Baltimore, Md.: Genealogical Publishing Co., 1983), 67, 69.

52. Richard Shiels, "The Feminization of American Congregationalism, 1730–1835," *American Quarterly* 33 (1981): 46–62; Bonomi, *Under the Cope of Heaven,* 111–15. See also Dunn, "Saints and Sisters," and Moran, "Sisters in Christ."

53. This paragraph is adapted from Goodfriend, "The Social Dimensions of Congregational Life in Colonial New York City," 257–58, 276. Women

formed a slight majority of the membership of the Tappan Reformed Church. Fabend, *A Dutch Family in the Middle Colonies*, 146–53.

54. Will of Sybout Claesen and Susanna Jans, CNYHS (1892), 107.

55. A. J. F. van Laer, "Deacons' Account Book, 1652–1654," in *The Dutch Settlers Society of Albany Yearbook*, 7 (1931–1932), 7.

56. Will of Margareta Selyns, 1711, CNYHS (1893), 115–16.

57. Kenneth Scott, "Contributors to Building of a New Dutch Church in New York City, 1688," *National Genealogical Society Quarterly* 49 (1961): 131–36.

58. Will of Judith Stuyvesant, CNYHS (1892), 139.

59. Van der Linde, *Old Dutch Reformed Church of Brooklyn, New York*, 101.

60. Will of Catherine Philipse, 1730/1, CNYHS (1894), 21–22.

61. On lay piety, see Jon Butler, "The Future of American Religious History: Prospectus, Agenda, Transatlantic *Problematique*," *William and Mary Quarterly* 42 (1985): 167–83; Gerald F. Moran and Maris A. Vinovskis, "The Puritan Family and Religion: A Critical Reappraisal," *William and Mary Quarterly* 39 (1982): 29–63; Patricia U. Bonomi and Peter R. Eisenstadt, "Church Adherence in the Eighteenth-Century British American Colonies," *William and Mary Quarterly* 39 (1982): 245–86. Mary Beth Norton synthesizes recent work on colonial women's history in "The Evolution of White Women's Experience in Early America," *American Historical Review* 99 (1984): 593–619.

62. In this connection, see Simon Schama, *The Embarrassment of Riches. An Interpretation of Dutch Culture in the Golden Age* (New York: Knopf, 1987).

ENGLAND AND THE NEW WORLD

Anglicans, Catholics, and Nonconformists after the Restoration, 1660–1720

Patricia Crawford

Background: Restoration to Toleration

After the Restoration, religious enthusiasm was suspect. Increasingly, those who refused to conform to the Anglican Church became more sober and respectable in their religious practices so that they could gain the right to worship in peace. After 1670, Quaker women who had been prominent in some of the wilder religious manifestations of the Interregnum found that a Quaker committee censored their writings for publication. At the upper social levels, increased emphasis on scientific explanations of the world and on reasoned belief enhanced the difference between the two sexes. As elite men turned away from revealed religion and adopted deism (or worse), the cultural gap between elite men and women widened. Enthusiastic religion was no longer a common cultural ground between men and women, and elite men distanced themselves from lower-class men as well as from women. The notion of woman as a creature of emotion remained unaltered after 1660. Indeed, the idea of woman as weak, unstable, and easily led astray was confirmed by the experiences of the revolutionary years. Men said that piety was especially good for women as a means of keeping them virtuous. Religion, insofar as it involved belief rather than reason, seemed natural to the less reasonable sex. From here it was easy to argue that women were naturally religious. By the eighteenth century, therefore, the role of religion in supporting the ideology of the good woman was enhanced. This essay discusses some of these changes.

The restoration of Charles II in 1660 effected a major alteration in the religious situation in England. Even while the Convention debated the religious settlement, Anglican squires were removing Puritan ministers from their livings. The Anglican Church was formally reestablished by the Parliament that met in 1661. Legislation restored its hierarchy and institutions, minus the court of High Commission, and imposed penalties on all who refused to conform.[1] However, in practice, the Anglican Church abandoned the belief that there was only one true church. Dissenters were persecuted but they were not burned as heretics.

Different religious groups were variously affected. For the first time, the Presbyterians found themselves among the Nonconformists. After their attempts to be included in the Anglican Church failed, they were forced to relinquish their belief in one church, to accept a position among the hated sects and to tolerate their fellow Nonconformists. The Independents either conformed or continued their separate worship in persecuted congregations. For them, no change of theology was necessary for they had always supported a degree of toleration and liberty of conscience. Nor were the Baptists or Quakers forced to alter their theology. The Baptists were once again persecuted, as they had been before 1640. For the Quakers, who had challenged the powers of the state during the 1650s, persecution was not a new experience, but the Restoration government was more committed to the eradication of Quaker views than Cromwell's government had been. Legislation singled out the Quakers, so Quaker women as well as men suffered more persecution after 1660.

Although Antonia Fraser suggests that the Restoration was a happy time for women—"the female clamor of the Commonwealth, both sonorous and serious, gave way to the merry prattle of the ladies of King Charles II's England"—its legislation had serious consequences for the admittedly small minority of women involved in sectarian activity.[2] After 1660 few new converts were made. Public religious activity for women was even more difficult, for there were widespread fears through the community that female disorder and rebellion went hand in hand. Women's public writings diminished sharply, even more than those of men.[3]

Ironically, the sects themselves, especially the Quakers, and the women prominent therein, contributed to the impetus toward the Restoration. The rapid growth of the Quakers in the 1650s and the amount of attention their activities received in the localities, in the news reports and tracts, all meant that many people looked to a restoration of the monarchy and the known ways as the only means of checking Quaker religious excesses.[4] Even an ejected Presbyterian minister celebrated the anniversary of Charles II's restoration two years later as "a stop to Anabapt[ists and] Quakers & others that were grown very high."[5]

Nonconformists have labeled the period from the Restoration to the accession of William and Mary as "the great persecution."[6] The legislation was harsh, although its enforcement varied depending on local circumstances. The attempts of Charles II to introduce toleration by royal prerogative were unsuccessful. The persecution was at its worst from 1681 to 1685. James II's accession to the throne in 1685 brought the very real danger to the Protestants of a pro-Catholic policy, which ultimately precipitated a better understanding between the Anglicans and Nonconformists.

The public situation of Dissenters altered in 1689. In 1688 prominent politicians invited King William of Orange to invade England on behalf of the Protestant religion. By the terms of the Toleration Act of 1689, Dissenters who took the oaths of allegiance and supremacy were allowed to worship freely in licensed meeting places. They were legally permitted to own property for religious purposes and to build chapels and meeting houses. Ministers who subscribed to thirty-six of the thirty-nine articles were no longer in danger of persecution. The historian Michael Watts has concluded that "The 'Glorious Revolution' thus gave orthodox Dissenters statutory freedom to worship in their own way, but it did not give them civil equality."[7] However, the Glorious Revolution affected Nonconformist men more than their female counterparts. All women, however orthodox their religious views, lacked certain civic rights. They could not serve on juries, nor on the bench as JPs, nor could they hold legal offices. By the late seventeenth century none could vote for Parliament, and they were certainly never elected as members.[8] A few women who held public offices, such as courtiers, midwives, or searchers for the plague, were required to take the oaths.[9] It can be argued that the position of women even worsened after the Glorious Revolution.[10] The language in which ideas of liberty were discussed was androcentric. Furthermore, as Mary Astell pointed out in 1700, "*If all Men are born free,* how is it that all Women are born slaves?"[11] Nevertheless, even if women's gains were nonexistent compared with those of propertied men's, there were some benefits. After the Toleration Act of 1689 women as well as men were able to worship openly in religious congregations of their own choosing and were free to witness to their faith in their daily lives.

Yet because women's lack of civil equality remained constant, in women's religious history the whole period from the Restoration to the early eighteenth century can be discussed as one. More important than the Glorious Revolution for women was the process of what has been called denominationalization, as the churches' need to survive in the world necessitated organization, clear membership qualifications, and rules for group behavior.[12] The transition from sects to denominations affected women, household religion, and personal piety.

ANGLICANS, NONCONFORMISTS, AND CATHOLICS

The majority of women in England probably thought the restoration of the Anglican Church a blessing. John Morrill's work has shown "the passive strength of Anglican survivalism" during the years of its persecution from 1646 to 1660.[13] Women had helped the Anglican faith to survive through the 1640s and 1650s. They had sought out Anglican ministers for the baptism of their children and for their marriages, and in many cases had attended Anglican services wherever possible. These services allowed women to participate more largely in corporate worship than did the Catholic Church. Women used the Prayer Book for their private devotions, and kept Anglican faith alive in their households.[14] The spontaneous celebration of Easter in 1660 even before the Declaration of Breda and the restoration of the king was a sign of popular support for the Anglican Church.[15]

Anglican ministers preached personal piety and morality. As one eighteenth-century commentator explained, all the best writers of the Anglican Church tried "to turn the Minds of People to the Practice of Moral Duties, and to cure them of that Madness and Enthusiasm into which they had been led . . . during the Times of Anarchy and Confusion."[16] Preachers urged gentlewomen to show a proper awareness of their social rank, to demonstrate "that one may be a Gentlewoman, or a Lady, & yet Elect." Women's role as mothers of pious children was stressed: the future of the church "in succeeding generations, is contained in these Infants yet un-borne."[17] Piety and religious conformity were the virtues emphasized for everyone after 1660. They had always been commended for women.

In later-seventeenth-century England a number of well-educated Anglican women gained the respect of their male contemporaries for their learning and piety. Ladies such as Anne Conway wrote theological treatises, which orthodox Anglican divines admired.[18] Women encouraged each other in godly conversation and behavior. The writings of Dorcas Bennet, for example, were published in the 1670s, in the hope that women would heed one of their own sex. "Preachers may say what they will," she alleged, but women refused to reform.[19] In the 1690s Mary Astell gained public recognition for her defense of the Anglican Church.[20]

After 1660 the Anglican Church resumed the task of disciplining the laity through the church courts. A woman who was excommunicated was refused the rite of churching if she gave birth.[21] However, many aspects of personal and sexual morality were increasingly controlled by the parish, and the church courts declined in importance later in the seventeenth century. Increasingly, the church courts prosecuted recusants and Dissenters, but failed to eradicate either.[22]

The burden of the legislation after 1660 fell heavily on the Presbyterian and Independent ministers who had accepted Anglican livings in the 1640s and 1650s. Unable to swear the oaths required in 1662, an estimated 2,029 ministers were ejected in 1662.[23] What followed was twenty-eight years of hardship of varying degrees. The Nonconformists accepted a Christian framework that made their sufferings bearable: "No Cross, No Crown" was a comforting text. But it was still a bleak, bitter, and unhappy time. Ministers had gifts that they could not exercise, and their surviving diaries bear witness to their frustration. As the ejected minister Philip Henry wrote in September 1663 of himself and other ministers: "Candles under a Bushel, lord set us up again yt wee may give light in thy house."[24] Dissenters were not able to preach openly until 1689. Teaching was difficult too, and it was impossible to plan for the future of God's kingdom on earth. Nonconformists were forced to concentrate on survival.

Nonconformist historiography has focused more on the ministers' sufferings than those of women or laymen.[25] Yet women continued to outnumber men in adherence to Dissent. Throughout the second half of the seventeenth century women comprised 62 percent of all members of Baptist churches, and 61 percent of Congregational churches. In London women made up 68 percent of both types of congregation.[26]

The wives of Nonconformist ministers suffered at the Anglican restoration. Women's private losses—of former homes, of friends and neighbors, of income and of social status and respect—have been little acknowledged. A wife did not make the decision about whether a minister could conform, but she could make it easy or difficult for her husband to follow his conscience by her attitude. One of the Baptists condemned at Aylsebury temporarily recanted, prevailed on by the tears and entreaties of his wife.[27] Poverty was more unbearable for married ministers, as Richard Baxter observed:

> it pierceth a Man's Heart to have Children crying, and Sickness come upon them for want of wholsom Food, or by drinking Water, and to have nothing to relieve them. And Women are usually less patient of

Suffering than men; and their Impatience would be more to a Husband than his own wants.[28]

Baxter's sympathy was deep for the poor man "that was fain to Spin as
Women do" to help support his family. Clearly the reversal of sex-
specific work roles added to the man's humiliation. Yet many ejected
ministers found support from their wives. Ellen Asty's cheerfulness
when her husband laid down his living was commended in her funeral
sermon in 1681: "in stead of repining, she said she was glad they had
such a house."[29] Similar testimony came from William Kiffin, a Baptist minister. His wife never uttered "the least discontent under all the
various providences."[30] A few months after his ejection, Philip Henry
found comfort in his home: "my wife is much my helper, present,
absent, & my heart doth safely trust in her, the lord's most holy name
bee blessed & praysed."[31]

When their Nonconformist husbands were in gaol, wives tried to
assist them. Wives of prisoners kept families and business going, and
also visited and supported their husbands. For example, when Joseph
Davis, a General Baptist linen merchant, was imprisoned, his wife had
the shop and three children to look after, and suffered personal ill-
health. Yet all the time that he was in gaol, she visited him, "During
which time her affections carried her sometimes beyond her ability, to
come and see me, when she was so weak I was forced to carry her
upstairs in my arms."[32] Women worked for the reprieve and release of
prisoners. At the Restoration Margaret Fell "was mov'd of the Lord" to
go to London to speak with Charles II about the Quaker sufferers in
gaol.[33] John James was sentenced to death for preaching to the Baptist
meeting in Bulstake Alley. His wife petitioned Charles II for his
reprieve. Other women, who had been present at his sermon, testified
on his behalf. They denied hearing the words of which he was accused.
Nevertheless, James was executed on November 26, 1662.[34] Other
women friends and supporters, former members of the congregation,
also supported the morale of the ejected clergy. For example, when
Philip Henry and Mr. Thomas and their wives dined with a Mrs. Has-
sell in 1663, Philip told her "tis much she is not asham'd of such poor
Outcasts . . . & shee answer'd they were ye best guests yt come to her
house."[35]

Family piety became more important to Dissent after 1662. When
the public ministry became impossible for some Presbyterians and Independents, the household became the one place where a man could exercise his gifts. For their wives and daughters the change after 1662 was
less marked. Women had no public roles in the church during the Civil

Wars and Interregnum to lose. What changed was that their husbands needed their support more than before. Furthermore, insofar as the future was bleak, the work of a good Protestant wife and mother in bearing and rearing children was vital in providing for the time to come. As women tended their households, educated their children, catechized their servants, and generally ensured that the family was a godly one, so they developed the ethos of family piety that was so important in later Nonconformity and ultimately in nineteenth-century English society. When the public ministry was persecuted, the role of wives and mothers in the family and household was correspondingly more important. By doing the work that the Lord had prescribed for women, they were serving the Lord in the present and providing for a godly future.[36]

Dissent still involved social disadvantages. Margaret Spufford has written of the isolating effect of religious nonconformity in Cambridgeshire villages during the seventeenth century.[37] After 1689 the social isolation affected the two sexes differently. Like the male Nonconformist laity, women came to be seen as a separate group, distinct from the remainder of the population. No Dissenting wife or daughter could be a member of the town's social elite. Nonconformist women experienced social ostracism. Since women in communities depended on the support of members of their own sex in their daily household tasks and domestic emergencies, the loss of neighborliness was a handicap. Increasingly, the rules of their own Dissenting congregations set them apart further. Standards of dress, for example, especially among the Quakers, were strict, and contempt for fashion and vanity excluded them from an important part of female culture. Many separatist churches frowned on social intercourse with outsiders, and the Quakers enforced endogamous marriage. By the early eighteenth century Dissenters were a narrow community, consisting, it has been estimated, of perhaps only 5 percent of the total population.[38] Endogamy further restricted women's sociability. Nonconformist women experienced the effects of outbreaks of public indignation against them at the times of riots, such as those associated with the trial of Sacheverell in 1710. As a consequence, the bonds between women in their own denominational churches may have been more intense.

For Catholic women the period after 1660 signaled some alleviation from persecution. Catholics continued to suffer limitations on the practice of their faith, but the sympathy of Charles II and James II meant that Catholics might look to the monarch for some assistance with personal hardships. Charles and James were anxious to remove the disabilities upon Catholics and did what they could to help individuals. However, the monarchs' attempts to alter public policies so as to allow toleration of Catholicism had contrary effects and aroused anti-Catholic hysteria, especially in 1679 when it was claimed that there was a Popish Plot. One Catholic woman, the prominent London midwife Elizabeth Cellier, was attacked for her pamphleteering and her support of the Duke of York.[39]

Records of the activity of Catholic women are fewer than for those of the Protestant Dissenters. Catholics tried to keep their worship secret, out of the public eye. We know that missionary activity by nuns continued. In 1669 one of the Sisters of Mary Ward's Institute, Frances Bedingfield, established a Catholic girls school at Hammersmith. A few years later another was set up near York. Although several of the sisters were imprisoned at the time of the Popish Plot, the sisters continued their work in England. In 1686 Bedingfield purchased a house near Micklegate Bar, York. There, at what became known as the Bar Convent, about twenty young women were accommodated to receive a Catholic education. The Bar and the sister-house at Hammersmith were the only two convents in England until the time of the French Revolution. Susan O'Brien suggests that despite the discontinuities in the history of the Institute, Mary Ward's educational ideals were known and upheld.[40] In the counties, Catholic women continued to shelter priests, hear mass, and try to avoid being presented for recusancy. As earlier, they kept their families loyal to their faith, and created an environment in which many sons and daughters found that their religious vocation was fostered. Women who wanted to become nuns still had to travel abroad, so only the wealthier families could allow their daughters to profess their faith. Among those presented for recusancy, women were a majority. While gentlewomen continued to marry within the Catholic elite, Catholic women of lower social status increasingly married Protestants. In Lancashire, Galgano calculates that at least a quarter of Catholic brides married out of their faith.[41]

Some Nonconformist women's sufferings were public. Quaker meetings and historians noted the Quaker women who were pilloried, whipped, or imprisoned.[42] Since the Restoration legislation singled out the Quakers, they were more likely to be imprisoned than other Nonconformists. Thus the experiences of women of different persuasions varied after 1660.

FROM RELIGIOUS MOVEMENT TO DENOMINATION: THE QUAKERS

Women's role in the Quaker movement changed after the first two decades, as Quakerism itself altered. Initially a dynamic movement, by about 1670 proceedings were more formalized, organization increased, and Quaker religion became more concerned with discipline and less with mysticism and ecstasy.[43] A number of factors may explain the changes in the nature of the Quaker movement. Sociologists of religion argue that most religious movements must come to terms with the world in order to survive.[44] After the Restoration, Quakers faced ruinous fines and imprisonments. Although they endured heroically, worship and religious meetings became very difficult. In addition, as the movement enlarged, the Quakers themselves were more vulnerable to the disorder of individuals, and so sought greater control. By the 1670s the Quakers believed that "the Enemy," Satan, was at work undermining the truth and the light, and sought to counter his attacks by a more intense public printed campaign and by the imposition of stricter discipline.

Women's visibility declined in the Quaker movement. From the first, Quakers had developed a policy about replying to printed attacks upon them, and of proselytizing through the press. In 1672 an all-male censoring committee was established, known as the Second Day Morning Meeting, whose purpose was to examine all proposed publications. Increasingly, the Friends chose to play down the prophetic element in their movement. By the 1690s women's publications, which had been numerous in this area, were fewer.[45] Judith Bowlbie, for example, submitted several manuscripts in the 1690s, which were returned to her as unsuitable for publication.[46] Meetings testified against those who published against the truth. The Upperside meeting of Buckinghamshire witnessed against Susannah Aldridge's publications.[47] Not all women accepted this censorship. In 1703 Abigail Fisher, whose papers were returned, protested because she said that some of the meeting's laws "do stopp the Passage of the Spirit."[48] She was right. All this censorship was far from the days of the early 1650s when women had spoken or published their messages as the spirit of the Lord moved them.

Quaker discipline of members became stricter. Women were in trouble more for offences relating to dress, "back biting," and gossip, men for drunkenness and violence. Records of meetings indicate that women's economic activities were scrutinized. For example, the Upperside meeting in Buckinghamshire advised a widow how to settle up "to yield up & deliver al she hath" to be divided among her husband's creditors. In 1674 the Upperside meeting reproved a female shopkeeper who had accumulated debts, but also resolved to purchase wood to help her husband to gainful employment.[49] The Swathmore women's meeting reproved two of their members for selling lace "which is needlesse."[50] Women's meetings also objected to their members' selling ale.[51]

Religious belief could make a single woman's economic circumstances even more difficult, even though some of the penalties affected men rather than women. Prior to the Toleration Act, goods could be seized in lieu of fines for attendance at religious meetings, and more men owned goods than did women. Nevertheless, single women might own property, and seizure of goods could threaten their livelihoods. In 1678 a widow in the Vale of the White Horse refused to pay tithes. Her livelihood was jeopardized when a quarter of her hemp was seized.[52] A servant maid in the Vale was transferred to parish relief in 1678, but she was forced to conform "(contrary to her conscience) for mere necessity of outward, needful things."[53] While men, too, were likely to experience poverty, the wages paid to women and the expectation of their economic dependence meant that they were more likely to be in poverty. Women needed more poor relief, and so Quaker women experienced more economic hardship for their faith. Quaker meetings provided supplementary relief, although their main aim was to make the poor independent.[54]

Quaker beliefs restricted women's occupations. Meetings tried to prohibit participation in the luxury trades. Lace making was judged to be unlawful in the 1690s. Both the Leeds and Brighouse meetings, for example, advised their members to forbear from those who persisted in the trade.[55] Since lace making, millinery, and fancy sewing were largely female occupations, these restrictions bore especially harshly on them. By 1728 the Friends' School at Saffron Walden was objecting to girls learning sewing. The Friends supporting the school wanted girls to be servants, not to get an independent living.[56] What had started in the 1650s as a desire for simplicity and an avoidance of waste and scandal in dress became a rigid code later. Again, women bore the brunt of this: "Away with your short black Aprons. . . . Away with your *Vizzards* whereby you are not distinguished from bad Women," wrote George Fox.[57] Ornamental dress for men was also disapproved of, but did not carry the same danger of sexual immorality.

The place of women in Quakerism became contentious in the 1670s. Three main issues were involved: separate women's meetings, marriage procedures, and women's speaking. Each issue involved women's exercise of authority over men, and thereby threatened male power.

The separate meetings of women Friends, which had begun in the 1650s, continued and expanded. The Society recognized that women's experiences and behavior were different from men's. Since in their daily lives women were closer to people in their communities and knew who was in need of relief, they could advise the men's financial meetings of suitable recipients of the Society's charity. Moreover, women's knowledge about young people made it appropriate for marriage proposals to be referred to the women's meetings. Although Quaker historiography has credited Fox with a major role in the development of separate women's meetings, it is more likely that he was responding to women's initiatives.[58] Certainly Fox was sympathetic to the idea of different roles for women and was supportive of their separate meetings. He argued in 1676 in defense of women's activities. Fox recognized that men felt threatened, fearing that women in the power of the Lord would be "too high." Even so, he knew that Moses and Aaron did not tell women to stay home and wash dishes "or such Expressions."[59] However, Fox still thought that women served the Lord in different ways from men, because they were fitter to look after families and to train children, and to be "mothers in Israel."[60] John Storey, one of the strongest antagonists of the women's meetings and of Fox, claimed that the whole notion of a separate women's meeting was monstrous among Christians. Others added that it was "ridiculous."[61]

Increasingly by the 1670s, Quaker meetings emphasized "orderly way of proceeding" in marriage.[62] Exogamy was not allowed, a policy which was more of a hardship to women because they outnumbered men in the Society. Meetings around the country censured those who married "out" to persons described as "a man of ye world" or a "Lass of the world."[63] Even for those who wanted to marry other Quakers, there was strict control. A couple who hesitated between the two meetings was to be "investigated" by five men. Another pair was instructed to delay their proposed marriage until they were more settled in "the truth."[64] Marriage procedure required that the couple appear three times before the Men's and Women's Monthly Meetings.[65] Meetings disowned those who married according to the standard English legal form. Since the civil courts recognized only those marriages performed by priests of the Anglican Church, the requirement that all Quakers marry according to the way of the society was a severe test of faith.

Male fears of the collective power of women can be seen in their printed attacks on women's participation in the marriage procedures. William Mucklow complained that if the women's meetings were allowed a veto, they could deprive a man of a person "whom he most dearly loves."[66] It was, said William Mather, "a very hard trial" for men to submit to female authority in matters of marriage. His arguments were contradictory. On the one hand, he thought that women were incapable of independent action. They were merely pawns in the male power struggles—their meetings were set up by men. On the other hand, Mather was haunted by the fear of female power, of the inappropriateness of women "ruffling" to the seat of counsel.[67] In 1680 Rogers mocked women who "pry" into marriages. He too saw the issue as one of female rule, and ridiculed the role of the women's meetings in relieving the poor as mere pretence.[68]

Women's speaking was also contentious. Since many women were inhibited in mixed meetings, separate meetings allowed women to speak more freely among themselves. But many believed that if the spirit moved through male and female alike, women should still speak in mixed meetings. Others sought to confine women's speaking to the extraordinary. Preaching and bearing witness were difficult to distinguish. Female modesty might inhibit both speaking before a large audience and talking of sexual matters in relation to proposed marriages. The issue was one of power: if women spoke in the power of the Lord, or if they decided to veto marriages, they were exercising authority over men, and some men found this intolerable.

Storey and his ally Wilkinson also objected to women's speaking in the mixed meetings. Margaret Fell had earlier defended the theoretical rights of women to speak. God himself had manifested "his Will and Mind concerning Women." Since the Quakers believed that those who lived under the gospel were in a prelapsarian state of freedom, Fell argued that it was only those under the law who should not prophesy. For others, the Lord had shown his power "without respect of Persons."[69] Opponents of women's speaking agreed that women who "received a Revelation from God" might speak. It was the old question of who had the power to label what was from the Lord, and what was mere will. Rogers's objection to the disorderly women who were "so rude in their Opposition" suggests that he at least had no difficulty in deciding which women were in the power of the Lord and which were troublemakers.[70] Allegations of sexual promiscuity featured, as always, in the debates about female participation. Mucklow alleged that there was "scandalous familiarity of the Prophets and Prophetesses" and wanton behavior generally.[71] Other comments revealed straight misogyny: women's singing, for example, was said to be "like caterwauling."[72]

All these issues relating to women's place in the Society of Friends—separate women's meetings, women's role in marriage procedures, and women's speaking—were central to a division in the Quaker movement in the 1670s. Some men objected to the women's meetings, because they conferred unscriptural authority on women over men. Some alleged that women's meetings were a kind of separation. Others argued that if the women's meetings were an accepted part of Quaker organization, then organization had triumphed over inspiration. Although the Society survived the Wilkinson-Storey split, and separate women's meetings continued, preaching was more regulated by 1700. The Box Meeting expressed concern at unlicensed women preaching, and there were complaints in London that women's speaking took up too much time.[73] Procedures developed whereby those who wished to speak were required to leave their names. Modesty Newman put her name down, but the London Morning Meeting put it out.[74] In 1702 and 1703 the London Morning Meeting told Mary Obee that she appeared too frequently at public meetings. The Meeting also vetoed her papers to Queen Anne, telling her "to be still and quiet in her mind."[75]

Thus, by the early eighteenth century Quakerism was more organized, and less open to active female participation. There was some compensatory development of protective impulses toward women. For example, if a man gained a woman's affections, or had had sexual relations with her, Quaker meetings pressed him to marry her.[76] Meetings also reinforced the conventional norms of married life. The Vale meeting disciplined a man who struck his wife and caused her to miscarry.[77]

During the later seventeenth century the women's meetings in various areas gained assurance and confidence. They issued yearly letters from their meetings, admonishing and advising from their own experiences.[78] But although the women's meetings continued, female rights to participate in preaching and witnessing in the mixed meetings were diminished. Individual women still became preachers, but they traveled in a more circumscribed manner and preached to meetings of Friends, rather than to outsiders. By the early eighteenth century the movement had lost much of its dynamism and was more concerned with formal piety rather than spirituality. It was a more pietistic, quietist spirituality that the Quaker movement offered to women.

THE PARTICULAR AND GENERAL BAPTIST CHURCHES, 1660–1720

After the Restoration members of the Baptist churches were set apart from the rest of society, as were other Nonconformists. The intensification of discipline affected women as well as men. Even during the 1650s, as we have seen, congregations assumed a supervisory role over many aspects of personal and family life and economic activity. In Baptist churches a higher proportion of people were excommunicated for their misdemeanors than in their counterparts in the Anglican Church. In the General Baptist Church at Fenstanton, for example, Watts calculated that of 178 members who were baptized between 1645 and 1656, 53 were excommunicated at some time during the same period. In one Congregational Church from 1690 to 1714, 795 members were added, of whom 199 were excommunicated.[79] While not all Nonconformist churches were so severe, the majority felt obliged to bear a strong witness to their gospel profession through the perfection of their personal lives.

Those who had power to discipline women in the church had power over their social roles. It is thus important to discover whether discipline was exercised by men over women, or whether women participated as members of congregations. The Baptist churches allow an exploration of this question. Unlike the Presbyterian churches, where discipline was normally exercised by the ministers, and thus fewer records survive, among the Baptists discipline was an important part of the congregation's collective duty. Baptist records were voluminous.

The records of the Maze Pond Particular Baptist Church from the 1690s show something of the contradictions and conflicts between theories about the ideal church and women's place in it, and actual practice.[80] Maze Pond formed after the church at Horsleydown divided over the issue of singing. Congregational singing, according to the minority, was formal, not "inspired" worship, in that it involved set words and a known tune. A minority of members resolved to forbear from fellowship, adding among their grievances that Horsleydown allowed a large role to women:

> you suffer Women to speake and sing, to teach and admonish in the Worship and servis of God in his Church, contrary to the Word of God, which commands women not to speak, nor to teach, but to learne in Silence 1 Cor. 14:34 1 Tim. 2:11, 12.[81]

Benjamin Keach, the Horsleydown pastor, insisted on discussing the issues with the minority group one at a time, coming last to "several sisters." The account of his discussion with Mary Leader, wife of one of the most prominent dissidents, raised in direct and vivid terms some of the issues that church members were forced to confront. Keach mocked Mary Leader's religious knowledge and then treated her as a puppet of her husband,

> saying to her, what have you to say . . . she replyed she could pass by all offences, but she would not keep Communion while they were in that way of singing, then he replyed quick upon her, and looking earnestly at her saying you have learnt a fine peace [sic] of Relidgion [sic] ha'nt you, I confess I am troubled to see that you that are but a Babe should pretend to such knowledg above others or to that effect, and then turning to her Husband Bro[the]r Luke Leader he said you have finely dragg'd her up.[82]

Keach both resented a woman having views and blamed her husband for teaching them to her, although Leader swore that her husband was not

responsible for her views. The irony is that although Keach's side gave
a large public participatory role to women, allowing them to bear witness, when Mary Leader opposed his views he dismissed her as a mere
adjunct of her husband. Horsleydown excommunicated the nine men.
The thirteen women decided they would continue attending, perhaps
to see what would happen. They pointed out that Horsleydown's attitudes to them were contradictory:

> you seemed not to look upon us as your Members or concerned
> with you, bidding us some times withdraw from you that you might
> doe your business without us, and at another time when we were
> come by your . . . desire, you named us to withdraw. [83]

Although the women were perfectly able to assert their views, they were
not theoretical defenders of the rights of women to speak and teach as
was the Horsleydown congregation.

When the newly separated group made a covenant to form Maze
Pond Church, six men and thirteen women signed as witnesses, in separate lists.[84] Women were in a different category of membership from
men. By 1694 the congregation had expanded enormously, to 52 men
and 126 women. At this date, when women formed more than two-
thirds of the congregation, the question of their participation in church
business became contentious. Around December 1694 "the Liberty of
the Sisters in the Church was largely discoursed" and after further dispute, resolved upon.[85] The church decided that women could neither
speak "in the immediate worship of God in his Church," nor could they
debate "equally as the men have power to do," nor be church officers.
Nevertheless, women had the right to vote:

> 4. We doe beleive [sic] the Sisters being equaly with the Brethren
> members of the misticall Body of Christ, his Church they have equall
> right Liberty and Previledge to voate with them by lifting up of their
> hands or as the Church sees meet, to shew their Assent or dissent for
> or against any matter or thing that is moued in the Church.
> 5. We doe believe that a Sister haveing signified her dissatisfaction
> in a voate may give the reasons for her dissatisfaction.

The church was not to proceed to a resolution until a woman had given
her reasons for her dissent, which she might do by a brother, unless the
necessity of the case required her "to deliver her minde her selfe."[86]
Thus, in addition to simply voting, a woman could argue her case.
Maze Pond may have been unusual, as Murdina Macdonald in her

study of the London Calvinist Baptists concluded that it was.[87] Nevertheless, it shows how even in the most liberal of churches there were practical confusions and theoretical inconsistencies inherent in women's membership of separatist churches.

In the selection of a pastor, the consent of the whole congregation was desired. The Cripplegate Baptist Church book recorded explicitly that if any men or women were dissatisfied with the nomination of David Crosley as their pastor in 1703, they were to hold up their hands.[88] But democracy could be limited, and class as well as gender could influence the politics. When the congregation voted in 1713 on Brother Mathews becoming an elder, there was a big majority against him, but because most of "the Antient and ruleing brethren" were not present, the business was deferred.[89] In 1714 there was a rumor that the church had passed an act that only those who contributed to the church's finances were to have a vote. Presumably it caused disquiet because it would have disenfranchised most of the women.[90]

Women's acquiescence in the proceedings of the Baptist Church was required, but their independent views were not. Sister Hopkins of the Cripplegate Church thought that the congregation was too severe in their censure of a wife in a domestic dispute, so she stayed away. Questioned, she said that she had consulted both her father and a minister at Abingdon who blamed the church for its proceedings. The church admonished her.[91] In another case, female criticism of a minister was disallowed. Honour Gould applied to Maze Pond in 1694 for admission because she was dissatisfied with the conduct of Hercules Collins as her minister: "his Preaching in her Judgment not being agreeable to the word of God, ner [nor] her owne expereirance [sic], neith can she profit thereby." She was not admitted, because Collins denied her allegations.[92]

One formal office was specific to women in the Baptist Church: that of deaconess, based on 1 Tim. 5:9 and 11. From 1656 widows assisted deacons in looking after the poor and sick. The Bristol Church appointed their first deaconess in 1662. On her death in 1673 another widow succeeded. In 1679 four widows over sixty were asked to consider becoming deaconesses. Only three were willing to serve, for on the basis of 1 Tim. 5:11 the church required the women not to marry. Thus, for the only church office open to women, celibacy was required. Since their duties were to visit the sick, and they could even speak a word of comfort, the Bristol Church book noted that this was probably the reason "why they must be 60 yeares of age, that none occasion may be given; and as in 1 Tim. 5:14."[93] Apparently Baptists shared the conventional assumption that women were insatiable for sex until well after menopause. However, concern for propriety did not operate in the same way when women were to be visited. Churches sent two brothers to admonish sisters, without a hint that this could compromise the women.

The Baptist churches upheld conventional views of women and the family. Since personal morality affected the public reputation of a church, the Baptist Church books of the later seventeenth century show congregations seriously concerned about domestic sins "whereby the name of God was greatly dishonored and our holy profession reproached."[94]

A discussion of the disparate standards employed to judge the marital and social conduct of men and women reveals the role of the Dissenting Church in enforcing traditional norms of social behavior. Baptists were to be respectful to parents. A woman's admission to the Baptist Church at Maze Pond was delayed until she acknowledged her fault in speaking unadvisedly of her mother.[95] Several churches punished husbands for cruelty to their wives. For example, in 1697 the Cripplegate Church disciplined Brother Simon, a journeyman shoemaker who lived near Clare Market, "for inhumanly beating his wife and giving himselfe to much idlenes not minding to be diligent in his calling and employment." He had gone into debt and failed to provide for his family. Since he refused to repent, the church cast him out.[96] In 1699 the Cripplegate Church disciplined Brother Leeson who was in debt to his father-in-law among others, and treated his wife, who was a nurse, "not in a loving but after an imperious scoffing rate." On the precedent cited from 2 Tim. 3:5, the church cast him out. The case also shows that the Baptist Church did not tolerate wifely insubordination. Leeson had complained of his wife's "very uncivill and barbarous language" to him. The church found that the story was an unhappy one: "shee had been very badly and inhumanely treated by her husband, That deep distressing poverty had afflicted her through his incapacity or negligence to gett a livelyhood or subsistence." Even though the church recognized that her husband had failed in his duty as a provider, they expected conformity to the ideals of uncomplaining womanhood. They admonished her, and refused her communion "till by a carefull meek conversation there may be seen a reall reformation."[97]

The more conventional sexual sins were also disciplined. The story of Brother Benjamin, a baker's servant who promised marriage to a maidservant and then had sexual relations with her was "publike to the neighbours to the great scandal and reproach of his holy profession." Benjamin admitted his offence, but complained "that he was unhappily drawn to it by the importunity of that wicked woman." The church cast him out.[98]

The church scrutinized the economic activities of both sexes. Although the lists of members of the Baptist Cripplegate Church give few clues as to economic status, the cases of discipline recorded from 1689 to 1699 occasionally mention occupations. These included shoemaker, waterman, chambermaid, and coachman. Women as well as men were expected to work for their living. In 1694 Sister Cooke was excluded for a series of offenses. Her case demonstrates the complex interlocking of women's financial affairs. Cooke persuaded one Mrs. Green, the nurse in her child bed, to lend £40 to Sister Webb on the promise that Webb would improve it to great advantage. After a long time the money was not repaid "though the poore woman was in great distress for want of it." As this was all the money that Mrs. Green had saved "to help her when her strength in labour might fayl her," she was completely undone when Webb failed to repay the money. Webb was repentant, but unable to meet her creditors. The church disowned her, recording that her actions had dishonored the name of God "and our holy profession reproached."[99] Although many Bapists paid poor rates, congregations undertook to supplement this relief.[100] Soon after the Maze Pond Church was formed in February 1694, arrangements were made for money to be collected for the poor, and a book to be kept for accounts.[101]

All denominations sought to practice endogamy. Surviving church books show that all were concerned about suitable marriage partners, to various degrees. Members of the General Baptist Assembly of 1668 resolved that while they would not call "marrying out" a fornication— that is, they would not totally deny that it was a marriage—nevertheless they saw it as "a marrying out of the Lord or out of the Church."[102] Again, women were more likely to offend because they outnumbered men in Baptist churches.

The churches usually acted to support the interests of masters against undisciplined servants. Records of the Cripplegate Baptist Church in the 1690s show that servants were disciplined for disorderly behavior.[103] Neighborly reputation was also important: two brothers were directed to enquire of a man's neighbors about his behavior before he could be admitted to the church.[104]

The relationship between a Nonconformist congregation and their pastor was frequently a close one, as the church books show. When it was suggested that Keach should be forbearing with the dissidents in his Particular Baptist congregation, he replied, "you had as good take a knife and stab me in the heart."[105] Sexual immorality was central to the dismissal of a Baptist pastor, David Crosley, from the Cripplegate Church in 1709. Complaints brought to light a series of incidents involving drunkenness and offenses with a number of women. To the sins of drink he confessed, but the sexual sins he denied. These—more serious because he was married—ranged from his kissing a woman in a tavern, being seen with a strumpet and going into a house of ill repute, propositioning various women, tongue kissing, and exposing himself. Since Crosley was reputed to be the largest man in his county, his behavior may have been especially offensive and menacing to women. Needless to say, there were counterallegations, particularly relating to the last two alleged offenses: one of the young women was said to be of dubious character—a liar, a drunkard, and a thief, and not to be trusted. The church was reluctant to conclude without consensus, but Crosley's subsequent actions led them to conclude his guilt. The whole case produced "abundance of heat, and disorder."[106]

To sum up, women's position in the Baptist churches remained ambiguous, although there were attempts to define it. As members of a congregation, women possessed certain freedoms and rights, which they could choose to exercise. Their assent to the business of the church was necessary, and they could put items on the church's agenda for discussion. They had the numerical strength, had they chosen to vote as a group, but they appear never to have done so. It should not be forgotten when we look at the records, as it must have been impossible to forget in the congregations, that women usually outnumbered men by two to one. This being the case, the exercise of discipline was not a simple case of men controlling women. Women had absorbed so many of the conventional norms of female behavior that they shared in the enforcement of these norms.

THE FEMINIZATION OF RELIGION

By the beginning of the eighteenth century, a process was observably under way in the American colonies by which the church became a more feminine institution. Ministers there observed with sorrow that male piety had declined and women in the congregations outnumbered men. Gender differentiation in religious life increased. Women's virtues were described in family terms, so that to be a good woman was to be a good Christian, while to be a good man was to be a good citizen. Mary Dunn has argued that such gender differentiation was a stage in the separation of church and state.[107]

Several factors mark the feminization of religion in England. A broad general movement away from emotional and intense belief followed the revolutionary period. Divines of the Anglican Church after the Restoration emphasized the importance of morality and sought to direct their congregations away from the religious enthusiasm that was blamed for the disorders of the Civil Wars and Interregnum. Increasingly, faith and reason were seen to be in binary opposition, as female and male always had been. Belief was for women, reason for men. Educated men sought to guide their conduct by the light of reason. Religion, based on emotion, was desirable for women as well as for men of lower status. This trend increased the separation between the sexes and the classes. Virtuous middle-class women became the good conscience of the family. Religion was for the household, where women taught their children personal morality. In the public sphere, educated men deemed secular values and virtues more appropriate.

By the later eighteenth century it was claimed that women's actual natures made them more susceptible to religion. As John Gregory argued in his *Father's Legacy to His Daughter*, women's "superior delicacy," modesty, and education preserved them from vice, while "the natural softness and sensibility of your dispositions . . . along with the natural warmth of your imaginations" made women especially susceptible to the feelings of devotion. Gregory advised his daughter to avoid perplexing works of theology and to concentrate on those books that were addressed to the heart, for "Religion is rather a matter of sentiment than reasoning."[108] But if religion was a matter of feeling, by the early eighteenth century extremes of feeling, such as religious enthusiasm, were deeply suspect in both men and women.

Among the Anglicans, Presbyterians, and Congregationalists, emphasis on family virtues for women, on their "relative duties" as daughters, wives, and mothers, influenced the patterns of female piety. Among some of the Dissenting churches, where women continued to outnumber men, the influence of female piety on the churches' morality was powerful, as mothers reared their children in the fear of the Lord. Household religion remained important for Nonconformists early in the eighteenth century. Yet there was a price to be paid for respectable piety. Nonconformists lost a missionary zeal and a widespread popular appeal. Converts were comparatively few in the eighteenth century, and the churches relied heavily upon the children of believers to continue the denominations. In this context, Nonconformist women could see religion as something especially their own. They could impose a regime of piety upon their households and educate their children in their beliefs.[109]

Women's numerical preponderance in Nonconformist congregations was a continuing feature of post-Restoration Dissent. Women may have outnumbered men in regularity of attendance at Anglican services, but I know of no evidence to test this hypothesis. Intriguingly, married women in the congregations were few, and single or widowed women were in the majority.[110] This, perhaps, accounts for the fact that the highest proportion of women in Baptist and Congregational churches were in London, where the increasing demand for servants attracted women to work in the capital. Historians have suggested a range of explanations for women's numerical predominance. Men risked more by Nonconformity, because of the civic disabilities imposed on Dissenters. Men had less time for active religious commitment; attendance at the Anglican Church placed fewer demands on them.[111] Yet the puzzle remains. Women's own statements from the earlier period speak of their determination to find spiritual satisfaction. In the smaller group of a Nonconformist congregation, the religious and social needs of some women may still have been better met.

An important shift had taken place by the eighteenth century. Religion was no longer what politics was all about, which is not to say that religion was no longer significant in politics. But the establishment of God's kingdom on earth had ceased to be the politicians' goal. Men were busy with public concerns, and religious belief was increasingly a private matter, or even a household matter, something for women and children. Men allowed women to be responsible for religion and piety in the home, but religion lost its prominence in English culture.[112] Insofar as religion was a matter of public concern, it was as a means of improving the behavior of the masses.

Early in the eighteenth century those who were disturbed at the relative decline of religious practices organized movements for reform. They established educational foundations to improve the morality of the public. In 1698 a number of prominent clergymen and laymen founded the Society for Promoting Christian Knowledge, and established fifty-four charity schools before 1704.[113] The curriculum of these schools was sex-specific. Boys were to learn arithmetic, writing, spelling, and reading, while girls were instructed "generally to knit their Stockings and Gloves, to mark, sew, make and mend, their Cloathes," and some to "learn to write and to spin their Cloathes."[114] Women's participation in subscribing and fund-raising was important for the success of the schools. The school for thirty poor girls at Chelsea was governed by female trustees and directed by Mary Astell.[115]

Within the Quaker churches women preachers seemed unnatural even to women by the 1700s. Even so, some women's testimonies show how they experienced the call to preach. They overcame the objections of their families and society, as well as their own. Margaret Lucas

(1701–1770), reared by a Presbyterian aunt and uncle, converted to Quakerism, and ultimately became a minister, although she recorded, "I had in my nature a great aversion to women's preaching."

> The first time I ever heard a woman preach, from a prejudice imbibed from my companions, and probably an aversion in my own nature, I thought it very ridiculous; and the oftener I had opportunities to witness it, the more I secretly despised it.[116]

During the later seventeenth and early eighteenth centuries many women followed mystics such as Bourignon and Jane Lead.[117] The prophet Anne Bathurst and Joanna Oxenbridg "were Two Principal Persons" who carried on the work of Lead's Philadelphian Society.[118] Early in the eighteenth century women were part of a religious movement known as the French Prophets. Women predominated among the prophets and leaders of this movement, but men as well as women prophesied when in trance. Schwartz, the historian of the group, has argued that men retained control by insisting upon judging the truth of an inspiration, and by restricting sacerdotal functions to men.[119] As in the 1650s, in 1707 a congregation of these worshipers was shocked when a woman stripped naked. She stood at the altar, and "did hold forth in a Powerful manner" for a quarter of an hour, and told them "she was come to Reform the People, and bring them to a right understanding."[120] Although the French Prophets numbered only around four hundred in 1708 in London, twenty thousand people assembled to witness a raising of a man from the dead.[121] Like many other religious groups, the French Prophets are known from the work of their enemies rather than from their own records. The opposition to the prophets, however, differed from earlier reactions to prophecies. There was more emphasis on the deception allegedly practiced by the prophets, and more explanations were offered in terms of madness.[122] Even so, the same sexual slanders as earlier were made.[123]

The most significant of the movements of religious enthusiasm and revival was that initiated by the Wesley brothers in the 1730s. Although Methodism is outside the scope of this book, it is worth noting that one of its characteristics in its early phase was the presence of women preachers. As a religion of enthusiasm, Methodism recognized that some women had special spiritual gifts, and the tradition of women preachers among some of the Dissenting churches served as an example to Methodist women.

The supposedly natural religiosity of women was a powerful part of the ideology of the eighteenth century. Female religious enthusiasts were marginalized, but still professed their faith, and participated in new religious movements. Within the established Anglican Church, and the Catholic and Nonconformist churches, many women continued to worship and find spiritual comfort. Many continued to find in religion a space of their own, a set of beliefs that were uniquely theirs, which provided comfort in their lives on earth and dreams and visions of a glorious life to come. Knowing God for themselves, they believed that they had found the most important thing in life.

NOTES

1. The main acts were as follows: the Corporation Act of 1661 debarred from office all men who did not take the Anglican sacrament. The Act of Uniformity of 1662 required all ministers to take oaths of loyalty, to accept the Book of Common Prayer, and to be reordained if they had not already been ordained by a bishop. The date of submission was St. Bartholemew's day, August 24, 1662. On that date many ministers bade farewell to their congregations. The Conventicle Act of 1664 struck at the religous liberty of the laity: no more than five people, apart from the household, were to come together for worship. By the Five Mile Act, preachers were forbidden to come within five miles of their former congregations. This legislation, collectively but incorrectly known as the Clarendon Code, deprived people of the ease for their consciences which Charles had promised in his Declaration of Breda. Historians have debated whether this was part of a deliberate plot by the Anglicans, or the inevitable outcome of Puritan division over comprehension or toleration. For an account from the Dissenting perspective, see Michael R. Watts, *The Dissenters: From the Reformation to the French Revolution* (Oxford: Clarendon Press, 1978).

2. Antonia Fraser, *The Weaker Vessel: Woman's Lot in Seventeenth-Century England* (London: Weidenfeld and Nicolson,1984), 263.

3. Patricia Crawford, "Women's Printed Writings 1600–1700," in *Women in English Society, 1500–1800*, ed. Mary Prior (New York: Routledge, 1985), 212 and 266.

4. Barry Reay, *The Quakers and the English Revolution* (New York: St. Martin's Press, 1985), 81.

5. Philip Henry, Stedman transcript of Diary, May 29, 1662. (I am grateful to Mr P. Warburton-Lee for allowing me to consult his manuscripts.)

6. Gerald R. Cragg, *Puritanism in the Period of the Great Persecution, 1660–1688* (Cambridge: Cambridge University Press, 1957).

7. Watts, *Dissenters*, 259–60.

8. Rose Graham,"The Civic Position of Women at Common Law Before 1800," in *English Ecclesiastical Studies*, ed. Rose Graham (New York:

Society for Promoting Christian Knowledge, The Macmillan Co., 1929).

9. Patricia Crawford, "Public Duty, Conscience, and Women in Early Modern England," in *Public Duty and Private Conscience: Festschrift for G. E. Aylmer*, ed. John Morrill and Paul Slack (Oxford: Oxford University Press, 1993).

10. Ruth Perry, "Mary Astell and the feminist critique of possessive individualism," *Eighteenth Century Studies* 23 (1990): 445. See also Lois G. Schwoerer, "Women and the Glorious Revolution," *Albion* 18 (1986): 195–218, esp. 217–18.

11. Mary Astell, *Reflections upon Marriage*, 1706, in *The First English Feminist*, ed. Bridget Hill (Aldershot, Hunts: Gower, Maurice Temple Smith, 1986), 76.

12. Michael Mullett, "From Sect to Denomination? Social Developments in Eighteenth-Century English Quakerism," *Journal of Religious History* 13 (1986): 168–91.

13. John Morrill, "The Attack on the Church of England in the Long Parliament, 1640–1642," in *History, Society and the Churches: Essays in Honour of Owen Chadwick*, ed. Derek Beales and Geoffrey Best (Cambridge: Cambridge University Press, 1985), 105–124. See also Patrick Collinson, *The Religion of Protestants: The Church in English Society 1559–1625* (Oxford: Clarendon Press, 1982), 192.

14. Sharon L. Arnoult, "'Deliver Us and thy Whole Church': Anglican Women during the English Civil War and Interregnum, 1640–1660," (abstract of paper, 1990 Western Conference of British Studies), 32–34.

15. Morrill, "Attack on the Church of England," 124.

16. E. Gibson, *Observations*, 1744, in *The Eighteenth-Century Constitution, 1688–1815. Documents and Commentary*, ed. E. Neville Williams (Cambridge: Cambridge University Press, 1960), 378.

17. John Oliver, *A Present for Teeming Women* (London, 1663), sig. a5v, a2v.

18. Carolyn Merchant, *The Death of Nature: Women, Ecology and the Scientific Revolution* (New York: Harper and Row, 1983), 253–68.

19. Dorcas Bennet, *Good and Seasonable Counsel*, (London, 1670), sig. a2.

20. Joan Kinnaird, "Mary Astell and the Conservative Contribution to English Feminism," *Journal of British Studies* 19 (1979): 53–75; Hill, *The First English Feminist*; Ruth Perry, *The Celebrated Mary Astell: An Early English Feminist* (Chicago: University of Chicago Press, 1986), 182–231.

21. Evan Davies, "The Enforcement of Religious Conformity in England, 1668–1700, with Special Reference to the Dioceses of Chichester and Worcester" (M. Litt, Oxford University, 1982), 181.

22. Martin Ingram, *Church Courts, Sex and Marriage in England, 1570–1640* (Cambridge: Cambridge University Press, 1987), 372–74.

23. Watts, *Dissenters*, 229.

24. M. H. Lee, ed., *Diaries and Letters of Philip Henry . . . 1631–1696* (London: Kegan Paul and Co., 1882), 147.

25. The tradition of the ministers' suffering began with the ministers themselves who preached farewell sermons, and was continued by Edmund Calamy with his account of the sufferings of those ejected; A. G. Matthews, *Calamy Revised* (Oxford: Clarendon Press, 1974).

26. Clive D. Field, "'Adam and Eve': Gender in the English Free Church Constitutency," *Journal of Ecclesiastical History* 44, no. 1 (1993): 63–79.

27. Thomas Crosby, *The History of the English Baptists*, 4 vols (London: printed and sold for by editor, 1738–1740), ii:183.

28. Richard Baxter, *Reliquiae Baxterianae* (London, 1696), pt. iii, 4.

29. Owen Stockton, *Consolation in Life and Death . . . A Funeral Sermon . . . Mrs Ellen Asty*, 1681, 14.

30. W. Orme, ed. *Remarkable Passages in the Life of William Kiffin* (London: Burton and Smith, 1823), 50.

31. Lee, *Diaries of Philip Henry*, 143.

32. *The Last Legacy of Mr Joseph Davis, Senr*, 1707, 1720, printed in A. C. Underwood, *A History of the English Baptists* (London: Carey Kingsgate Press, 1947), 100–102.

33. Margaret Fell, *A Brief Collection of Remarkable Passages* (London, 1710).

34. Thomas Crosby, *The History of the English Baptists*, 4 vols., (London, 1739), ii:165–71.

35. Lee, *Diaries of Philip Henry*, 147. Mr. Thomas was probably Zechariah Thomas, ejected August 1662; Matthews, *Calamy Revised*.

36. Patricia Crawford, "Katharine and Philip Henry and Their Children: A Case Study in Family Ideology," *Transactions of the Historical Society of Lancashire and Cheshire* 134 (1984): 39–73.

37. Margaret Spufford, *Contrasting Communities* (Cambridge: Sutton Publishing, 1974).

38. A. D. Gilbert, "The Growth and Decline of Nonconformity in England and Wales, with Special Reference to the Period before 1850" (D. Phil., Oxford University, 1973), 153.

39. Elizabeth Cellier, *Malice Defeated*, 1680. Bodleian Library Oxford, 1677 contains a collection of pamphlets on her case, including *Tho. Dangerfield's Answer to a Certain Scandalous Lying Pamphlet*, 1680.

40. Susan O'Brien, "Women of the 'English Catholic Community': Nuns and pupils at the Bar Convent, York, 1680–1790," in *Monastic Studies*, Volume 1 (1990) ed. Judith Loudes, 267–82.

41. Michael J. Galgano, "Out of the Mainstream: Catholic and Quaker Women in the Restoration Northwest," in *The World of William Penn*, ed. Richard S. Dunn and Mary Maples Dunn (Philadelphia: University of Pennsylvania Press, 1986), 119–21.

42. Joseph Besse, *A Collection of the Sufferings of the People Called Quakers*, 2 vols., (London: Luke Hinde, 1753).

43. Richard T. Vann, *The Social Development of English Quakerism, 1655–1755* (Cambridge, Mass.: Harvard University Press, 1969), 197–208. For discussions of this theme, see T. A. Davies, "The Quakers in Essex, 1655–1725" (D. Phil, Oxford University, 1986), 189–250.

44. Michael Mullett has reservations about this typology. Mullett, "From Sect to Denomination?" 169–91.

45. Louella M. Wright, *The Literary Life Early Friends 1650–1725* (New York: AMS Press, 1966), 97–107.

46. Friends' Library, London (hereafter FHL), Book of Minutes of the Second days Morning Meeting, transcript (hereafter LMMM), vol. ii:103, 19, 56.

47. B. S. Snell, ed., *The Minute Book of the Monthly Meeting of the Society of Friends for the Upperside of Buckinghamshire, 1669–1690* (Buckinghamshire Archaeological Society, vol. 1, 1937), 154–55.

48. FHL, LMMM, iii:124–28. Fisher was widowed in 1690.

49. Snell, *Upperside Minutes*, 34–35.

50. FHL, Swathmore Monthly Meeting, Women's minutes 1671–1700, f. 28.

51. Arnold Lloyd, *Quaker Social History* (Westport, Conn.: Greenwood Press, 1950), 116.

52. FHL, Vale of the White Horse Monthly Meeting Minutes, 1673–1722, transcribed by S. & B. Snell, part 2 (notes), 28.

53. Vale Minutes, part 1, 23.

54. Davies, "The Quakers in Essex," 130–61.

55. Jean Mortimer and Russell Mortimer, eds., *Leeds Friends' Minute Book, 1692 to 1712,* (Yorkshire Archaelogical Society), cxxxix, 1980, 12–13.

56. David W. Bolam, *Unbroken Community: The History of the Friends' School Saffron Walden, 1702–1952* (Cambridge: W. Heffer and Sons, 1952), 13.

57. William Mucklow, *Tyranny and Hypocrisy Detected* (London, 1673), 72.

58. William Charles Braithwaite, *Beginnings of Quakerism* (New York: Macmillan, 1912), 340–42; William Charles Braithwaite, *Second Period of Quakerism* (New York: Macmillan, 1919), 269–75; Bonnelyn Young Kunze, "The Family, Social and Religious Life of Margaret Fell" (Ph.D. diss., University of Rochester, 1986).

59. George Fox, *This is An Encouragement* (London, 1676), 25, 12, 20.

60. Ibid., 20, 95.

61. Storey quoted in William Rogers, *The Christian-Quaker Distinguished from the Apostate & Innovator*, 1680, pt. iv, 12; FHL, Swathmore MS, Women's Meeting, letter from Fox, 1675, f. 12.

62. Snell, *Upperside Minutes*, 130.

63. Ibid., 108–9, 133.

64. Ibid., 126–7, 99.

65. Isabel Ross, *Margaret Fell: Mother of Quakerism* (York: William Sessions Book Trust, 1984), 294.

66. William Mucklow, *The Spirit of the Hat* (London, 1673), 32.

67. William Mather, *A Novelty: Or, a Government of Women* (London, 1694?), 5, 22.

68. Rogers, *The Christian-Quaker*, pt. i, 64–66; pt. iv, 9–12.

69. Margaret Fell, *Women's Speaking Justified*, (London, 1666), 3, 9, 12. Selections of this work have been reprinted in various forms.

70. Rogers, *The Christian-Quaker*, pt. iii, 52.

71. Mucklow, *Tyranny*, 47–52.

72. Rogers, *The Christian-Quaker*, pt. iv, 12.

73. FHL, LMMM, iii:17.

74. FHL, LMMM, iii:332 (1709). She was required to bring a certificate from her previous meeting place.

75. FHL, LMMM, iii:79, 129, 135.

76. FHL, Vale of White Horse Minutes, 119.

77. Ibid., 18.

78. For a few yearly meeting letters, see Quaker women in my "Provisional Checklist of Women's Published Writings," in Prior, *Women in English Society*, 254.

79. Watts, *Dissenters*, 324.

80. Angus Library, Regent's Park College, MS 2/4/1, Maze Pond Church Book, 1691–1745.

81. Maze Pond, 44, October 1691.

82. Ibid., 44.

83. Ibid., 49.

84. Ibid., 4.

85. Ibid., 105, October 9, 1694.

86. Ibid., 108–9.

87. Murdina D. Macdonald, "London Calvinistic Baptists, 1689–1727: Tensions within a Dissenting Community under Toleration" (D. Phil, Oxford University, 1982), 91.

88. Angus Library, Cripplegate Church Book, 1689–1723, f. 22.

89. Ibid., ff. 69–70, December 10, 1713.

90. Ibid., f. 72.

91. Ibid., ff. 86v.–88v., 1716.

92. The only concession Maze Pond gave was to record that if indeed he had been guilty of the matters as charged, she had done right to leave; Maze Pond, 100, 102.

93. *Records of a Church of Christ in Bristol 1640–1687*. Roger Hayden, ed. Bristol Record Society, 27, 1974, 51, 208–9; Cripplegate, f. 72v.

94. Cripplegate, f. 10.

95. Maze Pond, 101.

96. Cripplegate, f. 10.

97. Ibid., ff. 11–12; printed in *Baptist Quarterly*, 1924–1925, ii:182–84.

98. *Baptist Quarterly*, ii:121.

99. Ibid., 113–15, 122–23.

100. Watts, *Dissenters*, 336–41.

101. Maze Pond, f. 93.

102. W. T. Whitley, ed., *Minutes of the General Assemby of the General Baptist Church in England*, 2 vols. (London: C. Griffin and Company, 1910), i:23.

103. *Baptist Quarterly*, ii:119–21.

104. Maze Pond, f. 102.

105. Ibid., f. 32.

106. Cripplegate, ff. 32–36v., 47v.–49.

107. Mary Maples Dunn, "Saints and Sisters: Congregational and Quaker Women in the Early Colonial Period," *American Quarterly* 30 (1978): 592–95.

108. John Gregory, *A Father's Legacy to His Daughters* (London, 1774), 9–25.

109. For a discussion of the importance of the family ideology of the good woman, see Crawford, "Family of Philip and Katherine Henry."

110. In 1703 there were only six couples in Heywood's Presbyterian congregation of fifty-one members; W. J. Sheils, "Oliver Heywood and His Congregation," *Studies in Church History* 23, 268–71.

111. Field, "Gender in the English Free Church Constitutency," table 3.

112. Dale A. Johnson, *Women in English Religion 1700–1925*, Studies in Women and Religion, vol. 10 (New York: Edwin Mellon Press, 1984), 13.

113. M. G. Jones, *The Charity School Movement: A Study of Eighteenth Century Puritanism in Action* (Cambridge: Cambridge University Press, 1938), 57.

114. Craig Rose, "Evangelical Philanthropy and Anglican Revival: The Charity Schools of Augustan London, 1698–1740," *London Journal* 16 (1991): 35–65; W. O. B. Allen and Edmund McClure, *Two Hundred Years: The History of the Society for Promoting Christian Knowledge, 1698–1898* (S.P.C.K. London, 1898), 138. Nearly twice as many boys as girls were enrolled by 1704; Allen and McClure, 140.

115. Perry, *Mary Astell*, 239.

116. "An account of the . . . call to the ministry of Margaret Lucas," in *The Friends Library*, vol. 13 (Philadelphia, 1849), 179–201.

117. See Patricia Crawford, *Women and Religion in England, 1500–1720* (London: Routledge, 1993), 106–112.

118. Desirée Hirst, *Hidden Riches: Traditional Symbolism from Renaissance to Blake* (London: Eyre and Spottiswoode, 1964), 103–5.

119. Hillel Schwartz, *Knaves, Fools, Madmen, and That Subtile Effluvium: A Study of the Opposition to the French Prophets in England, 1706–1710*, University of Florida Monographs no. 62 (Gainsville, Fla.: University of Florida Press, 1978), 19–20; Hillel Schwartz, *The French Prophets: The History of a Milenarian Group in Eighteenth-Century England* (Berkeley, Calif.: University of California Press, 1980), 146–47, 210.

120. "Lincoln's Inn Fields: The French Prophets," *Notes & Queries*, 6th ser. xi, 10 (January 1885): 21–22.

121. Schwartz, *Opposition to French Prophets*, 21–24.

122. Ibid., 31–65.

123. *Enthusiastick Imposters No Divinely Inspir'd Prophets* (London, 1707), 68.

THE ELOQUENCE

OF THE WORD AND THE SPIRIT

The Place of Puritan Women's Writing in Old and New England

Sylvia Brown

DEFENDING HER VIEW THAT THE MINISTRY OF NEW ENGLAND "did not teach the new covenant," Anne Hutchinson rehearsed before the General Court of Massachusetts Bay the hermeneutic steps by which she had arrived at that subversive position. Her interrogators asked her how she knew her interpretation of Scripture was correct.

> "How," responded Hutchinson, "did Abraham know that it was God that bid him offer his son, being a breach of the sixth commandment?"
> "By an immediate voice."
> "So," returned Hutchinson, "to me by an immediate revelation."
> "How! an immediate revelation."
> "By the voice of his own spirit to my soul."[1]

Anne Hutchinson left no extant writings. But her self-defense against the charge of "antinomianism" (literally, a refusal of law, especially the moral law given in the Ten Commandments) was transcribed at her examination before the General Court in November 1637. It is an instance of female eloquence justified, and at the same time made extremely dangerous, by the invocation of the Holy Spirit. Hutchinson's interrogators found her claim to immediate revelation shocking because, by it, she was asserting a divine authorization which set both her and her words outside human rules and structures, including those which placed the clergy over the laity and men over women. It was this claim to immediate revelation, taken up again in her trial before the Boston

Church the following March, which, more than any of the other accusations leveled at her, led to her excommunication and banishment.[2]

This essay will examine the paradoxical relationship between women's eloquence and the "authorizing" structures of Puritan culture, that is, those elements of Puritan culture that, like the Holy Spirit, could be used or invoked not only to give authority to a woman's pronouncements, but also to turn her into the "author" of influential speech acts, whether spoken or written. This relationship is paradoxical because, on the one hand, Puritanism shares the general misogynous assumption of early modern culture that the only good woman is a silent one, finding specific support for this position in the writings of its favorite authority, the Apostle Paul. "Let the woman learne in silence with all subiection," writes Paul, "I permit not a woman to teach, neither to vsurpe authoritie ouer the man, but to be in silence."[3] On the other hand, Puritan culture also, paradoxically, *values* women's words. Paul himself sends out contradictory messages on the subject. In certain circumstances he allows, and even requires, women to teach. The elder women are to be "teachers of honest things" and instruct the young women—especially that they should love their husbands and children. Anne Hutchinson quoted this very text back at her accusers to defend the meetings she held at her house.[4] But the same text was also used by women at the approved and exemplary center of Puritan culture. The Puritan Countess of Lincoln, Elizabeth Clinton, used it in a work of 1622 urging women to breast-feed their own children. "I beseech all godly women to remember," Clinton wrote, "how we *elder* ones are commaunded to instruct the *yonger*, to love their children."[5]

This ambivalence about women's words was related to an ambivalence within Puritanism itself regarding "the Word." Puritans are often understood as scriptural fundamentalists, but they were in fact uneasy about the Word by itself.[6] For Puritans, the Word never did stand on its own, but was infused, enlivened, and interpreted by the Spirit. The "letter killeth, but the Spirit giueth life."[7] Reading the Word by the light of the Spirit guaranteed both a true and a fruitful interpretation of Scripture, but it also detached interpretation from merely human hermeneutics based on logic or tradition. Indeed, the Protestant reformers' double emphasis on the Word and the Spirit, and particularly on private reading of Scripture guided by the Spirit, was aimed specifically at challenging the patristic tradition of learned scriptural commentary by which the Roman Catholic Church upheld its doctrinal authority and interpretive monopoly. Some of the most powerfully exemplary stories of the Reformation recounted the eloquence of unlearned Protestant women, who confounded Catholic interrogators by their intimate acquaintance with Scripture. Such women showed that the "true" interpretation of Scripture was evident, even to an unlearned woman, since the Spirit was ever-ready to guide the sincere reader.

But interpreting by the Spirit could come perilously close to "immediate revelation." Moderate Puritans were careful not to separate the Spirit, which enlivened and gave salvific potential to the Word, from the Word itself. The Spirit was present to help the godly understand, internalize, and reproduce the gospel in their own lives, whenever they heard a sermon or read the Bible. Radicals, however, were more willing to admit that the Spirit might act on its own, apart from the Word, dwelling entirely in the experiences of the believer.[8] Thus while both moderates and radicals agreed that what mattered was one's personal *response* to the Word as it was inspired and guided by the Spirit, radicals were more likely to claim direct, personal revelation. Radical teachers like Hutchinson were not so much operating outside normative Puritan practices and beliefs as following them to their logical ends. Hutchinson made visible not just the antinomianism but also the hermeneutic chaos which could follow from the experiential type of Protestantism upon which New England was founded. It was her articulation of a repressed, rather than a heretical, truth that made her so dangerous.[9]

Hutchinson and other eloquent women of the seventeenth century, whether they articulate religious teachings or experiences in speech or writing, are often understood as rebellious feminist foremothers, breaking out of the silent prison built by Paul's injunction that women should not speak in church.[10] On this reading, women's eloquence makes them prima facie religious radicals. In this essay, however, I shall argue that women's words intersected in more complicated ways with religious orthodoxy and radicalism. When were women's words acceptable, and when were they not? This essay will discuss instances of acceptable and unacceptable women's eloquence across a broad spectrum of Puritan culture: radical and orthodox, in New England and old England. While arguing for some common assumptions about women's words within Puritan culture, it will also examine the local contexts where the fine distinctions between dangerous and edifying words were drawn.

WOMEN'S WORDS:
WITHIN AND BEYOND THE PURITAN HOUSEHOLD

Puritan writers on marriage and household matters never failed to consider the question of women's words. Indeed, their widely circulated writings articulated the paradoxical status of women's words within Puritan culture. For them, the regulation of women's words in a marriage or a household unsurprisingly came to signify general good order and discipline. A woman's moderate, quiet speech, for instance, was a visible sign of acceptance of her divinely ordained inferiority, as well as a good example to children and servants, showing how *they* should behave with respect to their superiors. In his *Bride-Bush* of 1617, William Whately wrote: "No woman of gouernment will allow her children and seruants to bee loud and brawling before her; and shall shee before her husband bee so herselfe? What is become of inferiority then?"[11]

Whately, like many of his contemporaries, took Paul's injunction that women should "learn in silence" as his point of departure for thinking about women's words. "*Paul* commands the women to *learne in silence*. The word is, *in quietnesse*: wherein he not alone inioynes a publicke, but euen a generall silence to hold in the house and other like meetings." In *Of Domesticall Duties*, William Gouge commented on the same passage (1 Tim. 2:11–12), reading it not just as the enforcement of women's silence in church (which is arguably the exclusive meaning of this passage), but specifically of her silence in the presence of her husband. Her words to her husband must be "few, reuerend and meeke," which "implieth a reuerend subiection."[12]

Yet, for all their restrictions on women's words both in the church and at home, neither of these conservative Puritan commentators decreed absolute female silence. It is the *regulation* (and preferably the godly woman's self-imposed regulation) rather than the absence of women's words that mattered for Whately and Gouge. And, as is also true for Paul, they held that in certain circumstances a woman ought to speak, and moreover ought to speak with effect, in order to persuade. Whately, for instance, enjoined the wife of the man living in "any grosse sinne" to "labour by all kinde, louing, and Christian meanes to draw him out of it."[13] Other Puritan writers made very clear that this labor is preeminently rhetorical. A much reprinted tract on household government, for instance, advised women to use "gentle exhortation" to win their husbands from the alehouse. Robert Snawsel's *Looking-Glasse for Married Folkes* has a female character (named Eulalie, meaning "well-spoken") advising women that they may convert ungodly husbands by "gracious words and counsell, prayers and patience, your conference and community."[14] In his *Ornaments for the Daughters of Zion*, Cotton Mather advised a more assertive approach. The godly wife of a "Prayerless, Graceless man" should "not leave of her Ingenious Perswasions, till it may be said of him, *Behold he Prays!*" For such a woman, Mather even modified 1 Cor. 14:35 (which exhorts women to learn from their husbands at home): "Truly, though a Woman may not *Speak in the Church*, yet she may humbly Repeat unto her Husband at *Home* what the Minister *Spoke in the Church*, that may be Pertinent to his condition."[15]

Within Puritan culture, women's words were desirable and even powerful when they were, as Snawsel's Eulalie put it, "gracious," that is, when they extended the community of grace. Even for the most conservative of Puritan commentators, women had an evangelical role in building up the numbers of the godly. They not only converted ungodly husbands, but, preeminently, they brought their children into the family of faith. They were the first, and therefore the most influential, religious instructors.[16] In a section of his *Domesticall Duties* devoted to mothers' particular duty to give *"timely nurture"* to their children, Gouge asserted that the mother who feeds, clothes, and tends her infants, who is therefore "most in their sight," is also the most persuasive evangelizer at that impressionable age. "Her precepts therefore," wrote Gouge, ". . . are best heeded by the children, and she hath the best opportunity to perswade them to what she liketh best."[17] Gouge and other writers on Puritan pedagogy were emphatic about not letting this best time for persuasive nurture slip, as this first maternal instruction made a deeper and more lasting impression than any other. As another popular tract put it (in an oft-repeated conventional image): mothers "poure good liquour into their childrens tender vessels, the sauour whereof shall sticke in them a long while after: I meane, they may sowe in their mindes, the seede of religion and godlinesse."[18] As rhetoricians, godly mothers enjoyed ideal conditions, for they had near-exclusive access to and influence over their audience. That audience was, moreover, uniquely receptive—"tender vessels" waiting to be formed and filled.

This sanctioned persuasive role provided godly women, and particularly *mothers*, with an already authoritative mode in which to address their children, but by which they could also instruct, admonish, and even harangue a wider audience perceived as in need of basic instruction. In *The Countesse of Lincolnes Nurserie*, Elizabeth Clinton wrote as a mother to urge other mothers to nurse their own children. She did not argue from her own experience, except negatively: she voiced regret that she herself had used wet nurses, partly "overruled by anothers authority" (probably her husband's) and partly influenced by bad advice. She emphasized rather that she spoke *for* the godly community, for "if holy Ministers, or other Christians doe heare of a good woman to be brought to bed, and her child to bee living; their first question usually is, whether she her selfe give it sucke, yea, or no?"[19] Because of its formative influence in passing godliness from one generation to the next—in reproducing and extending the number of the godly—maternity in Puritan culture was never merely a private matter, and so maternal instruction could also, quite easily, modulate into public discourse relevant to the whole godly community.

One of the best examples of this modulation is Dorothy Leigh's *The Mothers Blessing*. First published in 1616, it was one of the earliest, most influential, as well as the most Puritan, of the genre of maternal advice. In the century after its first appearance, it was reprinted more often than any other book written by a woman.[20] Leigh addressed the work to her three young sons, showing them therein "the right way to heauen . . . truely obserued out of the written word of GOD." Ostensibly worrying that her youngest might "haue but little part in it" if she left her written advice to her eldest, Leigh decided to seek a wider audience by sending it "abroad" as a printed text. This was an extraordinary strategy, given that printed works by women were still a rarity in the first decades of the seventeenth century. But Leigh paradoxically found a legitimate route to the public "showing" of herself and her words through her "private" obligation to provide her sons with basic religious instruction. "Setting aside all feare," she wrote, "I haue aduentured to shew my imperfections to the view of the World, not regarding what censure shall for this bee laid vpon mee, so that heerein I may shew my selfe a louing Mother."[21] Nonetheless, when one reads Leigh's advice, it becomes apparent that she was writing not merely as a mother, but as one of the godly sort who feel that the Church has not yet been sufficiently reformed. Jacobean Puritans often fingered bad or insufficient preaching as the main reason for this imperfect reformation.[22] Leigh, too, after urging her sons to become preachers themselves, spent much of the second half of her book denouncing ministers who are negligent or too worldly. She urged an imagined readership clearly more extensive than her three boys to do something about this as part of a general program of reformation: "Moue the people to prouide themselues a Preacher, tell them of their wants, speake to the Magistrates, mourne to see the Alehouses full, and the Church of God emptie."[23]

Leigh's book was both popular and rhetorically powerful: its message may have influenced her son William's later career as a nonconforming minister in the 1630s.[24] In her case, the Pauline imperative to silence seemed to have been overridden by the evangelical efficacy that Puritan culture allowed maternal instruction. But again, the efficacy of women's words depended on certain preconditions or contingencies. Leigh, for instance, cast her work not only as maternal instruction, but also as a deathbed blessing, as she felt herself "going out of the world."[25] In his *Domesticall Duties*, William Gouge commented on the "deepe impression" made by the words of a dying mother or father: "The words of a dying parent are commonly most regarded. . . . If euer therefore there be a time seasonable for a parent to giue good instructions to his children, then is the time when parents are cleane departing from their children."[26] Leigh's writing was therefore supported by her approved maternal role as religious instructor and by the seasonableness of her utterance. The extraordinary circumstances of death lent not only permission to speak, but power to the words spoken.

Leigh also took care to align herself with a much admired symbol of both English and European Protestantism—Princess Elizabeth. Elizabeth was the daughter of the current English monarch, King James, and also the namesake of the previous queen who had restored and settled Protestantism in England after the Catholic reign of "Bloody Mary." In February 1613 Elizabeth had also married Frederick, Count Palatine, who was regarded as a bulwark against continental Catholicism: he was the first Elector of the Holy Roman Empire, but also a Calvinist and leader of the Protestant Union of Princes.

Leigh began her dedicatory epistle to this "Wife to the illustrious Prince" by further aligning herself with Protestant orthodoxy, grounding her own text in "the right way," which was of course the way grounded in Scripture. Leigh aligned her own words with the Word. What she had written had been "truely obserued out of the written word of GOD"; it was "the right and ready way to Heauen wel waranted by the scriptures of the olde and new Testament, which is the true word of God." Elizabeth Joscelin, in her own much reprinted mother's legacy, also urged the unborn child for whom she was writing to "bee obedient to theas instructions" because she had "learnt them out of gods word."[27] The evident approval which the legacies of Leigh and Joscelin enjoyed certainly depended on the authority of maternal instruction, but only because this instruction and their writing ultimately derived from a greater authority: from *the* Authority, from the teaching of Scripture itself. Their approved authorship, in other words, was not a matter of invention, but of reproduction. This kind of "authorship"— gendered by its association with maternity and reproduction—was not unfamiliar to Puritan culture. After all, godly mothers were exhorted to teach their children to repeat the words of orthodoxy. Alongside their ministers and their husbands, mothers were encouraged to catechize their children by such works as Robert Abbot's *Milk For Babes; Or, A Mother's Catechism for Her Children* (1646).[28] Some women, like Dorothy Burch in Kent and Sarah Fiske in New England, did write their own catechisms. Burch explained that she consented to a relative's pressure to publish her catechism, not only to honor God and help other

Christians by her knowledge, but also "that it may doe good to my children." Fiske composed her "Confession of Faith" at her admission into the church at Braintree, Massachusetts, circa 1652. It was published posthumously in 1704, as the title page put it, "for the Benefit of ALL, but more especially of YOUNG Persons; That they may Attain to a competent Knowledge, in Saving and Divine Truths."[29]

We might call these women, who reproduced godly, often maternal, instruction in textual form, "women of the Word," distinguishing them from the likes of Anne Hutchinson, whose spiritual "experiences" or personal revelations took them beyond the Word (or at least beyond orthodox interpretation). But although at the approved center of their own Puritan communities, women of the Word nonetheless articulated the critical, often downright dissenting, stance of their own group toward the unreformed majority.[30] I have been suggesting that their texts were "orthodox"; but whether a text is orthodox or radical depends on who is reading it, and when. A writer may also be "radical" in some respects, "orthodox" in others. Dorothy Leigh, for instance, explicitly endorsed women's subordinate status. Yet she violated "the vsuall order of women" by writing and publishing her maternal advice, and she unhesitatingly attacked anything she saw as a remnant of the unreformed Church—from praying the rosary to the belief in purgatory.[31] Within the moderate Puritan culture, which flourished largely unmolested by the Jacobean Church, she was entirely orthodox. From the perspective of a strictly conformist Church hierarchy, such as was to arise in the decades after her death, Leigh's writing might well have seemed excessively critical of the status quo.

It would also be a mistake to assume that the domestic authority of a godly woman's words was *necessarily* circumscribed—limited to a private sphere unconnected to wider political or national concerns. The Puritans themselves did not think so. In his popular *Poor Man's Family Book*, Richard Baxter conventionally imagined the evangelical and rhetorical duties of a mother toward her family. "She must be daily Catechizing them," he wrote, "and teaching them to know God, and speaking to them for holiness and against sin."[32] But for Baxter, writing in 1674, the year after the Declaration of Indulgence had been withdrawn and so put to an end a twelve-month period of toleration, the household propagation of godly religion must have seemed the only reliable site for true reformation. In such a situation, "when the churches are corrupted, and good ministers lacking, then godly families must keep up religion."[33] Particularly under persecution, the words a mother speaks and teaches to her children have not only evangelical, but powerful political potential. By helping their children "to that honest and holy disposition, which is the chief thing necessary in every relation to the Common good," by educating children "for Magistracie, Ministry and all publick services," godly mothers may, according to Baxter, "become chief instruments of the reformation and welfare of Churches and kingdoms and of the world."[34] For Baxter and his Nonconformist readers, the catechizing mother represented not only a "chief instrument" but also a last hope for political, godly reformation on a national, and even international scale. To be a "woman of the Word" under such circumstances was to reproduce words of orthodoxy, which were also words of activism and dissent.

COTTON MATHER'S LIBRARY OF WOMEN WRITERS

In specific contexts, then, women's words were both encouraged and powerful within Puritan culture. Nonetheless, Dorothy Leigh apologized for altering the usual order of women by writing. She expected her readers to marvel why she did not, "according to the vsuall custome of women, exhort . . . by word and admonitions, rather then by writing, a thing so vnusuall among vs."[35] Was it normally only through the spoken word, then, that Puritan women were encouraged to exhort and teach? Despite Leigh's worry (which may have been a conventional apologia), there are indications that, in some cases, women's *writing* may actually have been less problematic for Puritan culture than women's spoken words.

Among New England Puritans there is no more representative, nor more prolific, writer than Cotton Mather. The son and grandson of two famous ministers—Increase Mather and John Cotton, respectively—Cotton Mather was a well known minister himself, best known now as the author of an encyclopedic religious history of New England, *Magnalia Christi Americana*. Of his many other works, some were explicitly written with the female members of his congregation in mind.[36] In one of them, *Ornaments for the Daughters of Zion. Or the Character and Happiness of a Virtuous Woman*, Mather gave women what seems like an authorial stake in the Word itself. "God," he wrote, "has Employ'd many *Women* to *Write* for the *Church*, and *Inspir'd* some of them for Writing of the *Scriptures*." He cited the biblical songs of Deborah, Hannah, and Mary, the prophecy of Huldah, and, especially, the maternal instructions Bathsheba gave to her son Solomon in the last chapter of Proverbs. (Mather's book includes a serious discussion of the authorship of the last chapter of Proverbs, identifying which parts of the chapter are arguably Bathsheba's, and which her son's.)[37] Mather had his female audience in mind here, not so much to suggest that they too could write

Scripture, but rather to give them a stake in Scripture that would move them to zealous study of, and so subjection to, the Word: "how much does this oblige all *Women* to study that precious Bible, to the curious Workmanship whereof, the hand of a *Woman* has contributed?"[38]

Mather made clear that women who believed they were new Deborahs were disobeying the Word. Quaker women, for one, did believe this. Quakers believed their testimony to be no different from that given by the prophets and the apostles.[39] In *Little Flocks Guarded against Grievous Wolves*, Mather fulminated against these and other "*Strong Delusions*" propagated by the Quakers, not sparing Quaker women. ("*Baggages!*" was his comment on two who appeared stark naked at Puritan assemblies.) He also provided his readers with detailed refutations of Quaker arguments, recommending 1 Cor. 14:34–35 ("Let your Women keep silence in your Churches . . .") as a way of proving "why their *Women*, who *Speak* so much at their Meetings, may not be look'd upon as *Ministers*."[40] For Mather, such women belonged to an "Absurd Sect," which served to demonstrate just where the Pauline injunction to silence *did* apply. For, even though women certainly once did compose Scripture, "the Apostle does abundantly intimate unto us, that such *Inspirations* as compos'd the *Scriptures* are not now to be expected, when he gives the prohibition so much Transgres'd by the most Absurd Sect in our Days, *That the Woman may not speak in the Church*."[41] The transgression to which Mather referred was testifying—speaking when the Spirit moves—practiced by both women and men in Quaker meetings. It is significant that Mather connected Quaker women speaking out in church with the authoring of Scripture: both presumed immediate revelation, direct inspiration by the Holy Spirit. Thus, what made Quaker women absurd for Mather also made Anne Hutchinson a dangerous seducer for Mather's grandfather, John Cotton. The days of direct inspiration had passed.[42]

It was clearly the claim to immediate revelation rather than women's claim to authorship that bothered Mather. In both *Ornaments for the Daughters of Zion* and *Magnalia Christi Americana*, Mather cited a number of historical and contemporary female writers with admiration: women who, if they had not laid claim to prophecy, had nonetheless done "service for the *Tabernacle*" by their "Ingenious Writings."[43] Referring the reader to European catalogues of learned and devout women writers, he also mentioned by name, for instance, "that most accomplish'd Lady, *Anna Maria Schurman* [who] has in our Age adressed the World withal."[44] This erudite woman had died as recently as 1678 and was something of a prodigy. Even the men who praised her called her a "miraculum seu naturae monstrum," a miracle or a prodigy of nature—

with the implication, of course, that she had nothing to do with the rest of womankind.[45] But for Mather, van Schurman was but one of a library of talented women. These women, moreover, were to be found not just in Europe, but in the New World as well. "Books publish'd by *that Sex*," Mather declared, "were enough to make a *Library* far from contemptible; nor has even the *New-English* part of the *American* Strand been without *Authoresses* that would challenge a Room in such a *Library*."[46]

Which authors might Cotton Mather have been thinking of for this imagined library of published women's writing? And what made them "far from contemptible" rather than absurd? Mather himself evidently had a range of women writers in his real library. He might have known van Schurman merely by reputation, although his enthusiasm for her writing suggests a closer acquaintance.[47] He certainly read Elizabeth Joscelin's *Mothers Legacie*, for he mentioned Joscelin at least twice in his writings, praising her in both cases for her laudable desire to be "*a Mother to one of Gods Children*."[48] He introduced excerpts from his sister Jerusha's spiritual diary by citing the precedent writings of a young woman from Norwich, Mary Simpson, collected over sixty years before by John Collinges.[49] In *Magnalia Christi Americana*, Mather put forward Anne Bradstreet as his American example of female learning, praising her poems as having "afforded a grateful Entertainment unto the Ingenious."[50] In *Ornaments for the Daughters of Zion*, Mather also praised the learned Protestant martyr Lady Jane Grey, whose fragmentary writings and utterances were collected by John Foxe in his *Acts and Monuments*; a Frenchwoman who "a while since, published Homilies on the Epistle to the *Hebrews*"; and, finally, a Dutchwoman whose "Exquisite Pen" had "Celebrated the *Zeal* of a *Scotch* Woman, who for her *Zeal* having her Leg tortured in that cruel Horrid Engine call'd *the Boot*, bravely said, *My God I bless thee that thou hast given me a Leg to be thus used for thee!*"[51]

Mather's "library" of women writers reminds us that the horizons of New England Puritanism were not necessarily narrow or provincial. Mather relied heavily on the cultural resources of other reformed communities. But it is even more significant that these writers and martyrs from England, New England, the Netherlands, Scotland, and France were all *women*. Writing by women in the seventeenth century, particularly religious writing, has, until the recent past, almost automatically been assigned "marginal" status. Such a presentist judgment is complicated, though, not merely by the evidence that Mather certainly read godly women writers (and with some enthusiasm!), but even more by the fact that he made them *exemplary* in his own writings: they gave testimony of laudable zeal which was to be imitated. Here then is a model that Cotton Mather's female readers could use. While the quasi-mythical authoresses of Scripture gave them a stake in the authority of the Word, they could also follow the women of their own historical community in testifying to their own zeal. Doing so by writing was clearly acceptable, and women like Mather's sister Jerusha, for one, chose to avail themselves of this option.

As with the godly wives who could forgo wifely subservence and silence in the interest of converting an ungodly husband, Puritan female authorship was allowed, even encouraged, but it was also conditional. All of the approved writers in Mather's "library" were what I have called "women of the Word." I have already discussed how Elizabeth Joscelin aligned her own words with Scripture, with the Word. But Mather's female authors may also be considered "women of the Word" in that they propagated (what Mather considered to be) orthodox doctrine. Either they transmitted sound religious teaching from one generation to the next, as Joscelin, and as the prototype for all godly maternal instructors, Bathsheba, did. Or, they wrote in defense of orthodox religion under persecution, like Lady Jane Grey. One of the favorite texts by Lady Jane, one which Mather must certainly have encountered, was a letter written to her sister Katherine in a Greek New Testament, and purportedly sent the night before she went to the scaffold. Lady Jane's letter began: "I have here sent you (good sister Katherine) a book, which although it be not outwardly trimmed with gold, yet inwardly it is more worth than precious stones. It is the booke (deare sister) of the Law of the Lord."[52] This private document, which was later reproduced in several different places,[53] illustrates the carefully delimited kind of authority that women of the Word enjoyed. While daring to supplement the Word, Lady Jane, at the same time, subjected her own words to it. (It is noteworthy that she called the New Testament—and not the Old—the *Law*.) On the other hand, her decision to write her letter "in the end of the New Testament" was a modest one; yet it also gave her the last word, as an interpolation made powerful by its proximity to an especially philologically pure form of divine writ, and by its nearness to her own end.[54] But it was the act of passing on the Testament, as well as the exhortation to read it inscribed therein, that gave her words future evangelical currency. She became one of those orthodox writing "mothers" whose own words reproduced a reformed faith founded *sola Scriptura*. She was one who, literally, passed on the Word.

The orthodoxy of "women of the Word" was also guaranteed by the supervision of male editors and endorsers; or, to put it another way, these women's exemplary lives and writings were often pressed into service in the establishment of "orthodoxy." Beside Lady Jane's letter, for instance, Foxe inserted a marginal note directing readers to understand her as a "faithfull" woman—perhaps both a woman of faith and an upholder of the true reformed faith.[55] And, of course, Foxe's inclusion of Lady Jane in a martyrology which found its way into each parish Church made her one of the foundation figures upon which a Protestant national culture was erected. Some of the other "women of the Word" endorsed by Mather himself served a similar function for more local interests. Thomas Goad not only prefixed an "Approbation" to Elizabeth Joscelin's posthumous mother's legacy, but also altered it to conform more closely to his own brand of Protestantism.[56] The Independent minister John Collinges used Mary Simpson as an explicit case of how to overcome heretical opinions and arrive at what *he* considered an orthodox position. Simpson told of her effortful arrival at doctrinal clarity in an autobiographical piece (probably titled by Collinges): "A Short *Explanation* of her selfe, concerning divers *Articles* of *Faith*, especially such as are most *fundamentally* necessarie to salvation."[57] The beginning of Simpson's text has affinities to a creed or to the catechisms of Dorothy Burch and Sarah Fiske, but Collinges packaged even the autobiographical narrative so as to give both it and its "author" the seal of orthodox exemplarity. Like Foxe, Collinges added marginal notes, particularly where Simpson recounted her attempt to confirm or deny the opinions of certain "Instruments of Satan" by turning to Scripture. Through marginal annotation, Collinges endorsed her realization that merely reading Scripture herself was not enough. Scripture-reading needed the addition of "strong cryes" ("Observe the right way to profit by reading") as well as of prayer arising out of a sense of "wants" ("A right frame of spirit in seeking direction"). Through his notation, Collinges further emphasized that it was only after Simpson placed herself in a position of humility vis-à-vis Scripture that she was rewarded with orthodoxy: "God then shows her the truth."[58]

Interestingly, it is also at this point in Simpson's narrative that she described herself rewarded with *eloquence*:

Now when the Lord had revealed himselfe in this to me, I was earnest with God that I might not only *know* these truths, but I might be able to *hold* out these truths so as to stop the mouths of *gainsayers.* 2 dayes after Gods *revealing* himselfe, these parties came, and God gave me to speak that they were not able to answer.[59]

Simpson's remarkable eloquence was acknowledged by Collinges too. In the appended funeral sermon, Collinges went so far as to give Simpson the character of a preacher. "Grace had made her *eloquent*," he declared, so that when he went to visit her on her sickbed, "my eares silenced my tongue, and gave her leave to be the preacher, for the gain of those in the room, and that I myself might learn *Right-eousnes*." But Simpson remarked elsewhere in the same sermon, "I meane not that she was a *Pulpit-preacher*, No, . . . she preached as *Noah*, by *making the Ark*, nay more, as *Priscilla & Aquila*, by privately instructing others in the wayes of God."[60] For Collinges, and for Mather who implicitly equates Mary Simpson with his own sister Jerusha, this sort of acceptable female preaching builds an "ark" of personal example combined with orthodox utterance which will pass on an embattled faith. That these examples of female piety and eloquence were transmitted away from the domestic circle properly inhabited by women into the public realm of print seems, after all, not to have been as significant as their acknowledged power in propagating the "wayes of God."[61]

Female eloquence was necessary for the reproduction of Puritan orthodoxies. The flip side of this, however, was women's special involvement in doctrinal reproduction gone awry: in the Satanic propagation of heresies. Cotton Mather was no less vehement in his condemnation of demonic female persuasions as he was enthusiastic about the evangelical potential of the writings of godly women like his sister Jerusha. In his damning account of the "witchcraft" practiced by Goody Glover against the Goodwin children of Boston, Mather repeatedly emphasized the corruptness of Glover's language. She deviated from the English of godly Protestants, seeming to possess almost an excess of language: she could not avoid making nonsense of the Lord's Prayer (although as a Roman Catholic she could "recite her *Pater Noster* in Latin very readily"); she could only testify to the court in her native Irish; and when asked whether she believed there was a God, "her Answer was too blasphemous and horrible for any Pen of mine to mention."[62] The final section of this essay will return to a woman whose acknowledged eloquence the Puritan establishment of New England found disturbing and dangerous, precisely because they considered her words to have the power to reproduce Satanic heresies. I shall argue, however, that the danger lay not in Anne Hutchinson's difference from her orthodox sisters. On the contrary, it was her proximity to "women of the Word" that was the problem.

THE DANGER OF THE SPIRITED WOMAN

Understanding the centrality of "women of the Word" to Puritan culture enables us to see precisely why "women of the Spirit" were so threatening to that same culture. Women of the Spirit made visible the rather precarious scaffolding on which orthodoxy was erected. They did so not by repudiating the usual social and rhetorical structures that authorized female eloquence, but rather by mimicking them and so exposing the contradictions and subversive potential already present in orthodox Puritan culture.

I have classed Anne Hutchinson as a woman of the Spirit rather than of the Word. Yet in her examination before the General Court of Massachusetts, Hutchinson maintained the orthodoxy of her own behavior by grounding it in the Word. Attacked for holding subversive meetings, she cited the verse in Paul's epistle to Titus, which has already been discussed in connection with the legitimacy of women's teaching. "I conceive there lyes a clear rule in Titus," she responded, "that the elder women should instruct the younger and then I must have a time wherein I must do it."[63] Not unlike Dorothy Leigh, and not unlike the ministers who published the spiritual journals of godly women, Hutchinson went on to find in the imperative to instruct a wider public applicability for her words. When John Winthrop maintained that the female instruction allowed by Titus must not "cross" 1 Cor. 14:34–35 (the rule that women must keep silent in Church), Hutchinson demurred. She refused to limit herself solely to private or domestic instruction: "I do not conceive but that it [the verse from Titus] is meant for some publick times."[64] Hutchinson insisted on interpreting Scripture for herself. Moreover, she accepted contradictions within Scripture and the possibility of varying readings according to varying circumstances. This flexibility, no less than the bare fact of her disagreement with the New England establishment, revealed the potential for divisiveness within a theocracy founded upon the "self-evident" truths of the Word.

Amy Schrager Lang has defined the "problem" of Anne Hutchinson as essentially one of gender transgression: "in its simplest form, the problem was that Hutchinson stepped out of the role the community defined for her."[65] My argument takes a different tack in positioning Hutchinson at the disruptive center of her community—embodying its potentially explosive contradictions. Up to the very moment of her excommunication, Hutchinson was even *commended* for her abilities as a speaker or teacher. In her trial and excommunication from the Boston

Church, which followed her examination by the General Court and subsequent imprisonment, Hutchinson was praised by John Cotton, the most senior minister there, for her gift of instruction, even in the midst of being admonished for having "perverted" that gift. Like Mary Simpson, she was someone especially gifted in "instructing others in the wayes of God":

> I would speake it to Gods Glory you have bine an Instrument of doing some good amongst us. You have bine helpfull to many to bringe them of from thear unsound Grounds and Principles. . . . And the Lord hath indued yew with good parts and gifts fitt to instruct your Children and Servants and to be helpfull to your husband in the Government of the famely. He hath given you a sharpe apprehension, a ready utterance and abilite to expresse yourselfe in the Cause of God.[66]

Like any good woman of the Word, Hutchinson had been an "Instrument" for orthodoxy, reducing others to sound "Grounds and Principles." She had shown her fitness, moreover, for the role of godly mother, reproducing and disseminating the faith among her children and servants. However, she had not used her gifts well. She had spread heresy rather than propagating the Word. Winthrop's cruelly exaggerated account of Hutchinson's miscarriage—he accused her of giving birth to thirty monsters, equal to the number of her "misshapen opinions"— seems to me to betray Winthrop's fear that the reproductive gifts of godly women, on which Puritan culture so much depended, were *always* in danger of going awry.[67] In all of the rather mixed condemnations of Hutchinson, her talent for expressing herself was not the main problem, but was rather the "gift" that had made her useful; however, the very same eloquence that allowed her to do "some good" had also enabled her to propagate her heretical opinions with alarming efficacy.

As a powerfully eloquent woman, whose words had potential for both good *and* evil, Hutchinson dramatized the dangerous proximity of orthodox and heterodox utterance for Puritan culture. I have been suggesting that she was not all that different from other Puritan women. Like Dorothy Leigh, she modulated the domestic instruction that was expected of her into public utterance. Like Mary Simpson, she behaved like a preacher. Yet, in her own time and place, Hutchinson was judged as having gone too far. The minister Hugh Peters (who was later executed in England as a regicide) accused her of exercising authority not her own on three different fronts: "*you have rather bine a Husband than a Wife and a preacher than a Hearer; and a Magistrate than a Subject.*"[68]

Peters's accusation was broad rather than precise. He regarded Hutchinson as a comprehensive menace—a domestic, religious, and political cross-dresser. But what exactly was the threat she posed?

John Winthrop laid out the danger more explicitly at her examination before the General Court. According to him, the "ground work" of her beliefs was "the immediate revelation of the spirit . . . and that is the means by which she hath very much abused the country that they shall look for revelations and are not bound to the ministry of the word."[69] Hutchinson's speaking and teaching were not the problem; rather, it was the status she claimed for that speaking and teaching. Like the Quakers, she understood her words to flow from the present and personal revelations of the Spirit. This, as was also charged against her, gave her utterance the same status as Scripture.[70] Winthrop saw Hutchinson's wayward example undermining the whole country. If her claim to immediate revelation was believed, the interpretive monopoly of the ministry of the word, and so their ability to "set" orthodoxy, would be broken. (In his pronouncement of excommunication, John Wilson also saw Hutchinson's tongue as "a greate Cause of this Disorder." In accusing her of using it not to "set up the Ministry of the Word . . . but to set up her selfe," he, like Winthrop, was indirectly revealing the symbolic power of women's words and example within Puritan culture. The instrumentality attributed to them in the creation of disorder was, in a sense, the obverse of their part in "setting up" order.[71])

Again, the solution to the crisis was not merely a matter of repudiating the Spirit for the Word. If it were that simple, there might not have been a "crisis." But just as Anne Hutchinson found authority for her practices in the Word, so her "orthodox" opponents also allowed a place for the Spirit, and even for revelations. Her most intelligent interrogator, John Cotton, understood just how fine were the distinctions being drawn. Although he felt that "revelations" had been made "uncouth" in everyday speech, he nonetheless accepted that ordinary Christians might still receive them. Significantly, though, he took the precaution of (multiply) grounding them in the Word: not only are personal revelations sanctioned by Scripture, they are most often experienced when the Word is preached or read, and they *never* contradict it.[72]

Cotton's characterization of "lawful" revelations left ample room for another Anne Hutchinson—for once the breathings of the Spirit were allowed and idiosyncratic interpretations of the Word needed no external authorization, but could be referred to "experimental" faith.[73] It is perhaps not surprising that Hutchinson exempted only John Cotton from her blanket condemnation of the New England ministry. To her mind, he alone preached the covenant of grace; the others "had not the seal of the spirit."[74] We should also not be surprised at the determination with which the New England ministry condemned her. Hugh Peters's overdetermined charge of overturned hierarchies was but one crude attempt to reinstate lines of authority which Hutchinson's behavior had rendered so obviously and alarmingly permeable. Her condemnation by the General Court, and then her excommunication from the Boston Church, was a ritual rejection of the very real potential for disorder within New England Congregationalism and within Puritanism more generally. Drawing its energy from experiential faith and dissent, Puritanism needed nonetheless to set and reproduce its own orthodoxies. It also needed "women of the Word" to contribute to the orderly reproduction of orthodox doctrine. Perhaps, in a less direct way, it also needed "women of the Spirit" to contain the ever-present potential for deviation. For Anne Hutchinson—like other godly women who were literally or symbolically excommunicated for following their own lights—was not simply a rebel.[75] Rather, such women were dangerous precisely because they lived out too literally or too single-mindedly the sometimes contradictory beliefs of their own communities. "Women of the Spirit" and "women of the Word" were sisters after all.

NOTES

1. David D. Hall, ed., *The Antinomian Controversy, 1636–1638* (Middletown, Conn.: Wesleyan University Press, 1968), 337. According to Hutchinson, the New England ministry (with the exception of John Cotton) did not make clear enough that assurance of salvation was gained not by outward signs but by inward revelation of a "union" with Christ.

2. For an analysis of how the claim to immediate revelation clinched Hutchinson's conviction, see Edmund S. Morgan, "The Case against Anne Hutchinson," *New England Quarterly* 10 (1937): 647–48.

3. 1 Tim. 2:11–12. (Here and elsewhere, I quote from the 1602 Geneva Bible.) A parallel text is 1 Cor. 14:34–35: "Let your women keepe silence in the Churches: for it is not permitted vnto them to speake, but they ought to be subiect, as also the Law saith. And if they will learne any thing, let them aske their husbands at home: for it is a shame for a woman to speake in the Church."

4. Titus 2:3–4. See Hall, *Antinomian Controversy*, 315–16, and page 201 of this essay.

5. Elizabeth Clinton, *The Countesse of Lincolnes Nurserie* (Oxford, 1622), 16. Puritan tracts regularly urged women to breast feed their own children instead of following the more fashionable practice of sending them out to wetnurses.

6. It was the Presbyterian Thomas Cartwright who argued that the Word

needed to be supplemented by a preaching ministry; his opponent in controversy, John Whitgift, ironically accused him of popery for denying the all-sufficiency of Scripture. See Peter Lake, *Anglicans and Puritans?: Presbyterianism and English Conformist Thought from Whitgift to Hooker* (London: Unwin Hyman, 1988), 21, 38.

7. 2 Cor. 3:6. The Geneva commentary makes clear that Paul is writing primarily about the distinction between the Law (the letter) and the Gospel (the Spirit), but this verse came to be more widely applied, especially to distinguish "dead" formality from the "living" faith of the godly.

8. G. F. Nuttall summarizes the possible positions on Word in relation to Spirit in chapter 1 of *The Holy Spirit in Puritan Faith and Experience* (Oxford: Basil Blackwell, 1946).

9. Hutchinson's interlocutors themselves pointed this out without seeming to recognize the explosive consequences. Responding to her citation of Scripture, Roger Harlakenden, an assistant in the General Court, replied: "I may read scripture and the most glorious hypocrite may read them and yet go down to hell." See Hall, *Antinomian Controversy*, 316.

10. In her essay "'Discourse so Unsavoury': Women's Published Writings of the 1650s," in *Women, Writing, History 1640–1740*, ed. Isobel Grundy and Susan Wiseman (Athens, Ga.: University of Georgia Press, 1992), Elaine Hobby notes the coincidence of the frequent instruction that women be silent in churches and the rarity of the republication of women's religious writings. While agreeing with her general point that "a specific religious embargo was added to the general social pressures for feminine modesty to discourage women from writing such works" (p. 22), I think it therefore all the more interesting that certain works (like the mothers' legacies discussed below) *were* encouraged. Certainly they were frequently republished.

11. W[illiam] W[hately], *A Bride-Bush or Wedding Sermon* (London, 1617), 40.

12. Whately, *Bride-Bush*, 40. William Gouge, *Of Domesticall Duties* (London, 1622), 281–82. Gouge cites both 1 Tim. 2:12 and 1 Cor. 14:34 in the margin. For the parallel passage at 1 Cor. 14:34–35, which is explicitly about women's silence *in the church*, see note 3.

13. Whately, *Bride-Bush*, 11. If the woman fails, Whately goes on to say, "she must procure a Physician for his soule"—in other words, a minister. I find it significant that the wife's persuasive skills are the first recourse.

14. *A Godlie Forme of Householde Government: For the Ordering of Private Families, According to the Direction of Gods Word . . . Gathered by R[obert] C[leaver?]* (London, 1600), 187. Robert Snawsel, *A Looking-Glasse for Married Folkes* (London, 1631), 73. The wife's part in converting the ungodly husband is founded on another Pauline verse (1 Cor. 7:16), which Snawsel renders as, "What knowest thou O wife, whether thou shalt win thy husband?"

15. Cotton Mather, *Ornaments for the Daughters of Zion. Or the Character and Happiness of a Virtuous Woman* (London, 1694), 114. See also note 3.

16. For a wide-ranging discussion of mothers as active agents in their children's religious education, see Kenneth Charlton, *Women, Religion and Education in Early Modern England* (London: Routledge, 1999), 207–21.

17. Gouge, *Domesticall Duties*, 546.

18. *A Godlie Forme of Householde Government*, 61. Gouge used the same image to account for the efficacy of early instruction—"A vessell longest keepeth that sauour with which it first it is seasoned"—giving its origin in Horace ("Epistle to Lollius," ll. 69–70); *Domesticall Duties*, 545.

19. Clinton, *Countesse of Lincolnes Nurserie*, 16, 5.

20. On the popularity of mothers' advice books in the seventeenth century, and on Leigh's work in particular, see Sylvia Brown, *Women's Writing in Stuart England: The Mothers' Legacies of Dorothy Leigh, Elizabeth Joscelin, and Elizabeth Richardson* (Stroud, Gloucestershire, 1999).

21. Ibid., 16, 17–18. In the last passage quoted, Leigh also emphasized the origin of her writing in wifely duty, recounting her husband's dying wish that she take care for the religious instruction of their sons.

22. See Christopher Hill, "The Preaching of the Word," in *Society and Puritanism in Pre-Revolutionary England* (London: Secker and Warburg, 1964), 16–58.

23. Brown, *Women's Writing*, 68. Leigh's interest in keeping up the standards of a good ministry was echoed by Elizabeth Joscelin in her admiration for "true laboringe ministers"; Brown, *Women's Writing*, 110. Joscelin likely modeled her own mother's legacy on Leigh's work.

24. For William Leigh's troubles under Archbishop Laud, see Tom Webster, *Godly Clergy in Early Stuart England: The Caroline Puritan Movement c. 1620–1643* (Cambridge: Cambridge University Press, 1997), 208–9, 247, and Brown, *Women's Writing*, 8–9.

25. Brown, *Women's Writing*, 17.

26. Gouge, *Domesticall Duties*, 568.

27. Brown, *Women's Writing*, 16, 111. Like Leigh, Joscelin may have foreseen a wider readership than her own offspring. Even though she expressed a fear that her writing might "com to the worlds ey and bringe scorn upon my graue," this fear nonetheless could not "stay my hand from expressinge how much I couet thy saluation" (p. 111).

28. In a prefatory epistle to *Milk For Babes*, Abbot wrote to his "honoured Friends," Mary, Lady Baker and Unton, Lady Dering: "I am sure, that if it fall into either of your hands, you will reade, and reade, and make use of it, for the benefit of your good children" (sig. aa6r). For a discussion of domestic catechizing, see Ian Green, *The Christian's ABC: Cate-*

chisms and Catechizing in England c. 1530–1740 (Oxford: Clarendon Press, 1996), 204–29.

29. Dorothy Burch, *A Catechisme of the Severall Heads of Christian Religion . . . Intended Only for Private Use, but now Published for the Good and Benefit of Others* (London, 1646), sigs. A2v–A3r. Sarah Fiske, *A Confession of Faith OR, A Summary of Divinity. Drawn Up By a Young Gentle-Woman, In the Twenty-Fifth Year of her Age* (Boston, 1704). Fiske lived from 1627 to 1692.

30. Burch wrote her (orthodox Calvinist) *Catechisme* to counter the minister of her parish who, because she and other members of the congregation would not follow him in the way "descended from *Rome*," accused them of being "poore ignorant simple people" (sigs. A2r–v).

31. Leigh Brown, wrote that men should be given "the first and chiefe place," while women should "labour to come in the second"; Brown, *Women's Writing*, 24. For her consciousness of violating the usual "custome" or "order" of women, see 22, 24. For some of Leigh's criticisms of popery, see especially 30–31, 45.

32. Richard Baxter, *The Poor Man's Family Book* (London, 1674), 309.

33. Baxter, *Family Book*, 291. It was only after the Glorious Revolution that Dissenters were permitted to catechize in public congregations. See Green, *The Christian's ABC*, 209, and Michael R. Watts, *The Dissenters: From the Reformation to the French Revolution* (Oxford: Clarendon Press, 1985), 249–62.

34. Baxter, *Family Book*, 309.

35. Brown, *Women's Writing*, 22.

36. Examples are: *Elizabeth in her Holy Retirement. An Essay To Prepare a Pious Woman for her Lying In* (Boston, 1710), which Mather published for pious midwives, to give or lend to women preparing for childbirth; *Tabitha Rediviva. An Essay To Describe and Commend the Good Works of A Vertuous Woman* (Boston, 1713), based on a funeral sermon for Elizabeth Hutchinson; and *Memorials of Early Piety Occurring in the Holy Life & Joyful Death of Mrs. Jerusha Oliver* (Boston, 1711), a memoir of Mather's sister, with extracts from her spiritual journal. *Ornaments for the Daughters of Zion* (cited in this paper from the 1694 London edition) was first published in Cambridge, Massachusetts, in 1692.

37. Mather, *Ornaments for the Daughters of Zion*, 5, 6–7. Mather ignored the enunciatory nature of the biblical "writings" he cited; singing, prophesying, and advising could equally be associated with speech. Perhaps Mather considered writing more susceptible than speech to an orderly, and orthodox, inspiration of the Spirit.

38. Ibid., 3.

39. When interrogated by the Inquisition in the course of their travels, the Quakers Katherine Evans and Sarah Cheevers insisted that they had "no new Light, but the same the *Prophets* and *Apostles* bare testimony to." See *A True Account of the Great Tryals and Cruel Sufferings Undergone by*

those Two Faithful Servants of God, Katherine Evans and Sarah Cheevers (London, 1663), 11. In his "Prefatory Poem" to Cotton Mather's *Magnalia Christi Americana*, the minister Nicholas Noyes wrote of the Quakers, or "*Light-within-Enthusiasts*," who "boldly do pretend . . . If *Genesis* were lost, they could retrieve it." *Magnalia Christi Americana, Books I and II*, ed. Kenneth B. Murdock and Elizabeth W. Miller (Cambridge, Mass.: Belknap Press, 1977), 75.

40. Cotton Mather, *Little Flocks Guarded against Grievous Wolves. An Address Unto those Parts of New-England which are most Exposed unto Assaults, from the Modern Teachers of the Misled Quakers* (Boston, 1691), 103, 94–95.

41. Mather, *Ornaments for the Daughters of Zion*, 3.

42. At first John Cotton was one of Hutchinson's defenders (he was the sole exemption in her charge that the New England ministry did not preach the New Covenant). However, at her trial and excommunication from the Boston Church, Cotton not only publicly admonished her but also, more generally, the "Sisters" of the congregation, "many of whom I fear have bine too much seduced and led aside by her." See Hall, *Antinomian Controversy*, 370.

43. Mather, *Ornaments for the Daughters of Zion*, 3.

44. Ibid., *Ornaments*, 4. Mather referred to the catalogues of "*Berovicius, Hottinger*, and *Voetius*." Johan or Jan van Beverwyck was a Dordrecht physician who published *Van de Uitnementhyet des Vrouwelicken Geslachts* ("On the Excellence of the Female Sex") in 1639. Johann Heinrich Hottinger (1620–1667) was a professor of Semitic languages in Heidelberg. Gijsbert Voet was a minister and professor in Utrecht from 1634. In his *Sermoen van de Nutticheydt der Academien*, published in 1636, he argued that learning in women reinforced the path to salvation. For a discussion of van Schurman's contemporary and posthumous reputations, see the essays by de Baar, Rang, and Sneller in *Choosing the Better Part: Anna Maria van Schurman (1607–1678)*, ed. Mirjam de Baar et al., International Archives of the History of Ideas, no. 146 (Dordrecht: Kluwer Academic Publishers, 1996).

45. Louis Jacob, *Elogium* (1646), quoted in de Baar, *Choosing the Better Part*, 5. As well as "prodigy," *monstrum* would also have had our sense of "monster."

46. Mather, *Ornaments for the Daughters of Zion*, 3–4. See also Mather, *Magnalia Christi Americana*, 233.

47. In *Magnalia Christi Americana*, Mather declared that "The Writings of the most Renowned *Anna Maria Schurman,* have come over unto her [i.e., America]" (p. 233). Mather may have been thinking of van Schurman's celebrated 1641 *Dissertatio* in which she examined the question of whether women can be scholars, or perhaps her *Opuscula Hebraea Graeca Latina et Gallica prosaica et metrica*, first published in 1648 (Mather was himself a distinguished linguist). But she was also famous (and for some infamous) for a more "Puritan" work. In 1673 she pub-

lished the *Eukleria,* an autobiographical and theological tract in which she defended her decision to join the separatist community of Jean de Labadie.

48. Mather does not mention Joscelin by name, but the references are unmistakable. In *Elizabeth in her Holy Retirement,* she is referred to as "An Excellent Gentlewoman, who had a Strong presage, which prov'd a True One, of her *Dying* by her Travail" and who wrote a "*Legacy*... for her unborn Child" (p. 5). See also *Ornaments for the Daughters of Zion,* 120. Mather was thinking especially of the beginning of Joscelin's legacy, where she wrote, "Hauinge longe often and earnestly desired of god that I might be a mother to one of his children...": Brown, *Women's Writing,* 109.

49. *Memorials of Early Piety,* 1. Mather cites Collinges's work as *The Life and Death of a true Christian; deciphered in a Sermon, at the Burial of Mary Simpson;* it was published under the alternate title of *Faith & Experience: Or, A Short Narration of the Holy Life and Death of Mary Simpson* (London, 1649) (Wing C5316A).

50. Other published American women writers probably known to (and if known, likely approved by) Mather were Sarah Goodhue, whose posthumously printed book of godly advice, *Valedictory and Monitory Writing,* was printed by Samuel Green in Boston in 1681, and Mary Rowlandson, whose providential narrative of Indian captivity was also printed by Green the following year. Samuel Green was also a major printer of Cotton Mather's works. Green had taken over the printing press of John Foster, the publisher of Anne Bradstreet's *Several Poems.* See Benjamin Franklin V, ed., *Boston Printers, Publishers, and Booksellers: 1640–1800* (Boston, Mass.: Hall, 1980), s.v. "Samuel Green Jr."

51. Mather, *Ornaments for the Daughters of Zion,* 42–43, 29. I have not yet identified the French and Dutch writers, but from the context it seems clear that Mather considered them to have written in the cause of godly reformation. (Was the Frenchwoman perhaps a Huguenot?) "The Boot" was a distinctively Scottish torture, which would shatter the bones of the legs (*Oxford English Dictionary* s.v. "Boot" sb. 3.).

52. John Foxe, *The Third Volume of the Ecclesiasticall Historie: Containing the Acts and Monuments of Martyrs*... (London, 1641), 35.

53. As well as in editions of Foxe, Lady Jane's letter to her sister was reprinted with three other letters in 1554, 1615, 1629, and 1636 (see Short-Title Catalogue [STC] entries under Jane Dudley 7279—82).

54. Foxe, *Third Volume of the Ecclesiasticall Historie,* 35. The book was almost certainly Erasmus's first critical edition of the Greek Testament (1516). For its association with the literature of reformation, see John N. King, *English Reformation Literature: The Tudor Origins of the Protestant Tradition* (Princeton University Press, 1982), 44ff.

55. The marginal note reads: "A 'faithfull' exhortation of the Lady Jane to the Lady Katherine her sister, to read Gods word." See Foxe, *Third Volume of the Ecclesiasticall Historie,* 35.

56. For a discussion of Goad's alterations (which tended toward a strict Calvinism and a promotion of the interests of the ministry), see Sylvia Brown, "The Approbation of Elizabeth Joscelin," *English Manuscript Studies 1100–1700* 9 (2000).

57. Simpson's embedded text was dictated, taken from "her owne mouth" by "a faithfull friend," and probably ultimately shaped by Collinges. See Collinges, *Faith & Experience*, 69.

58. Ibid., 19–20.

59. Ibid., 21.

60. Ibid., 72, 67.

61. Mather published selections from his sister Jerusha's writings, not only because a "small Army of Neighbours" were calling for it, but because he hoped the "*View* of these Dispositions [of piety], may . . . be honoured with some Instrumentality, to produce or maintain the like in others; Especially in Persons of the same *Age* and *Sex*." See Mather, *Memorials of Early Piety*, sig. A2r, 44.

62. Mather, *Memorable Providences, Relating to Witchcrafts and Possessions* (Boston, 1689), 6, 7, 9.

63. Titus 2:3–5. See Hall, *Antinomian Controversy*, 315 and pp. 187–188 of this essay. Charles Hambrick-Stowe points out that Hutchinson's meetings took a recognizable form: it was common to meet to read over and discuss sermon notes (Hutchinson was accused of using this as a pretense for criticizing ministers). See C. E. Hambrick-Stowe, *The Practice of Piety: Puritan Devotional Disciplines in Seventeenth-Century New England* (University of North Carolina Press, 1982), 140. The interrogators at Hutchinson's first trial made clear that in condemning her they were *not* condemning women's meetings, except "in such a way and for such an end that it is to be detested." See Hall, *Antinomian Controversy*, 345.

64. Hall, *Antinomian Controversy*, 316. Winthrop's intervention was meant to point up Hutchinson's public intervention in church matters; for example, her criticism of the ministry.

65. Amy Schrager Lang, *Prophetic Woman: Anne Hutchinson and the Problem of Dissent in the Literature of New England* (Berkeley: University of California Press, 1987), 42.

66. Hall, *Antinomian Controversy*, 371. In his condemnation of Hutchinson, Cotton Mather likewise paid involuntary tribute to her verbal energy: "an haughty carriage, busie spirit, competent wit, and a voluble tongue." Quoted from Rufus M. Jones, *The Quakers in the American Colonies* (New York: Russell & Russell, 1962), 5.

67. John Winthrop, *A Short Story of the Rise, Reign, and Ruine of the Antinomians, Familists & Libertines, that infected the Churches of New England* (London, 1644), sig. **4r.

68. Hall, *Antinomian Controversy*, 383.

69. Ibid., 341.

70. One of the opinions laid to her charge before the General Court was that "her Revelations about futire Events are to be beleeved as well as Scripture because the same holy Ghost did indite both." Hall, *Antinomian Controversy*, 352.

71. Ibid., 384.

72. According to Cotton, revelations for (as opposed to against) the word of God "are such as are breathed by the spirit of God and are never dispensed but in a word of God and according to a word of God . . . being understood in the scripture sense I think they are not only lawful but such as christians may receive and God bear witness to it in his word, and usually he doth express it in the ministry of the word and doth accompany it by his spirit, or else it is in the reading of the word in some chapter or verse and whenever it comes it comes flying upon the wings of the spirit." See Hall, *Antinomian Controversy*, 340.

73. Mary Simpson's "Articles of Faith" contain a hedging similar to John Cotton's attempt to accommodate Spirit and Word. On the way that "God is made *knowne to us*": there is "a way of the *knowledge of God*, by the *Scripture*" and "there is a way of the *knowledge of God* in a more *speciall* way, wherein God [by his *Spirit*] revealeth himselfe to his people *experimentally*, yet according to *Scripture*." Collinges, *Faith & Experience*, 2. "[By his *Spirit*]" is perhaps Collinges' interpolation: another hedging.

74. Hall, *Antinomian Controversy*, 321.

75. One might begin a list of such women with the many female Quakers who were imprisoned for their beliefs, but also include figures like the Fifth Monarchist Anna Trapnel who recounted her arrest during her travels to Cornwall (along with her divinely inspired answers) in *Anna Trapnels Report and Plea* (London, 1654).

Gender and Religion
in England's Catholic Province

Debra Meyers

LORD BALTIMORE, WITH THE HELP OF OTHER recent English Roman Catholic converts, established the province of Maryland in 1634 to provide a safe haven where English subjects could practice their religion freely. The English Roman Catholic settlers brought both their wealth and their Anglican indentured servants to the New World in search of economic opportunities that the increasingly Puritan political climate in England denied them. Besides providing a refuge for Roman Catholics, Lord Baltimore's ecumenical nature enabled Maryland to become a haven for a variety of other religious groups in the seventeenth century; Anglicans, Labadists, Presbyterians, Puritans, Quakers, and other Nonconformists sought to establish themselves as landholders in the province. These religious sects lived in an interactive community in which, I would argue, one distinctive division occurred that influenced the way people behaved—"Predestinarians" versus "Free Will Christians." I have found it useful to group all of the Protestant sects that adhered to John Calvin's notion of predestination—namely, the Particular Baptists, Presbyterians, and Puritans—into the "Predestinarian" category for analysis purposes. And the "Free Will Christians"—made up principally of Anglicans, Quakers, and Roman Catholics—were grouped together because they shared a fundamental belief in freely choosing God and working toward their salvation by performing good deeds. Undeniably, these two groups had very different ideas about gaining eternal salvation, but they also had distinctive thoughts about their womenfolk as well. Predestinarian families limited their females' access to power and authority in the church, family, and society. Free Will

Christians, on the other hand, demonstrated a clear and consistent reliance on the female members of the family who were expected to be productive, active, and influential relations. The Free Will Christians shared a common ethos that both exalted womanhood and permitted women—like Henrietta Maria Neale—to play a central role in the church, society, and their families.

Described by one of her descendants as "the most beautiful and charming girl of her generation" Henrietta Maria Neale began her life as a member of a wealthy Roman Catholic English family that traveled extensively during her youth, finally settling in the English Roman Catholic province of Maryland in 1661.[1] Her parents, Captain James Neale and Ann Gill, both served the crown under Charles I and his Roman Catholic queen Henrietta Maria. As a token of her great affection for her maid of honor and as a symbol of their common devotion to the supreme matriarch, the queen gave Ann an oval pendant encrusted with diamonds and pearls depicting the Assumption of Saint Mary and agreed to be her namesake's godmother. When she reached maturity, Henrietta Maria Neale married Richard Bennett who met an untimely end when he drowned in Wye River, leaving her with an infant son to care for and a plantation to manage. She later married Anglican Philemon Lloyd and bore him several sons and daughters before he died.[2]

Blessed at birth with the wealth and land reminiscent of her godmother, Henrietta Maria Neale entered marriage with considerable power and moved freely within the civic arena as well as the Church. Her activities in the province of Maryland were as varied as they were numerous. For instance, she served as the executrix to her good friend John Londey's estate, legally responsible for distributing his property to his heirs in addition to collecting and paying off his debts.[3] She also built a Roman Catholic chapel on her property and maintained an important position within the Catholic community throughout her life. The Puritans who gained control of Maryland in 1689—as a consequence of the Glorious Revolution in England—recognized her position in the Catholic community and her ability to launch a military campaign against them when they targeted her home in a raid of her storehouse of firearms and ammunition.

Henrietta Maria Neale's power was predicated upon her ability to maintain and control real estate. As with all other adults in this early modern province, Henrietta Maria's status in the community, her church, and her family rested upon her ownership of land. Indeed, she purchased several parcels amounting to more than sixteen hundred acres during her lifetime that added to her already extensive holdings provided by her father and two husbands. Indicative of her authority over her dominion, Henrietta Maria named her tracts of land "Henrietta Maria's Discovery" and "Henrietta Maria's Purchase." As a consequence of her economic status, the priests granted her a voice in church affairs, she was accepted as a trusted associate in legal and business transactions, and she was respected as the family matriarch by her husband, her children, and the generations that followed. As a landholder she entered both her marriages as a financial partner expecting to be consulted by her husbands in decisions regarding land and labor usage and the allocation of property to their children. Additionally, she shared in the disciplining of their children and in decisions regarding their education. When Henrietta Maria wrote her last will and testament, she left her sons *and* her daughters real estate so that they too could secure positions of authority in their community, their church, and their families as marital partners.

Henrietta Maria's vast wealth suggests that the wealthy in colonial Maryland might have been disposed to bequeath females land when they died since the testator had more than enough property to allocate each of the family's children. While exact estate values are difficult to ascertain because the quality of land (rocky, fertile, swamp, meadow, forest) was rarely stipulated, cohorts grouped according to acreage reveal that married men who left wills between 1634 and 1713 did not treat their wives as partners based upon their wealth. John Allford of Dorchester County only left his wife less than one-third of his personal goods, and his two eldest sons inherited the nearly one-thousand-acre estate. Allford could have easily afforded to provide his wife with a small parcel of land, but he chose not to. After burying her husband, the widow probably continued to reside in the home she once shared with her husband. Now, however, she would be under the authority and care of her son who fulfilled his family duty as the new patriarch. Her daily routine probably changed little. She still washed and mended clothes, cooked, and tended the garden and livestock. She probably returned to childcare when grandchildren filled her son's house, or she may have moved into another man's house if she remarried.

Conversely, men with much smaller estates than Allford, like James Cheasum and Peter Mills, chose to acknowledge their wives as partners by allowing them to inherit land. James Cheasum of St. Mary's County owned a meager estate when he died in 1698. Yet, he gave his wife eighty acres, their eldest son sixty, and the other son and daughter fifty acres each. Since it took a minimum of fifty acres in Maryland for a family to live marginally well due to the twenty-one-year fallow required for growing the nutrient-depleting tobacco cash crop, Cheasum's legacy barely met the most basic needs of his family. It is important to point out that he could have given the land to the eldest son to preserve the estate, but instead Cheasum made sure that each of his living children—two sons and a daughter—had a piece of property on which to settle and begin new families of their own. Moreover, his wife and not his eldest son received the largest tract, indicating her important position in the family. Likewise, Peter Mills held a medium-sized estate of less than five hundred acres and he also made sure that his wife and each of his children, regardless of gender, had a piece of property to call their own. Both Cheasum and Mills treated their wives and daughters similarly to their sons; land was not the private domain of the male heads of the household. As a landholder, a widow with grown children could live by herself and not have to look to her eldest son for her upkeep or be forced to remarry in order to avoid living under her son's roof. If she had small children she usually managed her children's real estate along with her own property until they were old enough to leave home. Widows who controlled the children's holdings until they reached maturity could demand cooperation from their offspring as an authority figure.

The desire to provide land to both sons and daughters was not just a notion of elites that a few women like Henrietta Maria Neale could put into practice. Women and men of modest means willed land to daughters as well as to sons. Although this holds true for the vast majority of landholders who left wills between 1634 and 1713 (N=3190), approximately one out of every four testators denied females the freedom and responsibility of running their own estates, as did John All-ford, indicating an adherence to a patriarchal family model where men controlled the family's land, labor, and family decisions and where women were dependents.

If the size of one's estate did not determine the authority women exercised in the household economy, we might look to religion as a deciding factor. Interestingly, Allford revealed his Calvinist belief in pre-destination in his will, while Cheasum and Mills (like Henrietta Maria) professed their Roman Catholicism in theirs. Indeed, we find that a family's propensity to adhere to either the partnership or patriarchal model was tied closely with a family's religious affiliation.[4] On the one hand, Predestinarian families—including Particular Baptists, Presbyterians, and Puritans—tended to foster patriarchal family relations as we saw in Allford's treatment of his wife and sons. The powerful authority figure of the father assumed, for all intents and purposes, the sole responsibility for the welfare of all of his dependents, including servants, children (of his own flesh as well as those placed in his care), and of course his wife. When sons reached adulthood they assumed their rightful place as landholding patriarchs at the head of a household. Females, then, would have little need to inherit land since their family duties centered on childcare, food preparation, and washing. And as a landless family member, a wife exerted little if any authority in her family. A wife's position within a Predestinarian family was less authoritative than that of her Free Will Christian counterpart (composed of Arminian Anglicans, Catholics, and Quakers) when we consider that one out of ten Predestinarian husbands who left wills during the seventeenth century denied their widows the custody of their children if the wife chose to remarry. Free Will Christian husbands chose not to act in this way. This violation of a widow's natural right to her own children underscored a woman's subservient place within the Predestinarian family. In denying a widow the right to her children, a Predestinarian man believed that he was protecting his very young children, particularly his sons, from an unknown stepfather and his power as the family's new patriarch. Predestinarian men must have felt that it was their duty to protect their dependents from the uncertainties of life even after their deaths and they took this duty very seriously. These patriarchs cared for their dependents posthumously by naming male guardians (close friends or relatives) to look after their wives and minor children and the land the boys would eventually inherit, thus reinforcing the Predestinarians' notion of patriarchy.

William Crosse's preference for male heirs regardless of their blood relation to him, over his own daughters, succinctly illustrates the dynamics of the typical English Predestinarian family in Maryland. Crosse died in 1677, leaving his small estate to his only son William and a stepson. William received the bulk of the real estate, the stepson a small tract, yet his three daughters and wife shared only in the personal estate.[5] This marked propensity of the Predestinarians to support the patriarchal model reflected the fundamental cultural view of a woman as the bearer and nurturer of sons rather than an authority figure within the family. Maryland Predestinarians tended to embrace the patriarchal familial relationships presented in the English didactic tracts, such as *Several Discourses and Characters address'd to the Ladies of the Age: Wherein the Vanities of the Modish Women are Discovered.* The preponderance of seventeenth-century English marriage manuals, such as *Several Discourses and Characters address'd to the Ladies of the Age*, which called for a strong patriarch to head families, suggests that the Predestinarian families in Maryland adhered to an English ideal. In these volumes, husbands were advised to demand obedience from their complacent wives in order to enjoy a blissful marriage, just as they should demand it from other subordinate dependents, such as their children or servants. A husband, in every way innately his wife's superior, would decide all things and not tolerate insubordination from any of his charges for he alone knew what was best for the family, both collectively and individually. His ability to lead the family through the troubled waters of life also carried with it both the responsibility for the family's success as well as its failures. Because of this burden, husbands needed unquestioning obedience from their wives. Women who stepped out of this role threatened the well-being of their families. The author of *Several Discourses and Characters address'd to the Ladies of the Age* chastised English women for their general misbehavior including an entire chapter devoted to "Wives who usurp a governing Power over their Husbands, which is now so common, as it is almost become the general grievance of the Nation." He condemned wives "for usurping and practising and unlawful governing power over" their husbands. These disorderly women were acting "contrary to Magna Charta, and the fundamental Law of this Kingdom, and all other Laws whatsoever . . . both divine and human."[6] Consequently, a wife who acted illegally wielding authority within her family was going against human nature as well as English law and could, by implication, cause the social order ultimately to collapse. According to this prescriptive literature the ideal mode of behavior for a wife was to be subservient and obedient to her husband. Put in more universal terms, patriarchy was to inform the structure of the larger society that found its roots in the patriarchal family. If every master of the house could keep his dependents under his omniscient control, then social order would reign at the state level and all would be right in the world.

On the other hand, Free Will Christian families favored a more equitable distribution of family property suggesting that husbands and wives thought of themselves as marital partners. In these families, husbands and wives shared the responsibilities of child rearing and managing the agricultural business that would (hopefully, but not always) bring financial security to the immediate family and their heirs. Free Will Christian husbands consulted their wives in the important matter of dealing with the dispersal of family wealth, in the matter of substantive donations to the church, managing the family's property and servants, in addition to working together to raise and educate their children. Free Will Christian husbands and wives shared the work, risks, failures, and profits involved in running their estates and raising their children.

After a husband died, a Free Will Christian widow continued to exert authority over her children and the family business for she inherited much of the family's land. The widow's prerogative enabled her to manage her labor force more effectively. Generally, widows controlled their children's labor until their daughters were sixteen and their sons twenty-one. In addition to any servants or slaves a widow might employ she also garnered additional labor from her adult offspring. Children—both sons and daughters—eager to start families often agreed to continue to work for their mother if she allowed them to settle on the piece of property promised to them in their father's will.

Illustrative of the Free Will Christian husband's propensity to grant his wife considerable latitude in managing her own labor force, James Bowling did not wait until he died to place some of the family's most valuable assets in his wife's name. In recognition of his wife's contribution to the family's prosperity, Bowling gave his partner a "Deed of Gift" on September 5, 1684. He wrote: "for and in consideration of the Real Love[,] goodwill and great Affection that I beare unto my dear and Loveing wife Mary Bowling Do by those presents freely and Absolutely give . . . ffour slaves [namely] Ann a Malatta[,] Sara a Negroe and Elizabeth a Negroe all females together with a male Negroe named George all Children to a Negroe woman Called Mary to have and to hold the said foure slaves togither with their Increase."[7] There can be little doubt that Mary Bowling exerted her authority within her family—as the owner of her own labor force—just as she did over her new property. Moreover, James Bowling named Mary his sole executrix after his death with authority to distribute the legacies that he had outlined in his will. Significantly, she was left the family's dwelling plantation to manage for the rest of her life. Mary had a good deal of experience managing the family's assets while her husband was alive and thus was prepared to handle the estate after his death.

The notion of a marital partnership as exhibited by the Free Will Christian families in Maryland was alive and well in England too. In 1657 Edward Reyner published his marriage manual *Considerations Concerning Marriage, The Honour, Duties, Benefits, Troubles of it*, based on his reading of the Bible. He explained that the Bible cautioned potential marriage partners not to enter "rashly into it, but advisedly with due consideration for the choice of a fit yoke-fellow." These "yoke-fellows" ought to be equally matched in their religious fervor and share a common faith. Their compatibility was so important that he warned men and women that they must not "marry unequally . . . as a wise man to a foolish woman; or a vertuous woman to a profane wicked man" for it would be like shackling "the living to the dead; which was the cruellest Death invented by Tyrants, to make the living languish and die by the company of the dead." Having chosen a mate carefully, a wife could expect to be her husband's "yoke-fellow that stands on even ground with him." This implied that the partners were near equals and as such a husband and wife must respect each other, for a "wife is his companion," not his slave. This partnership, however, carried with it a tremendous burden as well. Reyner explained that a wife must "bear one end [of the yoke], and draw equally with her husband." As beasts of burden working as one unit, the couple faced the onerous responsibility of managing their property and their children. Thus, as yoke-fellows, husbands and wives shared equally in the economic and social risks and benefits that would befall them as partners. Reyner drew his inspiration for these thoughts from his Anglican belief system. These equitable unions were predicated upon the fact that "souls have no Sexes; and as they are in Christ they are both equal, male and female are in him all one."[8]

We can find evidence that Maryland women accepted these two marriage models in the wills that they left. Maryland clerks registered 211 female testaments between 1634 and 1713. Since women (and men) had little time to record their thoughts and daily routines in diaries, and few other documents expressing distinctly female views have survived, these wills provide us with an invaluable source for recovering the voices of previously ignored historical participants. Here these women reveal their most ardent final requests, desires, and beliefs. In order to assess their importance, however, we need to address the following: who were these women and why did they write wills? Most importantly, can they be identified as Predestinarians or Free Will Christians, and, if so, do distinctive patterns appear for the two groups? Were Predestinarian women relatively content with their positions as obedient wives under the control of powerful patriarchs, and did Free Will Christian women embrace the responsibility and duties associated with their demanding yoke-fellow positions? Or, on the contrary, did these women choose to rectify what they perceived were injustices by writing wills that allocated property in a different way than their male counterparts would have?

Women made up approximately one-third of the population, yet their wills make up less than 7 percent of the total wills left between 1634 and 1713 in Maryland. Why did so few women write wills? When women wanted legally enforceable contracts to ensure equitable distributions of their estates, they frequently persuaded their husbands to write a family will in order to provide for godchildren, grandchildren, other relatives, and children from a previous marriage. These family wills, by entailing much of the real estate, maintained the legacy for at least one subsequent generation. This fact helps to explain, in part, why there are so few females writing wills for the time period in Maryland.

Women who had their own wills drawn up did so for three reasons: to ensure their children's estates when considering remarriage, to provide a new executor and guardian for children when a father's will had not foreseen the early demise of his wife, or in order to circumvent intestate laws and customs by bequeathing property to extended and spiritual family members. Three out of four women who wrote wills did so after 1683, which can be attributed to their greater numbers in the province. Additionally, the majority of these women wrote their wills while sick "and in Danger of Death," just as the men in the province had.[9] The wills form a fairly even distribution across the oldest counties, namely, Anne Arundel, Calvert, Charles, St. Mary's, and Talbot. Thus female will writing did not tend to be a regional phenomenon. One hundred and three female estates provided enough information to estimate acreage cohorts, thus enabling us to confirm that women who wrote wills generally had significant estates to bequeath. Over one-third of these women owned more than five hundred acres of land and most of the others owned at least two hundred acres. A few women who left wills owned no real estate at all.

Using religion as an important variable, we find that Predestinarian and Free Will Christian women wrote wills that mirrored those of their male counterparts.[10] Significantly, Predestinarian women whose husbands were still alive never left wills. Since much of their marital responsibilities revolved around producing healthy sons, they left their families' financial affairs in the hands of the male head of the household. It was the husband's job to manage and maintain all of the family's property. If a wife brought real estate to the marriage, the land became her husband's property and it was his responsibility to allocate these resources to his heirs when he died.[11] If a Predestinarian wife died before her husband, the little personal property that she claimed as her own—such as clothing, cookware, dishes—might have been given to other women or to her daughters when she knew she was not going to recover from a grave illness. Having no debts of her own or significant property to bequeath, a Predestinarian wife could settle her affairs with a simple verbal request on her deathbed. And if she failed to make her last wishes known, we might assume that her protector (her husband) would give her cherished belongings such as gloves, petticoats, shoes, and so on to the appropriate heir.

One out of every four of the Predestinarian women who wrote wills was single, and the remaining three-quarters were widows. Yet we should remember that few widowed or single Predestinarian women in Maryland had a pressing need to write wills, hence their small numbers. Most Predestinarian women possessed only meager estates in personal goods, and their husbands allocated any dower they brought to the marriage to their eldest sons. Those women who felt a need to write a will in order to name a guardian for their children or an executor for their husband's will often disbursed the household items, slaves, and clothes to their children and other relatives, as did Widow Ann Smith and Widow Elizabeth Eareckson.[12] In the small number of cases where a Predestinarian female held real estate in her own name, she gave the responsibility of the administration of her estate to a male executor and the land to male friends or relatives, as did James Browne's widow Ann and the Widow Mary Aldry.[13] And since these widows believed that land should return to its proper place in the male domain, daughters and other females mentioned in these widows' wills nearly always received personal goods in the form of clothing, cookware, dishes, and livestock rather than land.

Thus Predestinarian widows concurred with their husbands and sons that females ought to inherit personal goods rather than realty and that males, in general, ought to have control over real estate as executors and administrators. Predestinarian women's lack of authority in controlling the families' most valuable property—land—indicates their overall lack of authority and power within the family. Moreover, individual Predestinarian women's pervasive reluctance to leave this property to their female heirs indicates that they too believed that the patriarchal family model was both natural and desirable.

Interestingly, Predestinarian women were much more likely than other women to have at least one female witness sign their wills. Nearly half of all their wills have such signatures (or "marks" in the case of women who could not write their names) compared to less than one-third of the Free Will Christians. This is significant when we consider that women only constituted roughly one-third of the population at this time. Why might Predestinarian women be more dependent upon other women? Since most of these testators were gravely ill when they wrote their wills, we can assume that other women in the community—relatives and friends—came to comfort and nurse the dying women. When it became apparent that a sick woman was not going to recover, these women in attendance served as witnesses to the testator's dying wishes. But why did women come to the homes of sick Predestinarian females in greater numbers than in other households? This pervasive reliance on other females might suggest a more vibrant female network than what we find in other households in Maryland. Could Predestinarian women have sought out female companionship more often than their Free Will Christian counterparts because of their subordinate positions within the family? It is quite possible that their lack of authority and power in a man's world may have encouraged them to seek out other females as equitable companions whose shared status served to bind them together in meaningful and supportive relationships.

Free Will Christian women tell a very different story. Their testaments indicate that they shared their male counterparts' ideas about marriages between yoke-fellows. A man and woman were joined together as a working team, managing their servants, children, and property. As partners they shared the work and risks associated with running a plantation during the early years of settlement faced with soft tobacco prices, the high costs of purchasing and providing for servants who might run away, and unpredictable weather. Simultaneously, some partners enjoyed the benefits too.

In a Free Will Christian family, status and power within a family had more to do with age than gender. In a society in which death often diminished the size of a family quite quickly, the older a child got, the more likely he or she would survive to become an adult. Consequently, birth order rather than gender often determined how much of the family's wealth would be left to a particular child. Older daughters, like the eldest sons, generally received sizable portions of the real estate, while younger siblings received considerably smaller shares. And these daughters grew up and became wives who brought their sizable estates to the new union. Significantly, these women tended to maintain control over their natal estates while they were married.[14]

Thus, we are not surprised to find Free Will Christian wives exerting their authority within the family as manifest in their ability and inclination to write a last will and testament. And since Free Will Christian husbands thought of their wives as partners with land of their own to control, approximately one of every five Free Will Christian women leaving a will was married. While Predestinarian married women had no reason to write wills, some Free Will Christian wives who owned and controlled significant parcels of land during their marriage wanted to bequeath their separate estates in their own wills when they died. Husbands readily accepted this action as a matter of course in these families or we would not see the discrepancy between the Predestinarian and the Free Will Christian wives leaving wills.

Like their Predestinarian counterparts, nearly three-quarters of all Free Will Christian female testators were widows and they used their wills in such a fashion that we are inclined to accept the notion that they held authority in their families when their husbands were alive and continued to do so after they became widows. Free Will Christian women tended to hold real estate in addition to personal goods throughout their lives. Widow Sarah Harris thought of herself as an "unproffitable servant of God" and wrote her will while "in perfect health and memory (praised be God) yet considering the certainty of death and the uncertainty of the time when it shall please Almighty God to call mee doe willingly and with a free heart render my Spiritt into the hands of my Lord God and Creator." Sarah had outlived at least three husbands—Walter Jenkins, Thomas Brookes, and Mr. Harris. She indicated in her will that Walter Jenkins had purchased the one-hundred-acre tract that she willed to her grandson John Ingram. Sarah bequeathed her daughter Hanna and her husband Christopher Goodhand the three-hundred-acre parcel purchased by the late Thomas Brookes. Additionally, she named her daughter and son-in-law joint executors.[15] Sarah assumed that the business acumen of her male and female heirs was largely equal. Therefore, she gave her daughter the responsibility for administering her will and the ownership and management of her own real estate. Sarah represents a typical pattern for Free Will Christian women of naming female and male beneficiaries in equal numbers. And they gave their daughters, granddaughters, and other females real estate as often as they gave it to male relatives, indicating their marked propensity for following the typical male testamentary patterns for Free Will Christians.[16] Thus, Free Will Christian males and females thought that the ability to manage real estate had little to do with gender.

A woman's propensity to follow the Predestinarian patriarchal or the Free Will Christian yoke-fellow inheritance patterns also determined whether or not she named female executors to her will. Almost without exception, Predestinarian women did not entrust the administration of their estates to females, while nearly one out of every five Free Will Christian women found female executrixes desirable, as did Blanch (Stanton Burle) Ryder. Blanch's first husband appears to have died intestate, owning at least four hundred acres.[17] Blanch inherited this estate and then married Thomas Ryder who died childless in 1703 leaving his wife executrix along with his entire estate to use during her life.[18] There is no way of knowing just how efficiently Blanch managed her growing estate, but she certainly cared enough about preserving the estate for future generations by writing a will that distributed her lands and goods to the people she thought most competent to act in her stead. The widow wrote her will when she took ill in 1707, asking that "all my Just Debts that I owe of Right be paid & Discharged."[19] Blanch named her son John and daughter Elizabeth Stanton "my whole & Sole [executors] of all the residue of my Estate after my Debts are Sattisfyed."[20] With this act, she gave her young, unmarried daughter a great deal of responsibility as joint executrix along with her brother. Blanch regarded both her son and daughter as yoke-fellows sharing responsibilities, in the words of Edward Reyner, "on even ground" expecting both to "bear one end [of the yoke], and draw equally." And if Blanch was willing to assign such responsibility to her children, we might assume that she thought that male/female partnerships were both normal and natural. On the contrary, Predestinarian women's reluctance to offer such positions of authority to their female relatives and friends attests to their belief that women—as subordinates beneath a patriarch—ought not to be in control of real estate or be responsible for its distribution.

Historians have suggested that, as a group, women tended to be more inclined to make charitable bequests than were men.[21] Yet this was not the case in seventeenth-century Maryland where both men and women left parts of their estates to the poor or their church approximately 7 percent of the time. Differences did exist, however. If the Predestinarian and Free Will Christian cohorts are considered, we see that roughly one out of every six Free Will Christian males and females left something to the poor, priests, or the church, while only one out of every thirty-three male Predestinarians did so. Strikingly, Predestinarian women never left portions of their estate to the poor or their church. This discrepancy between the two religious groups can be accounted for in large measure by the two cohorts' distinctive theological tenets. Predestinarians did not have to do "good works" to gain their salvation; their destinies were already determined. Long before they were born, God had decided who would be saved and gain eternal peace in heaven and who would be damned to an eternal life in hell. There was nothing human beings could do to change their destinies. Good works, such as leaving money to the poor or the church in a will, would not alter a person's condition as one of the damned or one of the elect and chosen saints. However, both the Roman Catholic and Arminian Anglican churches encouraged traditional requiems and a gift remembrance of the poor at the time of one's death. Quakers also were inspired by the Holy Spirit to do good deeds for the preservation of their souls. All of these Free Will Christian testators believed their material contributions to the poor or their religious groups assisted their entrance into heaven since eternal life in God's presence was predicated upon one's diligence in doing good works on earth. Thus, we are not surprised to see that the female benefactors in Maryland were Arminian Anglicans, Quakers, and Roman Catholics, and not Predestinarians.[22]

While religious ideology contributed to Free Will Christians' inclination to bequeath property to the poor or the church, other factors also played a role. Roman Catholic men often bequeathed their wives large portions of the family's real estate for life. Occasionally, husbands gave their wives land in freehold (in addition to movable goods) and that presented them with the opportunity to divest the property as they thought just.[23] This provided Roman Catholic women—who made up the bulk of female benefactors—with the means to make charitable donations. Unlike their Predestinarian counterparts, Roman Catholic women who left money to the church did so primarily to ensure the salvation of their souls, as did Elizabeth Diggs, Jane Green, Elizabeth Lindsey, Henrietta Maria Lloyd, Ann Neale, and Frances Sayer.[24] Additionally, Quakers like Elizabeth Balding and Arminians like Elizabeth Rigbye also bequeathed portions of their estates for the benefit of the poor of their communities or the support of their church.[25] All of the female benefactors were women of means; 60 percent had no living children when they died. Thus, we are not surprised to see that wealthy landholding Free Will Christian women without living children were much more likely to be charitable than other women.

The wills Marylanders left between 1634 and 1713 suggest a connection between religious groups and their adherence to either the yoke-fellow or patriarchy family models. It is beyond the scope of this essay to describe, in detail, the cause and effect relationships between the Predestinarian and Free Will Christians' theology and their propensity to adhere to the patriarchal or partnership models. However, some of the behavior toward women practiced by the Predestinarians and the Free Will Christians suggests possible connections between religious beliefs and family structures in seventeenth-century Maryland that can be briefly sketched here.

In addition to a common belief in the importance of "good works" for their entrance into heaven, Free Will Christians also shared a fundamental belief in female authority figures within the church. Unlike Predestinarian Anne Hutchinson and other women who were banished from John Winthrop's Puritan colony for propagating their beliefs, and the victims of witch-hunts in Puritan New England, English Roman Catholic women were encouraged to act as spiritual leaders by establishing religious orders. Moreover, the seventeenth century saw the remarkable emergence of the Virgin Mary to a status equivalent to that of Jesus Christ as the "*alter Christus*" in English Roman Catholic devotional literature, which might signify a magnified role for Catholic women in general in the early modern period.[26] Arminians joined the Roman Catholics in their embrace of female saints acting as intercessors on their behalf and paying them respect in their daily observances of the religious calendar that Catholics and Arminians shared. These powerful female intercessors of the English Arminians and Roman Catholics provided positive female role models; confident, assertive women were not witches as in Puritan New England, they were saints. Similarly, the Quakers extended virtual religious equality to their womenfolk by expecting them to serve as ministers during Sunday services and in converting others outside their community. The Free Will Christians also encouraged the inculcation of children at home by women, thus firmly cementing women's positions in the propagation of doctrine for the future welfare of the denominations.[27]

Certainly the most significant fact gleaned from the study of women's wills is the acceptance of patriarchal or partnership family models by Predestinarian and Free Will Christian women. The continuity between male and female will-writing Predestinarians on the one hand, and their Free Will Christian counterparts on the other, suggests that men and women reflected the distinctive gender roles associated with their particular religious belief systems. The few Predestinarian women who inherited real estate—with the right to dispose of it as they thought "fitting & convenient"—bequeathed it to males in their wills. Provided with what we might consider an opportunity to rectify any perceived injustice to their daughters, granddaughters, and nieces, these women, through their bequest patterns, tell us that they wished to sustain the Predestinarian patriarchal social order. Both Predestinarian men and women constructed and upheld the patriarchal social order. Conversely, Free Will Christian husbands and wives embraced the notion that marriage ought to be a partnership between yoke-fellows. They believed that men and women should share equally the work, risks, and benefits of raising a family, in addition to managing their real estate and labor force. Consequently, husbands regularly bequeathed their widows land and labor so that they could continue the authoritative position in the family that they had held while their husbands were alive. Similarly, when Free Will Christian women wrote wills, they too accepted and reinforced the notion that both males and females ought to control property. Religion, then, played an important part in the lives of early modern English men and women in Maryland.

NOTES

1. Francis McGrath, *Pillars of Maryland* (Richmond, Va.: Dietz Press, 1950), 88.

2. Colonel Lloyd served the province in several military expeditions including one against the Indians on the Eastern Shore. He also served Talbot County as a Burgess beginning in 1671 until he died. Christopher Johnston, "Lloyd Family," *Maryland Historical Magazine* 7 (1912): 423–24.

3. Maryland Hall of Records (hereafter MHR), Prerogative Court Wills, book 2, p. 260 (1693). (Hereafter cited as "Wills.")

4. For more information on how these two cohorts were determined, see Debra Meyers, "Religion, Women and the Family in Maryland, 1634–1713" (Ph.D. diss., University of Rochester, 1997), 143–49.

5. Wills, 5:325 (1677).

6. Anonymous, *Several Discourses and Characters address'd to the Ladies of the Age: Wherein the Vanities of the Modish Women are Discovered* (London, 1689), 53, 58–59.

7. MHR, Provincial Court Deeds WRC #1 f. 300 Deed of Gift dated September 5, 1684.

8. Edward Reyner, *Considerations Concerning Marriage, The Honour, Duties, Benefits, Troubles of it* (London, 1657), preface, 5, 7, 8, 11, 12, and 18.

9. Wills, 1:536 (1664).

10. Michael Graham suggested in "Meetinghouse and Chapel" that Catholic women inherited more than their dower more often than non-Catholics in the late seventeenth century. The data collected here argues that the vast majority of Free Will Christian women received more than dower rights. Graham further argued that both Catholic and Quaker women maintained prominent roles in the culture. Graham, "Meetinghouse and Chapel," in *Colonial Chesapeake Society*, ed. Carr, Morgan, and Russo (Chapel Hill: University of North Carolina Press, 1988), 271–73. However, the data presented here suggests that all three Free Will Christian groups respected the right of women to distribute their own property.

11. This was not the case for all women in Maryland. See Debra Meyers, "The Civic Lives of White Women in Seventeenth-Century Maryland," *Maryland Historical Magazine* 94 (1999): 322–25.

12. Wills, 6:29 (1688) (Smith) and Wills, 4:37 (1683) (Eareckson).

13. Wills, 7:377 (1697) (Ann Browne) and Wills, 6:239 (1697) (Aldry).

14. Debra Meyers, "The Civic Lives of White Women," 322–25.

15. Wills, 4:157 (1681).

16. For more biographical information, see Debra Meyers, "Verlinda Stone," in *Chronology of Women Worldwide: People, Places and Events That Shaped Women's History*, ed. Lynne Brakeman (Detroit, Mich.: Gale Publishers, 1996), 113.

17. Peter Coldham's *Settlers of Maryland, 1679–1700* lists Stephen Burle's four hundred acres in 1683 as "Burle's Park and Locust Thicket" in Anne Arundel County. Coldham, *Settlers of Maryland 1679–1700* (Baltimore, Md.: Genealogical Publishing, 1995), 24.

18. Wills, 11:403 (1703).

19. By the time she died, Blanch had five children: Stephen, John, a mar-

ried daughter Sarah, Blanch Wharton, and Elizabeth Stanton. Assuming Blanch influenced Ryder's will, all of Blanch's children stood to inherit Ryder's real estate when Blanch died, with the exception of Stephen. In her own will, she left her eldest son Stephen Burle a single shilling indicating either a wish to disinherit him, or, possibly, that he had received his share when his father died. Presumably owning enough real estate to support a family, Stephen married Sarah Gosling in 1709. Robert Barnes, ed., *Maryland Marriages, 1634–1777* (Baltimore: Genealogical Publishing, 1975), 26.

20. Wills, 12:14 (1707).

21. For instance, Suzanne Lebsock in *The Free Women of Petersburg* suggests that white women from 1784 to 1860 were more likely than men to free their slaves and leave money to orphans due to their divergent value systems. Lebsock, *The Free Women of Petersburg: Status and Culture in a Southern Town, 1784–1860* (New York: Norton, 1983), 137 and 241.

22. Forty percent of the men leaving charitable bequests were Roman Catholics.

23. Holding land in freehold allowed the owner to sell, mortgage, or otherwise alienate the land as he or she saw fit.

24. Wills, 13:96 (1705), 6:380 (1699), 5:342 (1676), 7:252 (1697), and 7:378 (1697). Elizabeth Darnell Diggs's epitaph can be found in Helen Ridgeley, *Historic Graves of Maryland* (Baltimore, Md.: Genealogical Publishing, 1967, original printed in 1908), 63. Elizabeth was the daughter of Col. Henry Darnell and his wife Ellinor Hatton Brooke. She had married Gentleman Edward Diggs and she was buried at St. Thomas graveyard at Chapel Point in Charles County. A reconstruction of the Darnell family's home plantation can be seen in Upper Marlborough, Maryland, today. Widow Frances Sayer of Talbot County gave five priests each 10 pounds sterling. Already having a chapel on her property, she ordered her executor to build an additional thirty-foot brick one over the joint grave for her and her husband: Wills, 6:166 (1698). Ann Neale, mother of Henrietta Maria Lloyd, was the heiress of Benjamin Gill who married Captain James Neale in 1636 and they traveled extensively with their many children to Amsterdam, Spain, and Portugal for personal business and as the proprietor's agent. Upon their return to Maryland in 1661, the family resided at "Wollaston Manor" and James was made a council member. Katharine Silverson, *Taney and Allied Families: A Genealogical Study with Biographical Notes* (New York: The American Historical Society, 1935), 228–37, and also McGrath, *Pillars of Maryland*, 74–90).

25. Wills, 2:217 (1687) and 11:10 (1700).

26. Patrick Malloy, "A Manuel of Prayers, 1583–1850" (Ph.D. diss., University of Notre Dame, 1991), 132.

27. Jo Ann McNamara, in "Wives and Widows in Early Christian Thought," looks at the effect of Christianity on women and finds that it was a positive change, a victory for women over Roman paganism.

She argues that women had increased rights and freedom of choice after the emergence of Christianity in late antiquity. A widow could only remain unmarried if past childbearing age in Roman law, but Christianity actually frowned on remarriage, thus freeing any woman of the inherent risks of childbearing. (McNamara, "Wives and Widows in Early Christian Thought," *International Journal of Women's Studies* 2 (1979): 575–92. Rodney Stark concurs with McNamara's provocative thesis, arguing that most of the early Christians were women who found the social implications of the new religion liberating. Stark, *The Rise of Christianity: A Sociologist Reconsiders History* (Princeton: Princeton University Press, 1996). However, many feminists see Christianity as an oppressive force, particularly Catholicism and its hierarchical structure, presumably producing a family structure based on women in a subordinate position. See, for instance, Margaret Miles, *Desire and Delight: A New Reading of Augustine's Confessions* (New York: Crossroad, 1992), and idem, *Carnal Knowing: Female Nakedness and Religious Meaning in the Christian West* (New York: Vintage Books, 1991); Robert Orsi, *The Madonna of 115th Street: Faith and Community in Italian Harlem, 1880–1950* (New Haven, Conn.: Yale University Press, 1985); and Elaine Pagels, *Adam, Eve, and the Serpent* (New York: Vintage Books, 1989).

CONTRIBUTORS

SYLVIA BROWN is Assistant Professor in the Department of English, University of Alberta, Canada. She has edited *Women's Writing in Stuart England: The Mothers' Legacies of Dorothy Leigh, Elizabeth Joscelin, and Elizabeth Richardson*, and is currently at work on a book about gender and writing in Puritan culture.

KATHRYN BURNS is Assistant Professor of History in the Department of History at the University of North Carolina at Chapel Hill. She works on colonial Latin America, and her most recent study is *Colonial Habits: Convents and the Spiritual Economy of Cuzco, Peru*.

MARYBETH CARLSON is an Assistant Professor in the Department of History at the University of Dayton. Her research focuses on working women and on poor relief in early modern Holland. She is currently completing a manuscript on domestic service in seventeenth- and eighteenth-century Rotterdam.

PATRICIA CRAWFORD teaches history at the University of Western Australia. Her most recent books are *Women and Religion in Early Modern England*, *Women in Early Modern England, 1550–1720* with Sara Mendelson, and *Women's Worlds in Seventeenth-Century England: A Sourcebook* with Laura Gowing.

SUSAN E. DINAN is Assistant Professor of History at Long Island University's C. W. Post campus. She has published articles in *Confraternities and Catholic Reform in Italy, France and Spain*, and *Variety and Vitality: Papers in Honor of John O'Malley, S. J.* Her current research includes a book manuscript on the Daughters of Charity in early modern France.

WILLIAM HENRY FOSTER III holds a Ph.D. in History from Cornell University. He is currently a Research Fellow at the McNeil Center for Early American Studies at the University of Pennsylvania where he is preparing a manuscript entitled *The Captors' Narrative: Catholic Women and Their Puritan Men on the Early North American Frontier*.

JOYCE D. GOODFRIEND is Professor of History at the University of Denver. She is the author of *Before the Melting Pot: Society and Culture in Colonial New York City, 1664–1730* and *The Published Diaries and Letters of American Women: An Annotated Bibliography,* as well as numerous essays on the colonial Dutch and early New York history. In 1999 she held an Andrew W. Mellon Senior Fellowship at the John Carter Brown Library of Brown University.

ELIZABETH A. LEHFELDT is Assistant Professor of History at Cleveland State University. Her publications include articles in *Renaissance Quarterly, Sixteenth Century Journal, Journal of Social History,* and *Archive for Reformation History.* She is currently working on a project examining gender and political legitimacy during the reign of Isabel of Castile.

DEBRA MEYERS is Assistant Professor of American History at the Ohio State University. Her most recent article entitled "The Civil Lives of White Women in Seventeenth-Century Maryland" appeared in the *Maryland Historical Magazine* (1999). Currently she is completing a transatlantic study of English women, families, and religion.

ALLYSON M. POSKA is Associate Professor of History at Mary Washington College in Fredericksburg, Virginia. Her first book, *Regulating the People: The Catholic Reformation in Seventeenth-Century Spain,* examined the impact of the Catholic Reformation on the Gallegan peasantry. She is currently working on an ethnohistorical study of Gallegan peasant women during the early modern period.

INDEX

Abancay, 48
abbesses, 29, 32, 43, 45, 46, 51–53, 54, 58, 61n. 2
Abbott, Robert, 193
Acarie, Madame, 76
activism. *See* religious activism
Africans, 54
Agreda, María de, 33
Ahlgren, Gilliam T. W., 40n. 16
Aiguillon, Duchess of, 83
Albany, New York, 141, 144
Alcalá, Angel, 41n. 31
Aldridge, Susannah, 165
Aldry, Mary, 222
Alfonso XI, King, 32
Algemeen Consistorie, 124
Allford, John, 215–16
Almonasi, Diego, 48
alter Christus, 226
Alumbrado Movement (Illuminism), 36, 37
Alvarez, Catalina, 48
Ambrosius, Isaac, 141
Amsterdam, 118, 120, 122
Anabaptists, 118, 119, 158
Andeans, 8, 9, 33, 44, 65nn. 32, 66n. 38
Andes, 49–50, 56
Anglican(s), 157–86, 213, 220; Church, 157, 160–61, 167, 169, 175, 177, 179, 225
Annecy, France, 77
antinomianism, 187, 189
Aragon, Spain, 38
Arbiol, Antonio, 60n. 1
Archbishop of Paris, 84

Arminian Anglicans, 13, 119, 217, 225–26
Arnauld, Antoine, 127
arras, 22
artisan class, 95, 98–100, 110n. 20
Asa, Andrés, 55–56
Asa, María Suta, 55
asceticism, 4, 75
Astell, Mary, 159–60, 177
Asty, Ellen, 162
Aubrey, Marie-Elisabeth, 89n. 29
Augustinian Black Sisters, 117
ayllus, 56

Baddia, Maria, 146
Bainton, Roland, 4
Balding, Elizabeth, 226
Baltimore, Lord, 213
Bancker, Elizabeth, 141
baptism, 136, 141, 160, 169
Baptist(s), 13, 158, 161, 172–74; Church, 161, 169–75, 177; Particular, 213, 216
Bar Convent, 164
Barcelona, Spain, 30, 32
Bathsheba, 195
Bathurst, Anne, 178
Bauer, A. J., 61n. 5
Baxter, Richard, 161–62, 194–95
beatas, 7, 21, 33–34, 36, 39, 72 (*see also* women, lay holy); false, 35
Bedingfield, Frances, 164
beggars, 79
begijnhoven, 116
beguines, 33, 72, 95, 116–17, 126
Benedictines, 27